Teaching Primary Science

PEARSON

We work with leading authors to develop
the strongest educational materials in teaching and
education, bringing cutting-edge thinking and best
learning practice to a global market.

Under a range of well-known imprints, including
Longman, we craft high-quality print and electronic
publications which help readers to understand and
apply their content, whether studying or at work.

To find out more about the complete range of our
publishing, please visit us on the World Wide Web at:
www.pearsoned.co.uk

Teaching Primary Science

Promoting Enjoyment and Developing Understanding

Peter Loxley
Lyn Dawes
Linda Nicholls
Babs Dore

Longman
is an imprint of

PEARSON

Harlow, England • London • New York • Boston • San Francisco • Toronto • Sydney • Singapore • Hong Kong
Tokyo • Seoul • Taipei • New Delhi • Cape Town • Madrid • Mexico City • Amsterdam • Munich • Paris • Milan

Pearson Education Limited
Edinburgh Gate
Harlow
Essex CM20 2JE
England

and Associated Companies throughout the world

Visit us on the World Wide Web at:
www.pearsoned.co.uk

First published 2010

ISBN 978-1-4058-7398-7

British Library Cataloguing-in-Publication Data
A catalogue record for this book is available from the British Library

Library of Congress Cataloging-in-Publication Data
Teaching primary science : promoting enjoyment and developing understanding / Peter Loxley . . . [et al.].
     p. cm.
   ISBN 978-1-4058-7398-7 (pbk.)
1. Science–Study and teaching (Elementary)   I. Loxley, Peter.
   LB1585.T436 2010
   372.35'044–dc22

                                        2009042112

10 9 8 7 6 5 4 3 2 1
13 12 11 10 09

Typeset in 10/13pt Din Regular by 35
Printed and bound by Ashford Colour Press Ltd, Gosport

The publisher's policy is to use paper manufactured from sustainable forests.

Brief contents

Contents

Part 1: Theory and practice   1

Contents

List of photos, illustrations and tables

Figures

Tables

Guided tour

This book is divided into two sections: Theory and Practice (Chapters 1–7) and Subject Knowledge and Ideas for Practice (Chapters 8–19) to develop your understanding of key scientific and teaching concepts.

Theory and practice

Chapter introductions begin by outlining the key themes of the chapter and highlighting the key topics that the chapter will explore.

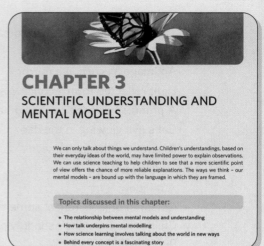

CHAPTER 3
SCIENTIFIC UNDERSTANDING AND MENTAL MODELS

We can only talk about things we understand. Children's understandings, based on their everyday ideas of the world, may have limited power to explain observations. We can use science teaching to help children to see that a more scientific point of view offers the chance of more reliable explanations. The ways we think – our mental models – are bound up with the language in which they are framed.

Topics discussed in this chapter:

- The relationship between mental models and understanding
- How talk underpins mental modelling
- How science learning involves talking about the world in new ways
- Behind every concept is a fascinating story

Part 2 Subject knowledge and ideas for practice

speed of light (300,000 km per second), the galaxy is so immense it would take about 25,000 years to reach the middle. Since time travel is not yet possible, scientists r on very powerful telescopes to explore the Milky Way.

Something to think about

What would the sky look like if we could see all the stars in the Milky Way from Earth?

Stargazing through the Hubble Telescope

Four hundred years ago Galileo was the first scientist to use a telescope to explo the night sky. Through the telescope he observed that Saturn had rings and Jupiter h moons. He also saw that the hazy patch across the centre of the sky called the Mi Way was not a cloud but an assortment of innumerable stars. The telescope chang forever our understanding of the nature of the universe and has enabled scientists take some amazing images of the stars.

Something to think about

What can we find out about the universe by looking at pictures taken by telescopes such as Hubble? What do these remarkable images tell us about the nature of the universe? You can view pictures taken by the Hubble Telescope at http://hubblesite.org/gallery/.

Example   Emperor penguins

A class of 10- and 11-year-olds were fascinated by a film showing colonies of emperor penguins huddling together to protect their chicks as they endured months of bitterly cold Antarctic weather. One group of children decided to find a way to investigate why penguins huddled in this way. They wondered about how to recreate Antarctic conditions until one child suggested they could make a model to simulate the penguins' behaviour. A simple model emerged; a large beaker was packed with successive rings of plastic test tubes each containing a thermometer. The test tubes were then filled with hot water and the whole apparatus left in the fridge for an hour. An hour later the thermometer readings confirmed that cooling was greatest in the outermost ring of test tubes.

The evidence the children collected helped them to think about what affects how quickly things cool. They concluded that temperature of the water fell more rapidly in the outermost test tubes because here the difference between the temperature of the water and the temperature in the fridge was greater than between the inner test tubes and the ones next to them.

Something to think about scenarios are designed to help you think creatively about key ideas to help you extend and develop your understanding. Found throughout the text, this feature asks you to pause and reflect, often posing key questions to consider or offering the opportunity to engage in a task.

Theory is applied to practice in short **Examples**, which present classroom situations, dialogs and stories that allow you to reflect upon best methods for teaching science.

Examples of children's art
Source: Peter Loxley

Part 2 Subject knowledge and ideas for practice

Greenhouse effect: human activity adds to greenhouse gases such as
carbon dioxide, methane and water vapour, which trap the Sun's energy
Source: Richard Ward / © Dorling Kindersley / DK Images

Problems with fossil fuels

There are relatively small amounts of carbon dioxide in the atmosphere. However,
when fossil fuels are burnt, carbon which has been locked inside the fuels for millions
of years is released in the form of carbon dioxide, causing the amount of this gas in
the atmosphere to increase significantly. Carbon dioxide is described as a greenhouse gas because it can absorb large amounts of heat and it acts like a blanket
surrounding the Earth. Although the Sun's rays are able to pass through it to reach the
Earth the heat becomes trapped. This is thought to be one of the causes of excessive
global warming and the resultant changes in our climate.
    The Earth has always benefited from the 'greenhouse effect' of its atmosphere

Photos and drawings illustrate the scientific
concepts explored and show how they are
implemented in the classroom.

---

ideas, we must provide children with opportunities to discuss and express their
thoughts. Meaningful discussion can take place during small-group work or
whole-class contexts. Children require clear guidelines to work collaboratively in
both small-group and whole-class situations (Chapter 4). They need to be awa
that their talk together is an important part of their work, and they need
taught the strategies and skills which will help every child take an active p
exploratory talk.

3. *Worksheets*
    The choice of resources can have a profound effect on the quality of the child
    learning and their attitudes to the topic. The disheartening phrase 'death by
    sheet' describes the dull nature of the learning experiences which such reso
    may provide! But well-designed worksheets can be a very useful way of o
    ising some activities. Worksheets should not be overused to the point
    children's activity is just focused on 'filling them in'. Whatever resources are
    practical or otherwise, they need to provide the children with something int
    ing to talk about.

Summary

Assessment is used to inform planning, and planning should outline how asse
will be carried out. Lesson plans should include key questions that can help ch
to articulate their knowledge and understanding. Questions should help child
think and share experience, and should not simply require children to guess
Children should be actively involved in the assessment process. Knowing the
ing objectives and knowing the steps needed to achieve them can help child
engage with their learning; but the main motivating drive is children's curiosi
helping children to ask their own questions and by ensuring that they realise that
is something interesting to discover, we can foster children's natural inquisiti
and satisfy their wish to learn.

Short chapter **Summaries** reflect on what
the chapter has covered, and will help you
to consolidate your learning.

Part 1 Theory and practice

when rigorously tested in the sixteenth century. Out of this period emerged a new
scientific age, with more rigorous methodology and greater freedom for people to
express their ideas. From that time onwards our understanding of how the natural
world works has developed at an ever increasing rate.

Further reading

Books

- Crump, T. (2002) *Science: As Seen Through the Development of Scientific Instruments*,
  London: Constable and Robinson Ltd.
- Brown, H. (1994) *The Wisdom of Science: Its Relevance to Culture and Religion*,
  Cambridge: Cambridge University Press.
- Fara, P. (2009) *Science: A Four Thousand Year History*, Oxford: Oxford University Press.
- Fortey, J. (2007) *Eyewitness Great Scientists*, London: Dorling Kindersley Ltd.
- Gregory, A. (2003) *Eureka: The Birth of Science*, Cambridge: Icon Books.
- Reed, A. W. (1993) *Aboriginal Myths, Legends and Fables* [compiled by A. W. Reed],
  Chatswood: N.S.W.
- Sobel, D. (1999) *Galileo's Daughter: A Drama of Science, Faith and Love*, London:
  Fourth Estate.

Primary Science Review Articles (Association of Science Education)

- PSR 96 (January/February 2007), 'Earth, air, fire and water, in our elements' by
  Tara Lievesley.

At the end of each chapter, **Further reading** offers
suggestions for books, journals and websites that will
to help you take your knowledge and understanding to
the next level.

Subject knowledge and ideas for practice

CHAPTER 16
ELECTRICITY AND MAGNETISM

Analogies are used to help visualise concepts such as electrical current, age and resistance. Analogies are an important meaning-making tool in s because they enable learners to use familiar images and experiences to make of unfamiliar scientific concepts. However, it is important to remember tha analogies presented do not provide exact representations of electricity and fore have limited explanatory power. When teaching electricity we need aware of the limitations of the analogies and discuss them with the children.

Topics discussed in this chapter:

- Historical context
- Static electricity

Part 1: Subject knowledge

Historical context

Around 2,600 years ago the ancient Greeks discovered that rubbing amber on lamb's wool produced **static electricity**. Once rubbed the wool attracted materials such as feathers and straw. If rubbed hard enough, small sparks could be generated.

Although static electricity was demonstrated in the times of the ancient Greeks, little progress was made until the eighteenth century when Benjamin Franklin (1706–90) demonstrated that electricity could travel between objects. He demonstrated that electricity acted like a fluid (current) travelling from what he called a positive object to a negative one.

In 1800 Alessandro Volta (1745–1827) discovered how to produce electricity using zinc and copper discs. This discovery was the forerunner of the dry-cell battery and was a dependable and safe source of **electrical current**. Hans Christian Oersted (1777–1851) demonstrated the relationship between electricity and magnetism. He realised that when electricity flows in a wire it creates a magnetic field around the wire which can be detected by a simple magnetic compass. André Marie Ampère (1775–1836) used this discovery as a way of measuring electric current, which led to the development of instruments such as the ammeter and voltmeter.

Static electricity

Why does rubbing create static electricity?

Rubbing a balloon against your sweatshirt will make you and a balloon stick together. How does this work?

Varied, theme-based science **Subject knowledge** covering such topics as the Earth and beyond, the diversity of life, health and well-being, force and motion, light and sound are presented in the first half of each chapter in this section and offer brief historical context and introduce some of the key scientists in the area being explored.

Part 2: Ideas for practice

Topic: Friction

Age group: Lower primary

Scientific view

Most things we do involve forces. For example, pushing forces help us jump and r Rubbing or sliding forces help us slow down and stop. Forces even help warm hands when we rub them together. Rubbing forces are also responsible for weari out our clothes. When we walk and run our shoes rub against the ground and b are torn off. Friction is another name for rubbing forces. Frictional forces can sl objects down and can scratch and damage surfaces. Friction can also help us to mo by providing 'grip' between surfaces.

Scientific enquiry skills

In these activities children will:

- raise and try to find answers to questions;
- put forward their own ideas and make simple predictions;
- make simple comparisons and identify simple patterns;
- compare what happened with what they expected would happen;
- plan a fair test with help from their teacher

Topic: Air resistance

Age group: Upper primary

Scientific view

Air is all around us. We live in a sea of air, like fish live in a sea of water. To move through air we need to push it out of the way, just like wading through water. Falling objects push air aside as they move towards the ground. The force with which objects push their way through air is called 'air resistance'. Air resistance is a force which impedes movement and is a type of friction.

Scientific enquiry skills

In these activities children will:

- raise and try to find answers to questions;
- think creatively to explain how air resistance works and to establish causes and effects;
- use first-hand experience to answer questions;
- use scientific knowledge and understanding to explain their observations;
- review their modelling to describe its significance and limitations.

Exploration stage

Children's talk involves trying out their own ideas

Setting the scene

In the second half of each chapter, **Ideas for practice** explore specific topics within the subject knowledge, for example in Chapter 8: Moon craters or phases of the Moon or in Chapter 13: healthy eating or the benefits of exercise, providing further information on the topic that offer innovative and engaging ways of bringing science to life in the classroom for Lower (ages 5–8 years) and Upper (ages 8–11) Primary Phases.

Scientific view

Light enables us to see and recognise different objects and to make sense of the world in which we live. Without light the world would be dark. Shadows are formed when objects block out light to create areas of darkness.

Scientific enquiry skills

In these activities children will:

- raise and try to find answers to questions;
- use first-hand experience and information sources to find answers to questions;
- make simple comparisons and identify simple patterns;
- compare what happened with what they expected would happen and try to explain it, drawing on their knowledge and understanding.

Exploration stage

Children's talk involves trying out their own ideas

Setting the scene

Read the extract from *Peter Pan*. Mrs Darling has just spotted Peter. Nana is a big d[...] who looks after the children Wendy, John and Michael.

Peter Pan

Mrs. Darling screamed, and, as if in answer to a bell, the door opened, and Nana [...] entered, returned from her evening out. She growled and sprang at the boy, who [...] leapt lightly through the window. Again Mrs. Darling screamed, this time in distress [...]

Formative assessment

Observational drawings – ask the children to draw an object and its shadow. They can annotate their drawing to show the direction of light and say how the shadow is formed.

Re-describing stage

Children's talk involves making sense of scientific ideas

The purpose of this stage is to help the children to visualise a shadow as an area of darkness where an object is blocking light.

Encourage the children to talk about why their shadows are always black or dark. Ask them to imagine what it would be like to stand inside a very dark shadow. Talk about the darkest place they have ever experienced. How did the dark make them feel? What could they see?

Scientific enquiry

Create a dark cave from opaque material and tables in the classroom. Put some dark, light and luminous objects in corners of the cave. Make it big enough for at least two children. Allow volunteers to go into the cave two at a time. When they come out ask them what they could see. Did they notice the objects in the corner? Did they recognise them?

By the end of the activity it is important that most of the children will have experienced the sense of dark and been able to talk about it. Ask the children to write about what it feels like to be in the dark. *Talk together* about why it was so dark in the cave. What would they need to do to see things more clearly in the cave? Establish that they need light to see. Allow them back into the cave with a torch to identify the objects. Establish that darkness is the absence of light; we need light to see things. Talk about how objects block out the light to form areas of darkness which are called shadows. What would it be like sitting within a giant's shadow?

Application stage

Children's talk involves trying out scientific ideas

Links to design technology and drama

Create a small shadow theatre using a box or a large one using a sheet suspended from the ceiling. Children can design and make shadow puppets to act a scene from *Peter Pan* or they can create their own stories. Use a range of opaque and translucent materials. Encourage each group to *work collaboratively* to design their own shadow scenery, props and characters. During rehearsals encourage the children to use their knowledge of shadows creatively. For example, sizes can be changed dramatically by moving the puppet closer to the light source. Giant monsters and carnivorous plants can be created this way. Talk to the children about the effects they want to create and help them put their ideas into action. Finally, children need to spend time preparing their script and rehearsing their performance.

Using the **Three-stage framework for teaching science**, specific concepts with practical ideas for making them come alive are presented.

- Introducing the framework, **scientific view** summarises the fundamental science behind the topic while **scientific enquiry skills** outline learning objectives to be explored.
- **Exploration stage** presents a range of teaching and learning strategies that set the scene for children in the classroom.
- **Re-describing stage** reinforces children's learning and understanding.
- **Application stage** offers ways for children to make use of their scientific learning in different contexts such as art, drama, poetry and creative writing.

Preface

The purpose of the book is to provide information which can be used by education students and qualified teachers to develop their subject knowledge and to gain insights into ways of teaching that promote the value of scientific understanding. The book focuses mainly on the teaching of scientific concepts and skills but, when appropriate, it sets science learning in technological contexts to foster an appreciation of how the two disciplines support one another. Cross-curricular contexts are used to help set the scene for children's science learning, including history, geography, art, drama, children's stories and poetry.

The design of the book is based on the belief that children are more likely to appreciate their science learning if concepts are presented as ideas or useful points of view, rather than facts or definitions to be remembered. A key feature of the book is the use of scientific ideas to solve theme-based 'puzzles' as part of a storytelling approach. As in all good mystery stories, the fascinating content of the story and its satisfying resolution provide pleasure and ensure interest. The advantage of narrative is that its familiar and engaging form can carry children along, helping them to generate a real understanding of science and to be able to remember what they have learned.

The book is arranged in two parts. Six of the seven chapters in Part 1 discuss generic issues and practices which are used to create a three-stage teaching and learning framework. Talking, listening and acting in scientific ways to solve a 'puzzle' underpin this framework. In each of the chapters we provide classroom-based exemplification whenever possible to help bridge the gap between theory and practice. Chapter 7 discusses the nature and origins of scientific knowledge. We have included this chapter because we believe that teachers' perceptions of scientific knowledge greatly influence their teaching. Teachers who envisage science as an amazing human achievement can more readily inspire similar feelings in children.

Part 2 presents theme-based science subject knowledge to help teachers develop their understanding of key concepts. It also presents what we have called 'Ideas for practice'. The 'Ideas for practice' exemplify how the three-stage framework can be used to teach particular topics to different age groups. The 'Ideas for practice' sections are not lesson plans but suggestions to illustrate how the teaching of particular topics can be organised.

Learning scientific concepts can be challenging and intellectually hard work for children. If we want them to make the necessary effort, we must ensure that they are rewarded with feelings of satisfaction and achievement. Chapter 1 looks at how learning in science can offer children pleasure and intellectual satisfaction, fostering their natural curiosity and helping them to develop sound scientific understanding.

Peter Loxley
Lyn Dawes
Linda Nicholls
Babs Dore

Acknowledgements

The authors would like to thank Mike Dore, Anna Loxley, Neil Mercer and Robert Nicholls for their patience and invaluable help with the book. We would also like to acknowledge the very positive and constructive feedback we received from our reviewers which helped to reinforce our belief in the value of the project:

Malcolom Anderson, University of Brighton
Karen Hartley, Edge Hill University
Jen Smyth, London Metropolitan University

Special thanks go to Catherine Yates and Joe Vella from Pearson Longman, who skilfully and enthusiastically nurtured us through the writing and publication of the book. We are also indebted to Gary Fuller, our science technician, for his patient and efficient support. Finally, we would like to say a big thank you to Julie Hill (Head Teacher) and the children from Green Oaks Primary School, Northampton, who made our science days such a delight.

Peter Loxley
Lyn Dawes
Linda Nicholls
Babs Dore

Publisher's acknowledgements

We are grateful to the following for permission to reproduce copyright material:

Photos and Illustrations

Pages 47, 51, 53, 56 and 59: Peter Loxley; 82: Copyright to the Ngarinyin clan estate Biyarrngongo of the artist Charlie Allungoy (Numbulmoore), Ngarinyin and Wilinggin Aboriginal Corporations and Mamaa The Untouchable Ones from Cave to Canvas art projects (explanation given by family member Yvonne Burgu as translated by Heather Winter). Picture supplied by the National Museum of Australia; 87: De Agostini Editore Picture Library / DK Images; 90: © British Library Board / Bridgeman Art Library Ltd; 92: © Bettmann / Corbis (left) and DK Images (right); 101: Courtesy of NASA; 102: © Dorling Kindersley / DK Images; 103, 105 (top) and 108: © Mark A. Garlick (www.space-art.co.uk); 105 (bottom): DK Images; 108: Courtesy of NASA; 110: Jamie Marshall / digitaleye / DK Images; 111: Mike Dunning / © Dorling Kindersley / DK Images; 112: Peter Bull / © Dorling Kindersley / DK Images; 113 and 114: Janos Marffy / © Dorling Kindersley / DK Images; 117, 120 and 121: Peter Loxley; 122: Courtesy of NASA; 126: © Dorling Kindersley / DK Images; 130: Richard Ward / © Dorling Kindersley / DK Images; 131: Linda Nicolls; 132: Dave King / © Dorling Kindersley / DK Images; 133: Andrew Beckett / © Dorling Kindersley / DK Images; 141: Linda Nicolls; 146: Peter Loxley; 152: Linda Nicolls; 155: © Dorling Kindersley / DK Images; 156: Mick Loates / © Dorling Kindersley / DK Images; 159: Linda Nicolls; 162: © Succession Henri Matisse / DACS 2009 / Tate Picture Library; 163: Babs Dore and Linda Nicholls; 167: Tim Ridley / © Dorling Kindersley / DK Images; 172 and 173: © Dorling Kindersley; / DK Images; 174: © Kim Taylor and Jane Burton (left) and Steve Gordon / © Dorling Kindersley (right) / DK Images; 177: Steve Shott (top left), Dave King (bottom left) and Tracy Morgan (top and bottom right) / © Dorling Kindersley / DK Images; 178: Peter Anderson / © Dorling Kindersley (top left); DK Images (top right); © Kim Taylor / Dorling Kindersley (bottom left and right) / DK Images; 182: Simone End / © Dorling Kindersley / DK Images; 185: Roger Philips (top left), Frank Greenaway (top right) and DK Images (bottom left) / © Dorling Kindersley / DK Images; 190: © The Gallery Collection / Corbis; 192: © Dorling Kindersley / DK Images; 193: © Dorling Kindersley / DK Images; 195: © Dorling Kindersley / DK Images; 197: Derek Hall / © Dorling Kindersley / DK Images; 198: Jerry Young / © Dorling Kindersley / DK Images; 199: Barrie Watts / © Dorling Kindersley / DK Images; 200: David Peart / © Dorling Kindersley / DK Images; 205: Peter Loxley; 207: © Dorling Kindersley / DK Images; 209: Peter Loxley; 213: © Dorling Kindersley / DK Images; 216: Kevin Jones / © Dorling Kindersley / DK Images; 217: © Dorling Kindersley / DK Images (top) and Dave King / © Dorling Kindersley / DK Images (bottom); 219: © Dorling Kindersley / DK Images; 222: Maximilian Stock Ltd / Science Photo Library Ltd; 224: Martin Brigdale / DK Images; 227: Tim Ridley / © Dorling Kindersley / DK Images; 235: © Dorling Kindersley / DK Images (left) © Leslie

Morris / Photographers Direct (right); 236: © Dorling Kindersley / DK Images (top left) and Dave King / © Dorling Kindersley / DK Images (top right); 236: © Dorling Kindersley / DK Images (bottom left) Andy Marlin / Getty Images (bottom right); 242: Peter Loxley; 244: © Dorling Kindersley / DK Images; 247: Peter Loxley; 251: John Woodcock / © Dorling Kindersley / DK Images; 253: Robin Hunter / © Dorling Kindersley / DK Images; 257: Steve Gorton / © Dorling Kindersley / DK Images; 258: Peter Loxley; 259: Peter Loxley; 266: Susanna Price / © Dorling Kindersley (left) and Mike Dunning / © Dorling Kindersley (right) / DK Images; 271: Peter Loxley; 272: © Dorling Kindersley / DK Images; 274: Dave King / © Dorling Kindersley / DK Images (bottom right); 275 and 276: Clive Streeter / © Dorling Kindersley / Courtesy of The Science Museum, London; 278: Janos Marffy / © Dorling Kindersley / DK Images; 279: Courtesy of Gary A. Glatzmaier (left) and Mike Dunning / © Dorling Kindersley / DK Images (right); 282, 283, 286, 293, 296, 298, 301, 306, 307: Peter Loxley; 311: Dave King / © Dorling Kindersley / DK Images; 313: Peter Gardner / © Dorling Kindersley / DK Images; 314: © Dorling Kindersley / DK Images; 315: Bjorn Rorslett / Science Photo Library Ltd; 316: © Dorling Kindersley / DK Images; 317: Robin Hunter / © Dorling Kindersley / DK Images; 318: DK Images; 319: © Rowan Greenwood / DK Images (top) and Kuo Kang Chen / © Dorling Kindersley / DK Images (bottom); 325 and 332: Peter Loxley; 334: © Dorling Kindersley / DK Images (top) and Peter Loxley (bottom); 335: John Woodcock / © Dorling Kindersley / DK Images; 336: Robin Hunter / © Dorling Kindersley / DK Images; 337: Jacopin / Science Photo Library Ltd; 338: Cyril Laubscher / © Dorling Kindersley / DK Images; 344: Frank Greenaway / © Dorling Kindersley / DK Images; 348: Peter Loxley.

Text

Page 119: Poetry from *The Moon* by Kjartan Poskitt in *Twinkle Twinkle Chocolate Bar: Rhymes for the Very Young* (Foster, J., 1993), Oxford University Press, p. 99. Originally published in *Pob and Friends* edited by Anne Wood. Reproduced with permission from Ragdoll Productions and author.

In some instances we have been unable to trace the owners of copyright material and we would appreciate any information that would enable us to do so.

PART 1
THEORY AND PRACTICE

CHAPTER 1
THE PLEASURE OF FINDING THINGS OUT

You see? That's why scientists persist in their investigations, why we struggle so desperately for every bit of knowledge, climb the steepest obstacles to the next fragment of understanding; [. . . it is] part of the pleasure of finding things out.

(Feynman, 1999)

During everyday experience, children observe and interpret for themselves the way the world works. As teachers, we need to find out what children have already experienced, imagined and concluded about scientific ideas. We have the challenge of helping them to come to a more scientific point of view. Children need access to established scientific information which is based on centuries of careful observation and research. At the same time, we must foster the curiosity which leads children to question theories, and the creativity which enables them to generate new thinking. The intrinsic interest of science is in thinking through and resolving the puzzles which are the ways the world works.

Topics discussed in the chapter:

- Children's attitudes to science
- Insights into effective science teaching
- The pleasure of finding things out
- Storytelling and science teaching

Children's attitudes to science

What children like about science

Children enjoy practical science; it is interesting to have a puzzle to solve, to set up your own investigation and find out something new. The resources we use in science are intrinsically fascinating – magnets, batteries and bulbs, snails and magnifiers. Excitingly, science happens outdoors, or offers a chance to measure or observe things around the school. Such practical activity is motivating and engaging, especially if there is a strong collaborative element. Working with a classmate ensures that there is someone to share ideas, and means that disheartening personal failure is less likely. Children who learn a scientific way of thinking based on reasoning about evidence are learning a life skill. Through the experience of school science, many children acquire an enduring interest in how the world works. Their curiosity is fuelled when they find out enough to know that there are still questions to ask and things to investigate.

Problems with learning concepts

Science is not just about exploration, but also about sharing the knowledge and understanding that people have accumulated over time. For children, the problem with science is having to 'learn facts'. There is a lot to learn and it is easy to get things wrong. This includes new words, or new uses of words, because science, like many other activities, has its own technical vocabulary. A further difficulty is that some scientific explanations are counter-intuitive. Children's everyday observations may lead them to hold firmly established ideas which turn out to be 'wrong' in terms of science. For example, a ball rolling along on grass will slowly come to a stop. If we think that the ball needs force to make it move, then it is reasonable to think that it stops because it has run out of force. A more scientific explanation would be that the ball eventually stops because the forces acting on it cause it to slow down. Children sometimes find science too abstract and separate from their everyday understanding. Force is an abstract idea; the concept of force is a strange notion for children, as is the idea that humans are animals made up of little cells, or that mass when affected by gravity becomes weight. Confusion arises because these scientific accounts do not map easily on to what children can see, feel and hear.

Something to think about

The Earth-centred model of the universe is an intuitive idea. When we watch the Sun rise in the east and set in the west common sense tells us that it must be travelling around the Earth. The idea that this is an illusion caused by the spin of the Earth is counter-intuitive. Many scientific ideas are counter-intuitive. What does this mean for the way we need to teach science? Is it feasible to expect children to discover scientific ideas for themselves?

In summary, children may see conceptual learning as hard work, dull and unoriginal. Although they like 'doing experiments', the children in Murphy and Beggs' (2003) study reported disliking writing, learning facts and technical vocabulary. Learning facts for examinations can have a negative effect on attitudes; children tend to enjoy and value science more when they have opportunities to discuss and debate ideas and issues. Research has shown that there is the need to teach concepts in ways which relate to everyday life and appeal to children's interests (Osborne et al., 2003; Simon, 2000; Cerini et al., 2003).

How can we make conceptual learning more rewarding?

In this book we offer a theory-based, practical approach to the teaching of science which we believe will help to overcome some of the difficulties children have with learning concepts. This approach involves teaching science as a collection of inter-related stories. Children are familiar with stories. They know that stories have a beginning, maybe with a puzzle or problem; a middle where events happen and may even become complicated or problematic; and a resolution, after which all becomes clear – although there may be other stories to be told subsequently. The process of science maps easily on to this narrative structure. The advantage of narrative is that it is a familiar and engaging form that can carry children along, helping them to generate a memorable understanding of science concepts, as ideas are framed in interesting and accessible contexts and explained in realistic terms.

A narrative approach to the teaching and learning of science can generate real enthusiasm for learning. Children can develop positive attitudes to the concepts they explore. A powerful mix of story and science can help children to develop a rewarding understanding of why and how things happen as they do.

Something to think about

What do you think the authors mean when they talk about presenting the scientific view as a narrative rather than a series of facts or definitions? What are the differences between the two approaches?

Insights into effective science teaching

Richard Feynman was one of the twentieth century's most brilliant scientists, achieving the Nobel Prize for Physics in 1965. He had an infectious enthusiasm for science and loved sharing his ideas with anyone who wanted to listen. His ability to talk about science in accessible ways made him a popular and entertaining public speaker. In a lecture for teachers Feynman spoke about the teaching of scientific definitions (Feynman, 1999). He thought that although children need to be taught certain scientific words and definitions, the learning of these words and definitions does not mean they are learning science. To illustrate the point he described a picture of a wind-up toy dog he had seen in a science textbook with the question *'What makes it move?'* written underneath. The answer the author of the book was looking for was that *'Energy makes it move'*. Feynman pointed out that this answer was meaningless for young people who are just learning about the concept of energy. He suggested that it would be equally meaningful to them to say that 'God makes the toy move' or 'spirits make it move'. He then asked what the teacher would do if the children said that they did not think energy made the toy move. He wanted to know how the teacher would persuade them that the energy explanation is valid. Why not God? Why not spirits? Why is 'energy' the best explanation?

The point Feynman wanted to make was that *'Energy makes things move'* is a definition which only makes sense to children *after* they understand the concept of energy. He suggested that children would learn more about how the toy worked by taking it apart to see how the spring is wound and how it releases to make the wheels go round. They could think about the effect of winding a spring, and what has to happen to create a wound spring. They could learn how the Sun enables plants to grow and how eating plants provides people with the capacity to wind up the toy and make it move. For Feynman, the answer to the question *'What makes it move?'* was that sunshine makes the dog move. And if children do not believe this, then teachers and children have a lot of interesting things to talk about.

Beware of mystic formulae

In his lecture Feynman used the term 'mystic formulae' to describe some of the explanations used in science books to answer questions. In particular he focused on the concept of friction and criticised the practice of using mystic formulae such as *'The soles of shoes wear out because of friction'* as scientific explanations. In his own words: 'Shoe leather wears out because it rubs against the sidewalk and the little notches and bumps on the sidewalk grab pieces and pull them off. To simply say it is because of friction is sad, because it's not science' (Feynman, 1999: 180).

Feynman's mini-narrative about how shoe leather wears out is the science behind the definition. Instead of labelling the wearing-out process as friction, he imagined the events which actually caused the shoes to wear out. To understand a concept we can create in our minds a representation or mental model of it – a kind of story.

Something to think about

Richard Feynman describes scientific definitions as mystic formulae. Can you think of any mystic formulae that you have been required to learn? Ask yourself what images come into your mind when you think of friction. What words would you use to describe it?

Talking concepts into existence

If you were preparing to teach children about friction, how would you start? To relate the idea of friction to the child's experience, you might start by encouraging the children to feel the sole of a shoe or rub their fingers on floor surfaces. They could talk about which surfaces give good grip and which surfaces are slippery, and try to explain why. Children could go on to talk about why they think shoes wear out. Can they explain why? What words would children use to describe how a shoe wears out? They might think of words such as rubbing or scratching – which are actions involving forces. The children could suggest which type of sole is likely to wear out more quickly and whether the shape and size of the sole affects how quickly they wear out. There are many things to talk about; and the more children talk about a concept and begin to see it as an everyday problem, the more likely they will be able to make sense of it.

Talking about how shoes wear out in this way enables children to construct meaningful pictures or images of the process in their minds. These internal representations or mental models are discussed in more detail in Chapter 3. Drawing pictures also helps children to create mental models of scientific concepts.

The key to developing children's understanding of friction is to help them see that all surfaces are uneven. Even the smoothest surfaces have irregularities which are not visible to the naked eye. An analogy using a familiar scenario, such as a car travelling over a rough road, can be useful. Children can visualise how the tyres collide with the bumps and holes in the road. Children need to be helped to visualise 'friction' – how the uneven surfaces rub up against each other – by employing a combination of drawings, analogies and figurative language until the most evocative images are constructed. Ultimately the intention is to construct an explanation in words and pictures which describes how friction works.

This joint oral construction of understanding between teacher and children has the outcome of 'talking the concept into existence' (Ogborn et al., 1996). In this case, seeing the science means visualising how friction works and understanding how it applies to the practical situation. When we as teachers are able to 'see' the science, we are more able to manage the children's conceptual learning in ways which stimulate and maintain their interest (Asoko, 2000). Helping to 'see' the science is the purpose of the teaching and learning framework set out in Chapter 2, and the examples of theme-based plans presented in Part 2 of the book.

Something to think about

Talking a scientific concept into existence requires us to use words to create an image or representation of the concept in our mind. Think of a scientific concept which you can picture in your mind (friction, electricity, photosynthesis). What words would you encourage children to use to enable them to visualise the concept in their minds?

The pleasure of finding things out

It is not surprising to find that children may not enjoy memorising facts and learning how to spell complex scientific words. If we are to promote positive attitudes to science, the experiences which stimulate children's conceptual development must be rewarding both intellectually and emotionally. Feynman provides an elegant account of how as a child he first came to appreciate the value of scientific knowledge and the pleasure which can be gained from finding out that the world wasn't as he first perceived it to be. On regular walks in the countryside, the young Feynman would be tantalised by his father's questions about the animals and plants which they observed, and challenged to explain reasons for their behaviour (Feynman, 1999). Feynman describes one occasion when the conversation focused on the behaviour of a bird.

> During the walks in the woods with my father, I learned a great deal. In the case of the birds, for example: Instead of naming them, my father would say, 'Look, notice that bird is always pecking in its feathers. It pecks a lot in its feathers. Why do you think it pecks the feathers?'
> (Feynman, 1999: 181)

Feynman was encouraged by his father to suggest a hypothesis, offering what seemed to him to be a logical reason. His father would help him test if he was right. In this case he hypothesised that the bird was straightening its feathers because it had just landed. He was encouraged to test this idea by checking to see if other birds preened their feathers on landing. Noting that this did not usually happen, they looked for another reason. Eventually his father introduced a new way of 'seeing' the event by suggesting that the preening bird could be removing parasites. The experience created a real opportunity to think together about the idea of *interdependency*.

> he went on to say that in the world whenever there is any source of something that could be eaten to make life go, some form of life finds a way to make use of that source; and that each little bit of leftover stuff is eaten by something.
> (Feynman, 1999: p. 182)

Interdependence is a 'big idea' in science because it applies to a wide range of events and situations. It is a powerful idea which helps us understand how life on earth has developed and how it is sustained.

> ## Something to think about
>
> Charles Darwin developed the concepts of adaptation and interdependence to explain how all living things in the world are related to each other. These ideas explain the origins of all living things on the Earth – they are 'big ideas'. What everyday examples of interdependence or adaptation are immediately available to the children in your class?

New ways of seeing the world

By considering the concept of parasites Feynman was able to think of the events he had observed in a different way. Initially he had been encouraged to explain his personal point of view, but when the account proved unreliable there was a need to imagine, discover or find out about a new way of seeing the events. The explanation of a more scientific point of view, coupled with the pleasure he gained from being actively involved in the telling of a story was very rewarding. For children, discovery involves creative thinking. Things that they have never realised and which are new to them require the exercise of creativity to imagine and understand – and 'finding out' can be very exciting.

> Now the point of this is that the result of observation, even if I were unable to come to an ultimate conclusion, was a wonderful piece of gold, with a marvellous result. It was something marvellous.
> (Feynman, 1999: 182)

The story of the birds reminds us that we can teach children by stimulating curiosity, asking interesting questions, and providing key information at the point it is required. An important purpose of science education is to share with children the amazing visions of the world that science has discovered. If shared through rational and evocative dialogue, children can experience the pleasure of learning science which comes from the wonder and awe of finding out that the world is not always as we first perceive it to be. In addition children can learn that accurate scientific explanations 'hold water' when tested and questioned, which their own everyday descriptions of events might not. The child begins to realise that its developing knowledge is cumulative and can be put to use, whereas everyday understandings may not be sound or robust when tested.

Storytelling and science teaching

In his anecdote Feynman was reminiscing about an experience which was unique and very special to him. Producing similar rewarding intellectual and emotional experiences for a class of primary children may not be so easy. The more general and important point about the value of scientific knowledge is that the usefulness of science resides in its power to transform the way we see the world. To achieve this, learning has to be set in contexts which require the need for a scientific explanation. Contexts for science learning need to be familiar to children, yet hold the potential to produce dilemmas or problems which the development of conceptual understanding can help to resolve. Children commonly ask questions. In classrooms, they may find it harder to do so. A first step is to establish puzzles or encourage questions about the natural world. We can then organise science learning in meaningful stages so that children can have access to scientific ideas, can work through activities which help them to make meaning from experience, and then go on to use their new understanding to solve problems and answer questions.

In Feynman's narrative, his father pointed out a puzzling event. He then took on the role of the expert to model the scientific skills of hypothesising, observation and investigation necessary to construct an explanation for the behaviour of the birds. Practising these scientific ways of thinking led to conflict between how Feynman initially visualised the event, and the empirical evidence. This added tension and an imperative to consider alternative ideas. In effect, the puzzling event pushed Feynman's existing knowledge to its limit and created a desire to learn more. It stimulated his curiosity and fostered motivation to discuss ideas. The ensuing conversation enabled Feynman to re-describe aspects of nature in more scientific ways (Sutton, 1996). Eventually his active participation was rewarded with a sense of pleasure and satisfaction as the puzzle was resolved. He was able to see the event in a new and more powerful way. The story ends with the child's heightened interest likely to create opportunities for more questions and stories. The pleasure of finding things out helps children want to go on to find out even more.

Something to think about

Think about a story which has had an influence on you – not necessarily to do with science. What did you like about it? Did it develop around some issues? If so, were these issues resolved? Did it help you resolve some personal issues? Did it make you think about the world in a different way? Would you describe it as an empowering story? Do you know any empowering scientific stories?

Storytellers arouse curiosity, create tension and provide the satisfaction of answered questions and an interesting resolution. Teachers can adopt this straightforward narrative sequence to help plan stimulating lessons. The difference between traditional storytelling and science teaching is that in the latter we want the audience (children) to take an active part in the storytelling. We want children to tell the story using their own voices, each with its own unique interpretation of the theme, but each based on sound science.

To facilitate a storytelling approach science lessons need:

1. A theme which can be communicated to children in narrative form.
   Feynman's narrative was developed from the theme of interdependency.

2. A context which is relevant for the theme and also familiar to the children.
   A woodland setting is an ideal place to observe the behaviour of birds.

3. Events and/or activities which set the scene against which the narrative can unfold.
   An adult set the scene by drawing attention to what the birds were doing.

4. A 'hook' or puzzling event which arouses children's curiosity.
   Why was the bird pecking its feathers? This was cast as a puzzling event which needed explanation.

5. A complication which indicates there is more to the event than the children may imagine.
   Feynman's initial suggestion proved incorrect and he was keen to find out what was really happening.

6. A resolution with the help of a well-informed adult who can provide relevant guidance to help solve the dilemma.
   Feynman's father introduced him to the idea of parasites. As a result Feynman's understanding of the behaviour of birds changed and he learned to see the world in a new way.

7. Opportunities for children to develop further understanding of the theme.
   Feynman and his father went on to talk about the concept of interdependency, applying it to the behaviour of other living things in the woods.

The way Feynman learnt science greatly influenced his love of the subject and influenced his thinking about what constitutes effective teaching. We suggest that primary science teachers can usefully draw on established storytelling techniques to create similar stimulating learning experiences for their children.

Summary

Teaching science as facts and definitions is unlikely to promote effective learning. Meaningful and memorable learning requires the children to be intellectually and emotionally stimulated. This is more likely to happen if we plan learning settings in which children can experience the pleasure of finding out things about the natural world which surprise them and satisfy their desire to know. We suggest it is possible to apply storytelling techniques to science teaching in order to arouse and satisfy children's natural curiosity about the world in which they live.

The next chapter presents a framework for organising children's learning based on a storytelling approach. The framework provides opportunities for children to express and test their own ideas before exploring the value of the scientific point of view.

Further reading

Books

- Feynman, R. (1999) *The Pleasure of Finding Things Out*, London: Penguin Books.
- Oliver, A. (2006) *Creative Teaching Science*, London: David Fulton, Chapter 1: The importance of teaching science creatively and Chapter 2: Creative science teaching.

Primary science review articles (Association of Science Education)

- PSR 105 (November/December 2008), 'What makes children like science?' by John Leisten.
- PSR 89 (September/October 2005), 'The pleasure of finding things out' by Peter Loxley.
- PSR 83 (May/June 2004), 'Conversations in primary science: advice for "older learners"' by Neville Evans.
- PSR 71 (January/February 2002), 'Science is for life' by Sandra Eady.

CHAPTER 2
ORGANISING HOW CHILDREN LEARN SCIENCE

The close link between science and narrative can help us to stage the way that we teach science to children (Chapter 1). This chapter explains how we can usefully structure children's learning in stages, so that they become engaged with a puzzle, work through relevant experiences to resolve it and, finally, apply their newly developed ideas.

Topics discussed in this chapter:

- A three-stage framework for learning science
- An outline of the three-stage framework
- An example of how to stage children's conceptual understanding
- How the framework supports a storytelling approach

A three-stage framework for learning science

Children like stories. Stories have gripping openings, and then perhaps a complication or a puzzle; they involve characters actively engaged in a series of events to unravel the puzzle, before finally coming to a satisfactory resolution. Science can be like this too. A question about the way the world works sets us off on a trail of enquiry; we generate a theory and test it; finally we find a satisfactory explanation which helps us understand the world better.

The value of stories is not only in their ability to entertain, but also in their power to persuade. For children abstract scientific ideas can at first seem to have little relevance to how they usually visualise the world. Everyday experience stimulates children to develop their own ideas which they trust and are reluctant to change. For example, a child may visualise a battery as a container full of electricity which slowly empties out when connected to a circuit. This is not scientifically accurate but it is useful because it enables the child to explain why batteries go flat over time. It is consistent with the child's experiences and enables them to predict how a circuit will behave.

Because children place so much trust in their own intuitive ideas, they are often reluctant to engage meaningfully with more complex scientific ideas. Children need to be persuaded that the scientific ideas provide useful ways of visualising how the world works. As Clive Sutton points out:

> To involve someone else in your science is not just a matter of telling them what you have found; it involves persuading them of the usefulness and validity of the view you adopt, and the relevance of the evidence you present.
> (Sutton, 1996: 146)

Teachers can use a persuasive, narrative approach to help children visualise the world in more scientific ways. This chapter sets out a three-stage framework which is designed to help teachers to teach science in persuasive ways (Loxley, 2009).

Something to think about

What does Sutton mean when he says that teaching is not just a matter of telling children what they need to learn? Read Feynman's account of how he learnt about the concept of interdependence in Chapter 1. Would you describe the approach taken by his father as questioning or persuading?

The framework is built on firm foundations

During the 1980s researchers at Leeds University developed a framework for science learning through the Children's Learning in Science (CLIS) project. The CLIS project was based on the constructivist view of learning which emphasised the way children construct their own understanding from their interactions with the physical world. The first step in the CLIS approach is called 'elicitation'. This involves providing opportunities for the children to make their own ideas explicit, exposing any misconceptions. Further stages involve activities which are designed to help children recognise the limitations of their everyday ideas when confronted with empirical evidence. Outcomes of the project suggest that children rarely completely abandon their initial ideas. They are more likely to construct hybrid ideas based on their own ideas and the parts of the scientific view which are most useful to them. (See Chapter 3.)

The use of empirical evidence in persuading children to adopt the scientific view as an alternative to their own ideas was an important part of science education research in the 1980s and early 1990s. Less emphasis was placed on the influence of context, culture and social interactions. In recent years the focus on how children come to understand scientific concepts has changed. Rather than the emphasis being on children making sense of phenomena through practical enquiry, it has shifted to the types of cultural and social interactions which help children appreciate scientific ideas as someone else's point of view (Chapter 3). This sociocultural approach to learning focuses on persuasive ways of presenting and talking about established scientific ideas. To understand scientific ideas children need to use their own cultural language to help create representations of the ideas in their minds (Loxley, 2009). By talking about abstract scientific ideas in interpretive ways, children can use their own words to give the ideas some physical reality. In other words, to talk them into existence (Chapter 1).

Something to think about

What do you think the authors mean when they refer to scientific ideas as someone else's point of view? Think of a topic of interest, not necessarily to do with science. How would you persuade another person that your point of view is valid and worth listening to? Is just telling them that you are right enough?

The process by which learners use language and other interpretive tools such as drawings, pictures and 3-D models to create images of scientific concepts in their minds is known as mental modelling. The three-stage framework set out below is designed to help teachers to organise the way children construct mental models of scientific ideas. (A more detailed account of the relationship between scientific understanding and mental modelling is provided in Chapter 3.)

Outline of the three-stage framework

1. **The exploratory stage** sets the scene for the children's learning by providing a puzzle or dilemma which they need to resolve. Activities in this stage should encourage children to share ideas and work collaboratively towards solving the puzzle. Complications help children recognise a need for a scientific explanation.

2. **The re-describing stage** encourages the children to rethink their ideas in the light of evidence and the scientific view. Coming to appreciate the usefulness of the scientific view is the goal of this stage. This involves talking about and interpreting the scientific ideas in ways which enable children to make sense of them and to see their value with regard to solving the puzzle or dilemma.

3. **The application stage** allows children to try out and experience the explanatory power of their newly acquired scientific ideas in other contexts. The more widely the children apply the scientific ideas, the more likely they will make them their own.

How progression is built into the three-stage framework

The purpose of the three-stage framework is to help children develop reliable and useful understanding of the topic and theme. This may involve modification of their initial ideas or simply an extension of what they already know. The diagram below, 'Progression in the three-stage framework', indicates the cyclic nature of the framework through which children's ideas are progressively developed into 'bigger ideas' which provide more explanatory power (Chapter 3). The term 're-describing stage' was first used by Sutton (1996) to emphasise the role language plays when a learner is developing a new way of visualising an event or phenomenon.

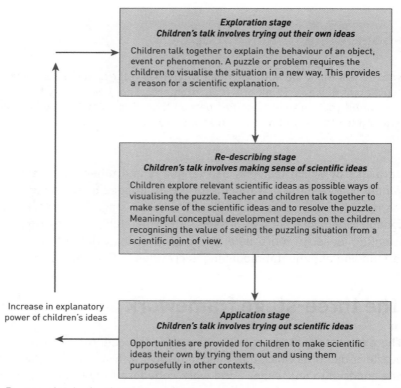

Exploration stage
Children's talk involves trying out their own ideas

Children talk together to explain the behaviour of an object, event or phenomenon. A puzzle or problem requires the children to visualise the situation in a new way. This provides a reason for a scientific explanation.

Re-describing stage
Children's talk involves making sense of scientific ideas

Children explore relevant scientific ideas as possible ways of visualising the puzzle. Teacher and children talk together to make sense of the scientific ideas and to resolve the puzzle. Meaningful conceptual development depends on the children recognising the value of seeing the puzzling situation from a scientific point of view.

Increase in explanatory power of children's ideas

Application stage
Children's talk involves trying out scientific ideas

Opportunities are provided for children to make scientific ideas their own by trying them out and using them purposefully in other contexts.

Progression in the three-stage framework

Something to think about

The authors describe progression in children's science learning as developing children's existing ideas into bigger ideas with more explanatory power. What do you think they mean by explanatory power? Can you think of a big scientific idea which has explanatory power?

An example of the three-stage framework

This section provides an example of how to stage the development of children's understanding of the concept of dormancy. We do not provide a teaching plan but a brief outline to exemplify how the framework can be used in the classroom. This topic can be adapted for use with KS1 or KS2.

Topic: Dormancy

Many living things have evolved in ways which enable them to make best use of the environment in which they live. For many organisms this mean remaining in a state of dormancy until the conditions are right for growth and development.

Title: Sleepy autumn

Scientific view

Living things have evolved in ways which best enable them to survive and reproduce. Living things in a particular habitat compete for available resources. At times of the year when the weather is cold and food is scarce, some living things find that it is an advantage to remain dormant until conditions improve. Both plants and animals are sensitive to changes in temperature in ways that induce or end dormancy.

Exploratory stage

Children's talk involves trying out their own ideas

Setting the scene

Set the scene for the children's learning by taking them to a local park or woodland to find out what happens to plants in autumn. Before setting out, children can talk together about what they would expect to see on their walk. The following statements can be used as talking points. Ask children to discuss in groups whether they think these ideas are true, false or if their group is unsure. Admitting uncertainty should be highlighted as being very useful because it helps to establish what we need to find out. (For further information about talking points see Chapter 4.)

Talking points

- We would expect to see lots of plants with flowers growing in autumn.
- In autumn leaves turn brown because the trees die.
- In autumn bushes create berries and seeds for birds to eat.
- In autumn we would expect to see birds building their nests to keep warm in winter.
- There will be no insects or other small creatures in the wood.

Discuss children's responses to the talking points. Examine the reasons for their answers and assess what the children know about woodlands during autumn.

Scientific enquiry

On the walk collect a range of berries, seeds and different coloured leaves. Take tree/plant identification cards and find out names of trees which shed their leaves or produce seeds and fruits. Take photographs of a variety of trees, bushes and any animals which are around. Check under fallen wood and in leaf litter for evidence of animal life.

Things to talk about on the walk:

- Why are some trees losing their leaves? What could be happening to them?
- What is going to happen to the berries on the bushes? What is inside the berries?
- Why are there so many seeds on the ground? What's going to happen to them?
- What will the park/woodland look like later in the winter?
- How do the plants know it is autumn?

Back in the classroom, children can make autumn displays from their photographs and objects they collected on the walk. Children can talk together about what they saw on their walk. Compare with their responses to the talking points. Were children surprised by what they observed? Can they identify anything they have learned, or ask a question to share with other children?

Puzzle

What will happen to the woodland berries and seeds as the weather becomes colder in the winter? When will the seeds start to grow (germinate)? How can seeds tell when to germinate?

Scientific enquiry

Encourage the children to suggest solutions to the puzzle. Using fast-growing seeds such as bean sprouts or cress, some questions and ideas can be tested in the classroom. Help children to identify key variables such as temperature and water availability. Encourage children to think how they can simulate winter, spring and summer temperatures. Children can establish through guided enquiry that seeds need water, air and a specific range of temperatures to germinate.

Formative assessment

Encourage the children to interpret the results of their enquiry in ways which can help solve the puzzle. Talk together about children's ideas and assess what they know about deciduous trees, and the concept of dormancy.

Something to think about

What do you think is the purpose of the 'talking points'? Can you think of any other talking points which you would want to add?

Re-describing stage

Children's talk involves making sense of scientific ideas

Use children's ideas as points for discussion. Solving the puzzle depends on children coming to understand that seeds can respond to changes in the world around them. Seeds are sensitive to changes in temperature in a way which determines when the conditions are right to grow. Different seeds need different conditions for germination and growth, but most seedlings would not thrive in winter conditions of low temperature and little light. Introduce the scientific word 'dormant' to describe seeds which are living, but inactive until the conditions are suitable for germination and growth. Help children to articulate their interpretation of the term. What words would they use to describe the inactivity of seeds during winter? What other living things exhibit dormancy? How does this advantage or disadvantage them?

Scientific enquiry

Children can use information sources to find out conditions which seeds in different parts of the world require to germinate. They can investigate the role that smoke and fire play in the germination of some types of seeds. Children can present findings in ways that help them to communicate their ideas and establish new questions that arise.

Assessment and further learning

Use the children's interpretation of dormancy and their presentations to assess their progress. What else would they like to find out? Children can raise and investigate their own questions.

Something to think about

Children may not use the word 'dormant' to explain the seeds' condition but they may use equivalent words. What other words could they use which would not represent misconceptions? Explain why.

Something to think about

The purpose of the re-describing stage is to help the children solve the puzzle by thinking about it from a scientific point of view. How would you organise and manage the children's learning in this stage?

Application stage

Children's talk involves trying out scientific ideas

Return to some of the original talking points

In autumn the leaves of deciduous trees turn brown and fall. Encourage children to apply their understanding of dormancy to explain what they think is happening to the trees. What conditions will cause the trees to grow again? Why do some trees not lose their leaves in autumn/winter?

Exploring dormancy in common animals

Children can explore other types of livings things which use dormancy as a survival strategy. Many cold-blooded animals such as snails and frogs hibernate over winter until spring brings a plentiful supply of food. Children can use a range of information sources to enquire into the behaviour of the animals in the local woodland which hibernate. They could present their findings in the form of a news report with a title such as, 'The mystery of the abandoned woodland: where have all the animals gone?'

Link to music and dance

Children can use music and dance to depict the coming of spring when the dormant animals and plants once again start to become active. Animals returning from warmer climates can be included. The performance could be entitled 'The awakening' which could be a whole class activity or performed in smaller groups.

Something to think about

Do you think understanding the scientific view could change the way children perceive autumn in the local woodland? Explain why. How would you assess their understanding of the topic?

How the framework supports a storytelling approach

Exploratory stage: children's talk involves trying out their own ideas

The exploratory stage sets the scene for the children's learning. It is important that the context for science learning is both interesting and familiar and provides opportunities for the children to talk about the topic in their own words. During this stage children consider ideas to the point where they begin to recognise a need for a scientific explanation. Observations on the walk can lead to questions about what happens to seeds during winter and what conditions encourage growth. Understanding the concept of dormancy will help children to solve the puzzle of what happens to the woodland in autumn.

It is useful to think of the exploratory stage as the opening chapter of a short story in which the scene is set for the action to come. The context, events and activities in this part are arranged to arouse children's curiosity in the topic and to introduce a dilemma that requires resolution. It is important when planning the exploration stage to choose contexts which enhance the significance of the scientific view. Both storytelling and science teaching are dependent on the skilful use of language and context. When talking about successful story writing, Carver (2005) points out the importance of providing unique ways of describing the world and finding the right contexts in which to express them.

> Some writers (teachers) have a bunch of talent; I don't know any writers (teachers) who are without it. But a unique and exact way of looking at things, and finding the right context for expressing that way of looking (understanding), that's something else. (Carver, 2005: 32; our brackets for emphasis)

Contexts play an important role in both storytelling and science learning because they add meaning to the events and ideas involved. When presented in inappropriate contexts ideas can seem irrelevant and worthless. The same ideas when used in another context can appear insightful and inspirational. Choosing a context which has the potential to promote a scientific view of the world is an important part of planning a science lesson. Suitable contexts are those which are familiar enough for children to talk about from their own experiences, but also produce puzzling situations which scientific ideas can help to resolve. Activities in the exploration stage should focus on an event or phenomenon which is explored practically and discursively to the point where a scientific explanation is required to satisfy the children's curiosity.

Something to think about

Context plays an important role in children's science learning. Think how context has influenced your own science learning. Do you think an autumn walk in woodland is the right context in which to teach children about dormancy? Can you think of other contexts?

Re-describing stage: children's talk involves making sense of scientific ideas

In this stage, children explore scientific solutions to the dilemmas identified in the exploration stage. In the exploration stage, children have opportunities to use their personal ideas to explain the relevant events or phenomena; in the re-describing stage they are encouraged to see and talk about the same events from a scientific perspective.

> A new scientific insight involves a re-description of the phenomenon which is being studied. Whatever the topic of interest, there is a problem in making sense of it, and then progress is made when someone starts to visualise it in a new way, drawing on language which has not been used in this context before. Taking words from some other area of experience, then try them out in the new context, and use them as an aid to figuring out what is going on.
> (Sutton, 1996: 144)

Something to think about

Sutton suggests that when making sense of new phenomena, children need to draw on language from some other area of experience. What other areas of experience could children use to help them understand the concept of dormancy?

In our storytelling analogy the re-describing stage is the part of the story when conflicts and disagreements are resolved. In the science class this means revealing a scientific way of seeing the phenomenon or event which was the focus of discussion and enquiry in the exploration stage. The challenge for teachers is working out how to help children interpret this new vision in a way that will prove useful to them. Abstract ideas may be represented and communicated through words, symbols, gestures, actions, pictures, diagrams, physical models and mathematical formulae (Asoko and de Boo, 2001). These are mental modelling tools which children need to learn to use to make sense of scientific ideas (Chapter 3). In this stage children may need to use a combination of different representations or modelling strategies to help them appreciate the scientific view.

When planning for conceptual development, the choice of modelling strategies needs to be carefully matched to the scientific ideas being taught and to the children's existing knowledge and experience. The key is to choose representations of scientific ideas which link to and enrich existing mental representations which children already hold. This is why analogies are important tools for science learning. Analogies enable children to use their existing understanding to make sense of a new way of visualising the world. Strategies for modelling scientific ideas can be found in Chapter 6 and are part of 'Ideas for practice' presented in Part 2 of the book.

Something to think about

In your own words describe the purpose of the re-describing stage. What are the children re-describing? How should they be doing it? What should be the outcomes of the re-describing stage? How important is it that the children speak aloud; would writing achieve the same result?

Application stage: children's talk involves trying out scientific ideas

To personalise scientific ideas, children need to be persuaded that they can be applied usefully in a range of situations. The more often children use new ideas and language in appropriate contexts, the more meaningful these ideas will become. The learning goal is for children to develop their own accurate and functional mental models of the relevant scientific concepts so that they can make use of them in other contexts. For example, if a child understands the concept of dormancy in seeds, they should be able to apply this knowledge to explain why some trees lose their leaves in autumn and why certain animals hibernate. The bigger the scientific idea, the more widely and extensively it can be used to make sense of how the world works. The concept of gravity is a big idea because it not only helps to explain why things fall to ground, but is also useful when explaining how the solar system works and even how the universe was formed. Big ideas can change the way children visualise the world and provide much more powerful ways of interpreting events than their own intuitive models. The purpose of the application stage is to provide an opportunity for the children to apply their new knowledge in another context in order for them to experience and hence develop an appreciation of its explanatory power. In this stage, children use their new scientific knowledge to construct explanatory narratives about situations which they have not previously explored.

The ability to apply ideas in different contexts is a measure of children's understanding; the application stage provides opportunities to assess children's progress.

Something to think about

What does the word 'functional' mean to you? How can scientific ideas be functional? Compare a scientific idea which you think is useful with one which has no use. Is functionality just about the idea or is it more to do with context? Could one idea be useful to one person and useless to someone else?

The application stage can be set in a wide range of contexts, both scientific and cross-curricular. Cross-curricular contexts need to be chosen carefully so that they help to promote the value of the scientific ideas (Chapter 7). The 'Ideas for practice' in Part 2 provide a range of examples of how scientific ideas can be used in cross-curricular settings.

Summary

Effective teaching involves persuading children of the value of the scientific ideas we want them to learn. This can be done by organising children's learning so that they become engaged with the resolution of a puzzle. To resolve the puzzle, children can work collaboratively to share ideas and make sense of the scientific view. Meaningful learning depends on the children appreciating the explanatory power of the scientific view and how it can provide them with useful ways of thinking and talking about the world.

Summary of stages

1. *Exploratory*: children are puzzled, intrigued and involved in a quest for understanding.
2. *Re-describing*: children explore ways of resolving the dilemma by developing an understanding of the situation from a scientific point of view.
3. *Application*: children are provided with opportunities to appreciate the usefulness of their new scientific understanding by applying it to other contexts.

The next chapter looks at the nature of understanding and why meaningful learning is dependent on children recognising the usefulness of the scientific ideas we teach them. The chapter emphasises the role language plays in teaching and learning science.

CHAPTER 3
SCIENTIFIC UNDERSTANDING AND MENTAL MODELS

We can only talk about things we understand. Children's understandings, based on their everyday ideas of the world, may have limited power to explain observations. We can use science teaching to help children to see that a more scientific point of view offers the chance of more reliable explanations. The ways we think – our mental models – are bound up with the language in which they are framed.

Topics discussed in this chapter:

- The relationship between mental models and understanding
- How talk underpins mental modelling
- How science learning involves talking about the world in new ways
- Behind every concept is a fascinating story

Mental models and understanding

What do we mean by understanding?

Our ability to talk about an object, event or phenomenon is dependent on our understanding of it (Borges and Gilbert, 1999). This may seem self-evident; but what do we actually mean by 'understanding'? Imagine what goes through your mind when on entering a room someone asks you to 'pull up a chair'. To understand this request you need to have in your mind a picture or model of the state of affairs these words represent. You need to know what a chair looks like and how it is used. You also need to have a mental representation of the actions which relate to the word 'pull' within this context. That is, you can create a representation or simulation of how you are required to act in your mind (Greca and Moreira, 2000).

We have in our minds representations of a vast array of states of affairs, objects, sequences of events and processes which help us understand and make sense of how the world works. These 'mental models' help us to make predictions, to understand phenomena and events, to make decisions and control our actions. Our ability to talk about and explain an event or phenomenon depends on the nature of the representation inside our brains. To fully understand a situation so that we can explain it to others, we must have a working mental model of it (Borges and Gilbert, 1999).

Now imagine you are an alien, visiting Earth from the planet Rijal IV and you have never seen a chair; but you have owned a dog. Both have four legs. Your dog barks and uses its legs to move. Based on this model, it is possible that you may expect a chair to do the same. Experience would soon tell you that your understanding of how a dog behaves is not a very useful model for predicting the purpose and behaviour of the chair. You would need to think about it in a different way with the help of someone who understood more about chairs than you. This is perhaps an extreme example, but helps to show that we use existing mental models as a basis for making sense of new situations. If we apply inappropriate mental models then we are likely to misinterpret key aspects of a situation.

Example   A muddled mental model

A teacher was at the pond with three under-5s from the Reception class when this conversation took place with one of them.

T: Ducks. What do you think they are covered in, Cerelia?

C: Silk.

T: Silk, hmm. And how do they float?

C: They swim. But when they get out you can only see their back legs.

T: Back legs? How many legs do they have?

C: Four.

T: *(astonished but suddenly visualising all the ducks doing doggy-paddle)* Well! Only two really. They've turned their front legs into wings I think.

C: *(amused)* Hah!

Comment

The child had looked at the ducks' shape and with little experience of birds (indeed maybe not knowing that ducks are birds) had imagined they had four legs like a cat or a dog. Confronted with the teacher's idea of two legs, she was not yet ready to change her mind. The child required further experience of how birds differ from other animals in order to develop a reliable mental model.

When it comes to understanding the natural world, children's mental models can be very imaginative, but also limited and unreliable. The purpose of science learning is to help them develop mental representations of the natural world which are reliable and therefore more useful than their existing models.

Something to think about

Picture in your mind how electricity flows through wires. What do you imagine? Do you picture electricity as sparkly things in the wire or perhaps like a flash of lightning from the battery? Draw a picture of your mental model. Do you think your model is muddled or clear?

Children need to be persuaded of the usefulness of the scientific view

Children come to understand the world by constructing working representations of it in their minds (Johnson-Laird, 1983). These models may not be accurate or complete but are useful to the individual who uses them. A child may visualise a battery as a container full of electricity which slowly empties out when connected in a circuit. This is not scientifically accurate but it is useful because it enables the child to explain why some batteries light up bulbs more brightly than others and why a battery goes flat over time. It is consistent with the child's experiences and enables them to predict accurately how a simple circuit will behave. This is why misconceptions are often so hard to redress. Children are often reluctant to replace a simple and trusted mental representation with a more complex model unless they can be persuaded that it is more useful, or that their own model is untrustworthy.

The problem with simple intuitive models is that they can only adequately explain a small range of effects. For example, the model of the battery as a reservoir of electricity cannot fully explain why we need a circuit; why this must be connected to each battery terminal in order to light up a bulb. Why do we need a path in and out of the battery if the electricity is stored in the battery and used up in the bulb? For this model we only need one path for the electricity to flow along. The child's intuitive model cannot explain this. Scientific concepts are representations of the natural world which can be relied on in a wide range of situations. In other words, they have more explanatory power than children's intuitive models. Teaching science involves promoting the usefulness of the conceptual models that science has produced and striving to show or persuade children that it is worth making the effort to understand them. Persuading children that scientific models are useful tools for interpreting, explaining and exploring events and phenomena in the natural world is an important part of effective science teaching.

Something to think about

What happens inside the filament of the bulb to cause it to glow? Can you use your mental model of electricity to explain this or is it starting to let you down? How functional is your mental model? How much explanatory power does it provide? Do you think you need to amend it?

Talk underpins mental modelling

The ability of a child to talk about a concept is linked to their understanding of it. Therefore talk should underpin conceptual learning in the classroom. To help children develop a useful way of visualising a concept we need to encourage them to talk about it and to listen to different explanations. For example, consider the transcript 'The pupil' below, a teaching episode in which a group of children are discussing how the pupil in the eye works.

Example   The pupil

A group of children discuss whether or not it is true that the pupil in the eye opens wider in the dark.

Alex: *(reading)* 'The pupil of the eye opens wide in the dark.' Hmm.

Bryn: Yes.

Alex: Opens wide *(using hands to show opening)* like, what opens wide, a door, your mouth . . .

Bryn: The pupil, what, what is . . .

Alex: The black round bit. That bit *(points to B's eyes)*.

Bryn: Hey! mind out.

Alex: Shh, and so when it's dark, it opens it says here, opens . . .

Samia: But look, I think untrue, because your eyelids open, not your eye . . .

Bryn: Yes *(blinks rapidly a few times)*.

Samia: . . . and anyway you open your eyes in the day not in the dark.

Bryn: Yes.

Samia: You shut them to sleep at night and open them in the morning.

Alex: Hmmm. The pupil. How can it open *(group are quiet for a few moments)*.

Samia: False then. We say.

Comment

As part of a topic on light, children were presented with the talking point 'The pupil of the eye opens wide in the dark' and were asked to discuss whether they thought it was true or false. The purpose of the discussion was to encourage the children to think together about how their eyes work in different light conditions. (See Chapter 4 for the uses of talking points and the nature of *exploratory talk* which they are designed to promote.)

Children's ideas

The children consider their understanding of how the pupil opens, in comparison with that of their group mates. The word 'open' in this context causes some confusion. Alex's image of the pupil opening like a door on a hinge is misleading and cannot explain how the pupil works. Since opening and closing of the eyelids is more obvious, this is the focus for the children's talk. In the absence of a reliable model for how the pupil opens, the children conclude that the statement is false. This conversation helps the teacher to find out what the children need to know. They need further experience or explanation of the mechanism by which the pupil opens and closes, and to think about reasons why it does so.

Helping children to re-describe how the pupil opens

In response to the children's ideas the teacher intervened to help them rethink how the pupil could open and let in more light. The teacher encouraged all groups to share a wider range of ideas. She used a simulation to explain how the pupil allows light to enter the eye. She encouraged the children to continue talking about their understanding of the concept; could other vocabulary provide more useful representations? The teacher continued to prompt the children to critically reflect on their description of the pupil and encouraged them to provide alternative ideas. As the transcript 'I think expand' indicates, she prompted the children to describe what they observed in their own words. This intervention was intended to help the children to choose words which provided clearer or more insightful ways of describing and talking about how the pupil works.

Example   I think expand

Teacher intervenes to help children choose useful words to re-describe how the pupil opens wider in the dark

Teacher: OK let's try to use another word instead of 'pupil'. Now you've had a look what other words could we use? Bryn?

Bryn: Well it's the dark bit of the eye.

Alex: It's dark and round.

Samia: Like a dark hole.

Teacher: That's interesting Samia. Why do you say it's a hole?

Samia: It looks like a hole.

Teacher: OK a hole is a good way of thinking about it, a hole which lets light get into our eyes. But now do you think holes open and close? What other words?

Alex: Well holes do open and close.

Bryn: Open wider.

Alex: I think expand.

Teacher: OK expand. We might be able to see if we can make it change . . . we could blindfold one of you and one of you could look at a book in bright light . . . what do you think?

Comment

When Samia described the pupil as a hole, the teacher reinforced this useful idea and used the same vocabulary to explain how light enters the eye. The description of the pupil as a hole enabled the children to imagine that it could get bigger and smaller – it could open wider or expand. This is a 'change of mind' from their earlier conception of a door opening and closing. The children went on to use mirrors and magnifiers to observe how the size of their own pupil changed in different light conditions. The conversation continued using the children's words to describe their observations. During the plenary discussion the teacher introduced the scientific terms 'contraction' and 'dilation' to describe the changes that the children had observed.

This example highlights the crucial importance of spoken language as a mental modelling tool. In this case, the topic was taught over a series of lessons using a range of different strategies. The intended outcome of the lesson was to enable the children to visualise how the pupil controlled the amount of light entering the eye. Once the children had a useful mental model, the use of physical models, analogies and carefully explained vocabulary could develop deeper understanding.

Something to think about

In the transcript 'I think expand' the teacher intervened to help the children choose useful words to describe how the pupil works. Why are these words effective? What difference did the discussion make to the children's developing ideas? Is it helpful to describe spoken language as a tool for mental modelling?

The differences between the children's initial ideas and the scientific view represent the changes that need to occur in the children's thinking if effective learning is to be achieved (Scott, 1998). In this case, conceptual development required the children to rethink their original understanding of how things can open. Once they were able to re-describe the concept in terms of widening or expanding, they were able to develop a useful mental model of how the pupil works.

Something to think about

In the first two chapters we point out the need for children to talk concepts into existence. What does this mean when we consider mental modelling? Can you explain or give an example to illustrate this idea: 'Children need to talk science concepts into mental models'?

Big ideas have more explanatory power

In a later activity the children drew pictures to show how the pupil controls the amount of light entering the eye. This involved talking about how light travels in straight lines. The concept of light travelling in straight lines is a 'big idea' because it can be used to interpret and explain a wide range of phenomena. It can be used to explain how the behaviour of light enables us to see and locate objects. It can also be used to explain shadows and how images are formed in mirrors and lenses. Conceptual development involves providing children with progressively more explanatory power by helping them interpret and learn to use some of science's big ideas. Using newly acquired scientific ideas for different purposes helps children to become more familiar with such ideas and to adopt them for their personal use. Once scientific ideas are personalised as mental models they can become part of the way children perceive the world.

Something to think about

Understanding how light travels in straight lines is a big idea because it offers much explanatory power. In other words, it can be used to explain the behaviour of light in a wide range of situations. What are the big ideas associated with sound? Which ideas have the most explanatory power?

Learning to talk about the world in new ways

The two transcripts exemplify the idea that an exploration of language is just as important for children's understanding of scientific concepts as is practical exploration. Science educator and philosopher Joan Solomon evocatively describes the process of science learning for children as similar to 'arriving on a foreign shore, or struggling with a conversation in an unknown language' (Solomon, 1994: 16). She describes science learning in terms of a child listening in on a family conversation and trying to make sense of what the adults are talking about.

> Imagine an alternative picture of pupil learning. A young student sits outside a circle of disputing scholars picking up fragments of conversation and trying to piece them together. Once we were all that child, the family were the circle and we turned over phrases that we heard until they built up into an idea. We tried out the sense of it, and occasionally we were amusingly wrong. If we were lucky no one laughed. Then it was explained once more in helpful ways and with good games to go with the learning of it. When we tried again and the half-formed idea seemed to be accepted by others, it became stronger. Kindly adults encouraged us to use it in new ways: our understanding and pride in using it grew. The idea gradually became ours and, by the same token, we became a part of the privileged and knowing circle who uses it.
> (Solomon, 1994: 17)

Something to think about

What do you think of Solomon's description of science learning as 'struggling with a conversation in an unknown language'? Is this as a useful analogy? What implications does it have for the way we teach science?

Children's language and scientific words

Solomon's description of science as an alien culture implies that children need to learn the language of science as they engage meaningfully in science activity. But learning how to speak a different language is not the same as simply learning words. A word becomes part of a child's language when they 'populate it with their own intent and adapt it for their own purposes' (Wertsch, 1991: 59). To make sense of a scientific word children must use their own language and ideas, creating a representation or model in their minds. Fostering this process in the classroom involves organising conversations in which children can put new ideas into their own words, trying out recently heard vocabulary. They need opportunities to engage with new thinking and to articulate their tentative understandings. Learning does not happen at the instant a new idea is encountered, but is a cumulative process in which previous conceptions, vocabulary and images are tested and amended over time. The use of scientific vocabulary is important if a child is to gain confidence in their ability to express complex ideas with clarity and accuracy. The accumulation of a wide vocabulary requires chances to understand words in action and to use words with other learners. Such events as forgetting words or using them erroneously are invaluable experiences when they happen in supportive classroom contexts. Children may never hear particular words used in a scientific context anywhere else; we need to provide every opportunity for children to hear, speak, read, write, describe, explain and query unfamiliar words such as *photosynthesis*, *respiration*, or *invertebrate*; or familiar words in unfamiliar contexts, such as *force*, *material* or *energy*.

Something to think about

What do you think Wertsch means when he says that a word becomes part of children's language when they 'populate it with their own intent and adapt it for their own purposes'? Consider the three-stage framework in the light of Wertsch's view. Does it provide opportunities for children to make sense of scientific words and then to adapt them and use them for other purposes?

Talking to develop a shared point of view

Scientific words have meanings linked to their origins. For example, the word 'pollen' is derived from the Greek word meaning 'fine flour'. This analogy was a useful way for the ancient Greeks to visualise and talk about the substance they found inside a wide range of flowers. Pollen, like flour, is a light and dusty material which can be dispersed by wind or animals. Children can observe and examine flour, pollen and other fine powders such as talc, and use their own words to describe them. They can think of different ways to describe or label pollen. They can share their individual ideas and evaluate which offers the most meaningful explanatory power; what is the best way to describe, explain and clarify the purpose of pollen. Children need opportunities to use spoken language to make their ideas explicit – to one another and to themselves. This type of classroom discourse is what Sutton (1996) describes as 'talking around a topic'.

> To persuade someone into your point of view requires talking around the topic until shared meanings are developed. The teacher's personal voice is important, but learners must also have freedom of re-expression. In order to be able to hear scientists' language as expressions of thought and not just 'description' of nature they must understand language as an interpretive tool, and that means having experience of using it in that way themselves.
> (Sutton, 1996: 147)

Behind every concept is a fascinating story

The German physician and botanist Rudolf Jakob Camerarius (1665–1721) is credited with describing sexual reproduction in plants. He identified stamens and pollen as the male parts and style, stigma and ovaries as the female parts. He described the mechanism of pollination. Charles Darwin interpreted pollination as 'acts of contrivances' between plants and animals, envisaging a profound and mysterious collaboration between plant and pollinator.

To these scientists the act of pollination wasn't simply the transfer of pollen from the anther of one plant to the stigma of another: it was far more exciting and intriguing than that. Pollination can be explained as a story which describes the intricate and vital relationships between specific plants and animals. Such stories raise their own questions. How did the relationship develop? Why does it continue? What happens to the pollinator if the plant dies out, and vice versa? Pollination is a real-life drama which children can narrate in their own words. But pollination is also a rather abstract scientific concept. In the classroom, it can be 'talked into existence' in ways that help children understand its explanatory power.

> Words can have a power and influence quite out of proportion to their triviality as mere marks on paper or vibrations in the air. When circumstances are right they can excite people's minds and move their imaginations, in science as in any other area of human activity.
> (Sutton, 1992: 1)

Something to think about

The 'Goldilocks Zone' is a term that present-day scientists use to describe extremely distant solar systems which could support life. The Goldilocks Zone contains planets which are not too hot or too cold to support life; they are just right! What is your favourite scientific term? Can you find out the story behind it?

Summary

Children create in their minds complex working models which help them to talk about and explain their experiences. These mental models can be useful but are often unreliable when applied more widely. Scientific concepts offer more reliable ways of visualising how the natural world works. Effective science teaching helps children to make sense of the scientific view and learn to appreciate its explanatory power. Talk is the child's most powerful tool for understanding the scientific view. In the next chapter we examine the nature of classroom talk and look at how different kinds of talk can help children understand the world in scientific ways.

Further reading

Books

- Mortimer, E. F. and Scott, P. H. (2003) *Meaning Making in Secondary Science Classrooms*, Buckingham: Open University Press.

  A secondary science book relevant to primary science teaching.

- Sutton, C. (1992) *Words, Science and Learning*, Buckingham: Open University Press.

- Sutton, C. (1996) 'The scientific model as a form of speech', in G. Welford, J. Osborne and P. Scott (eds), *Research in Science Education in Europe*, London: Falmer Press.

CHAPTER 4
TALK FOR LEARNING IN SCIENCE

**A great deal of education is to do with learning how to use language –
to represent ideas, to interpret experiences, to formulate problems
and to solve them.**
(Mercer, 1995)

Why do we need to give speaking and listening – talk – special attention when
we think about teaching science? And having focused on talk, what sort of talk is
of most educational value? If we are convinced that talk is important for science
learning, how can we ensure that children's talk is educationally effective? And
finally, what are the implications for talk between ourselves as teachers, and the
children we teach?

Topics discussed in this chapter:

- The importance of talk for learning in science
- Exploratory talk and its ground rules
- Dialogic teaching and children's ideas
- Talking points: a strategy to promote effective talk

The importance of talk for learning in science

Piaget tells us that children learn through interacting with the world. Play and exploration start with children's curiosity and their (maybe unspoken) questions: 'What happens if I keep squashing this plasticene?' 'What if I touch ice – how will it feel?' The chance to play provides the child with information from which they make meaning. The child adds newly gained experience to what they have already understood. If new experience doesn't fit, the child accommodates their new experience by changing what they think: that is, they learn from the experience. They develop a story or model that fits with what they 'know'. If new experience does not fit previous models, the child may rethink. For example, a child who has never played with jelly, seen a hamster or banged a drum will attend to the new input from their senses and find that it does not match with what they already know. This 'failure' to understand prompts the child to generate new ideas (such as, some red materials are sticky; small furry creatures are not all inanimate toys; if you hit round things they bang). Piaget envisaged the child as a 'lone scientist', engaged in constant enquiry and continually faced with the puzzle of new experience and evidence which creates questions in the mind. The child engages in empirical enquiry; up against problems of understanding, they resolve these by reconsidering or, as Huxley puts it, by *giving up their preconceived notions*.

> Sit down before fact as a little child, be prepared to give up every preconceived notion . . . or you shall learn nothing.
> (Thomas H. Huxley, biologist, 1825–95)

But children are rarely alone; and they learn from one another, and from adults, as they talk. As the child acquires language, experience of how the world works can be shared and speculated about to reach tentative conclusions. The child's wish to communicate their experiences pushes the limits of language and enables development. The Russian psychologist Lev Vygotsky, studying children's interactions, recognised that the use of spoken language helps us to interpret experience, to explain and describe our ideas to one another and, in doing so, to learn from and with one another. The child's quest for meaning is radically altered by speaking and listening. Children learn about the world through talk with others; simultaneously they are developing their capacity to use the medium of language. In science classrooms we can organise particularly powerful ways to think and speak. Learning to talk like scientists provides children with a transferable learning tool with which to question, assert, explain, hypothesise, reflect . . . and more.

It is the link between speaking, listening, thinking and learning which makes talk so important in science classrooms. We can provide children with fascinating experiences and thoughtful resources; but unless we also provide them with opportunities to discuss what they are doing, their chance to learn is diminished. But there is a problem for the classroom teacher. Learning depends on talk focused on the task in hand, and it is very easy for children to distract one another. What will drive the talk, the need to be social, or the need to learn? Will children engage with one another's minds openly, or will they fiercely defend their own ideas with no thought of others? Will they withdraw and let others do the talking; or, while others talk, will their minds be entirely occupied by formulating their own next contribution? As teachers, we know how easy it is for children to lose concentration, and how enticing are the distractions offered by others. But our concern about talk should not mean that we silence children. It should remind us that children need help to understand the importance and purpose of their discussion, and that we need to provide them with the language tools which will help them to think and learn through talk.

Something to think about

Are children aware of the value of discussing ideas? Do they understand how to provide their opinion, with reasons, and how to negotiate what they think with other children? What do they say when asked these things? Do they recognise the importance of talk for their own learning? Can we teach them this?

Exploratory talk and its ground rules

What makes a good discussion? What are the features of the children's interaction which will really help them to think and learn? Asked these questions, both teachers and children commonly agree that those taking part in a discussion should:

- listen attentively;
- include everyone in the discussion;
- ask questions;
- share all relevant information openly;
- challenge one another's ideas and opinions with respect;
- ask for and give reasons for ideas;
- seek to reach a group agreement before proceeding.

Science educator Douglas Barnes, listening to group work in science classrooms (Barnes, 1976), described hearing the sort of talk detailed above, in which children were hesitant in their thinking yet confident to speak out. Their views were aired and examined, and all seemed to be engaged in a joint quest for understanding. He described this as exploratory talk. Exploratory talk is talk in which everyone is invited to give their ideas and to challenge one another respectfully, share information, and give and ask for reasons. Contributions may be hesitant but children are confident to articulate their new thinking. There is active listening and interest in different points of view. Children are aware of the importance of the discussion and know that it is a strength to change their mind in response to a good reason or line of thinking. Everyone seeks to reach an agreement.

Exploratory talk is educationally effective talk, because it enables children to share their thinking, and helps groups to do better than each child could have done alone. It is this sort of talk that we want to hear in science classrooms.

Class ground rules for exploratory talk

Classes benefit from devising a set of 'rules' which help everyone to remember that talk is crucial for learning, and that the invaluable chance to discuss their science with each other can only happen in the special setting of the classroom. We can ask the children what rules they would use to ensure 'a good discussion'. Collect a short list of rules, making sure that these embody the principles of exploratory talk (for example, 'We will all listen carefully' – and not, for example, 'Don't speak until you are asked'). Ask the class to sign up to using their rules during science. Have the rules visible and refer to them often. Ensure that they are used as learning intentions and discussed in plenary sessions. Adapt them if they are not working. Unless teachers help children to share these rules, they will talk to one another as if they were in a social setting, with all the ensuing problems including that of learning falling away. This is not because children are wilfully difficult, but because each has a different understanding of what 'talk together . . .' means.

Outcomes of teaching talk for learning

Children taught how to discuss things with one another, and who have an understanding of exploratory talk, can be heard to make more use of such phrases as 'What do you think? Why do you think that?' The words 'think' and 'because' are more frequently used. Learning proceeds through joint enquiry. Children in science classrooms need to be awarene of their importance to one another – their responsibility for ensuring that time is spent on productive discussion. In science, we can teach children that spoken language is not just for giving information but for 'interthinking' (Mercer, 2000). Interthinking is the use of spoken language to support thinking together – collectively making sense of experience and solving problems. It enables the dynamic interaction of minds, and is the best use of the social nature of human thinking. Talk is the child's tool for interthinking and every child can learn to use talk this way.

Dialogic teaching and children's ideas

So far we have considered the child's discussion with their classmates. But much learning depends on whole-class sessions led by the teacher. How do the ideas of exploratory talk and interthinking fit with what happens in whole-class talk? Psychologist Jerome Bruner noticed that teachers provide learners with a special sort of help as they tackle a new task or idea. He described the help as 'scaffolding', a powerful metaphor to indicate the way that support could be provided, and gradually withdrawn as a learner becomes more independent (Bruner, 1986).

A child may be able to read a thermometer, but may not know what is being measured. The thermometer in a mix of ice and salt may read −8°C. The child may say, 'It's measuring the cold'. We, as teachers, know what it is that the child needs to know; we also know that to provide a lecture on thermodynamics would not help them at all. We know that small steps and a clear context for new vocabulary is a good way to proceed, and that modelling a task can help. We know that talking the child through the process or concept means that at any stage the child can put to use the safety net of questioning. So this is what we do. As Bruner puts it, we reduce the degrees of freedom so that success is possible – whether in acquiring a skill, or understanding a concept. This is scaffolding. We use scaffolding, through talk, to break down the task into achievable steps and move the child through it, then check if they are able to do it alone.

> The essence of the concept of scaffolding is the sensitive, supportive intervention of a teacher in the progress of a learner who is actively involved in some specific task, but who is not quite able to manage the task alone. [. . .] A crucial quality of scaffolding is that it is the provision of guidance and support which is increased or withdrawn in response to the developing competence of the learner.
> (Mercer, 1995: 74 and 75)

Exploratory talk tends to happen amongst groups of equals – it is symmetrical. Teacher-led discussion is *asymmetric*, in that the teacher is expected to organise and shape the talk. Whole class dialogue between a teacher and class is like exploratory talk in that it may be grounded in children's experience, conducted with respect, and show visible questioning and reasoning throughout. It is different from exploratory talk in that it has the teacher's idea of what children might accomplish built in. We can describe a particularly productive sort of talk between teachers and their classes as *dialogic teaching*. Dialogic teaching is particularly effective in science.

What is dialogic teaching?

> Dialogic teaching harnesses the power of talk to engage children, stimulate and extend their thinking, and advance learning and understanding.
> (Alexander, 2006: 27)

Dialogic teaching is described by educational researcher Robin Alexander as teaching that leads to effective classroom discussions and, ultimately, to deeper learning. Through dialogue, teachers find out what children think, engage with their developing ideas and help them to overcome misunderstandings. We can recognise dialogic teaching when we hear sustained contributions from children, with children listening and responding to their classmates. Another characteristic of a good dialogue is that the teacher helps children to express their ideas and generates a linked discussion. Children have time to think. They have access to one another's ideas in the same way as they might during exploratory talk, but the ideas are ushered in a purposeful direction by the teacher's intervention.

In summary, by talking about their science in small groups, or taking part in a whole-class dialogue, children can:

- articulate their everyday ideas;
- hear a range of alternative points of view;
- ask for and listen to reasons and evidence;
- create and elaborate on a science story;
- ask questions and express uncertainty;
- consider new ideas and change their mind.

As a bonus for the teacher, the chance to hear children talking is an invaluable assessment opportunity.

Something to think about

What are the barriers that stop children from contributing to whole class discussion? Do all children feel that they can say what they have found out, describe their confusion, elaborate on ideas, or ask a question stimulated by their science activities? Are children directly taught how to do these things and, if not, why?

The transcript 'Thicker wire' is an example of a dialogue in a Year 6 classroom. The class had spent two sessions studying circuits, including considering electrical resistance. The extract begins as the teacher, drawing a circuit on a flip chart, provides information and then checks for understanding of specific scientific vocabulary.

Example   Thicker wire

T: This is a kind of, um, virtually an electronic whiteboard here, you have to imagine . . . So when this current is going along a wire there's a certain sort of, well, what do you think resistance means? Can you think of a good sentence with 'resistance' in that's *not* to do with electricity? What do you resist doing, Logan?

L: I resist tidying up my room.

T: Perfect example. There's some friction about it, you resist tidying your room, the wire resists the current – so a very thin wire like that, in a light bulb [. . .] because it's resisting so much, it's giving out loads of light, and a bit of heat. OK, have a think about this; if you've got this *thin* wire here with a *high* resistance, what would we do to create a low resistance, if we want the current to flow easily? Beatrice?

B: Um, have a thicker wire.

T: We could have a thicker wire couldn't we? And we'd have a low resistance.

→

K: Why low?

T: Because it lets the current flow more easily. If, if you've got *low resistance* to tidying your bedroom, that means your Mum said to you 'I'll give you £20 if you tidy your bedroom' and suddenly the resistance all goes away, doesn't it? 'Oh yes, I'll tidy my bedroom.' Thicker wire, lower resistance. Fletcher, in a minute I want to hear from you but not just now. We've got some thin wires and some thick wires over here, long wires and short wires. What difference do you think length will make? Daniel, what were you going to add?

D: I was just going to say we could, we could do some investigating on that.

T: You fancy having a go at trying out – investigating to see if you can see different resistances by looking at how well our bulbs light up. Right – is it important Fletcher?

F: I know another example of resistance. Sam's resisting to learn.

T: Oh, Sam's good at that.

Comment

The teacher asks for children's everyday ideas about resistance, reminding them that she would like to hear their thoughts. K asks for clarification (the confidence to show uncertainty is a feature of good dialogue) and the teacher provides a direct answer, reusing the familiar context of tidying a room suggested earlier by a classmate. One child (D) anticipates the teacher's suggestion and is already thinking ahead about setting up an investigation, while another takes the chance to make a joke about his friend. Knowing the child Sam to be both bright and hard-working, the teacher accepts this and moves on. Such dialogues, in which the class are relaxed but on task, commonly happen when a teacher and their class share an interest in science. In addition the children know that their suggestions are highly valued by the teacher and by one another. This is not perfect dialogic talk: for example, no child takes an extended turn. But it is a dialogic episode, helping to develop the children's thinking and learning.

Talking points: a strategy to promote effective talk

The idea of using a narrative approach to science necessarily involves creative thinking. Teachers have to create contexts which relate to children's everyday experience and simultaneously address learning intentions. Teacher and children between them must create the stories that will carry the narrative line of science thinking. Children need to be creative in the way they consider their own ideas and compare them with the ideas of others. Much of this groundwork for understanding science goes on through talk.

Some resources usefully promote talk in science. These may be concrete resources like magnets or electrical circuits or snails; a particular piece of software; Concept Cartoons (Naylor and Keogh, 2000); science poems or stories (Rosen, 2000); non-fiction books, or a classroom visitor such as a firefighter or dental nurse.

A particular resource which can promote talk in primary science is 'talking points' (Dawes, 2008a; 2008b). Talking points are designed to provide groups of children with starting points for their discussion. Talking points suggest a range of ideas, giving children a chance to match these with their own thinking while attending to what their classmates think. Children can express ideas which may be misconceptions, enabling the teacher to plan relevant future experiences. They can consider the limits of their own understanding in a 'safe' forum where it is acceptable and even interesting to admit, 'I don't know . . .' Working in a small group allows every child to speak and means that the group can support one another during subsequent whole-class discussion.

Teachers can generate, or teach children how to generate, their own talking points. Below are two examples. Children familiar with exploratory talk can be asked to work with others to decide if they agree or disagree with the ideas – or if they are unsure. Subsequent whole-class discussion orchestrated by the teacher helps everyone to consider a range of points of view, share their thinking, establish areas of uncertainty for further work, and generally develop their vocabulary and ideas.

Talking points Example 1: small creatures

What does your group think of these ideas? Are they true or false, and why do you think so?

1. All creepy crawlies are insects.
2. Insects eat plants.
3. Spiders are insects.
4. A woodlouse has more legs than a spider.
5. Slugs are snails which are out of their shells.
6. There is more than one sort of worm.
7. Ladybirds lay eggs and tiny ladybirds hatch out in summer.
8. Insects have six legs, so a caterpillar is not an insect.
9. Dragonflies are carnivores.
10. Some insects use camouflage to protect themselves.

Talking points Example 2: force

Talk together to decide if these statements are true or false, or is your group unsure?

1. A small object falls to the ground at the same speed as a large object.
2. Things stop when they run out of force.
3. A biro has a gravitational field and attracts other objects.
4. There is no gravity above the Earth's atmosphere.
5. The weight of an object measures how much stuff it's made up of.
6. A larger object has more air resistance.

7. A falling stone pulled by gravity is pushed up by air resistance.
8. You can reduce pressure by spreading weight out over a larger area.
9. The air is too light to be affected by the Earth's gravity.
10. Steel ships float because they have air in them.

Summary

Children use talk to explain their ideas, listen to others, ask questions, and develop their thinking. By talking with a science focus, children can develop science concepts and at the same time practise ways of talking which will stand them in good stead in other contexts. By sharing ideas, asking for and giving reasons, and keeping the talk on task, a group of children can make meaning from the experiences science exploration offers. Exploratory talk is educationally effective talk which enables interthinking. Teachers use talk to offer the careful support of scaffolding, and to generate classroom dialogue. Dialogic teaching involves teachers taking the lead in orchestrating whole-class discussion, encouraging children to elaborate, explain and link their contributions, and helping the whole group to attend and engage with ideas. By creating science stories, and moving between a more authoritative, explanatory style and episodes of dialogue, teachers can engage children in thinking about their everyday ideas of science towards a more scientific point of view. Talking points are a particular resource which can help to generate exploratory talk and provide a useful basis for closing plenary dialogue.

Further reading

Books

- Asoko, H. and Scott, P. (2006) 'Talk in science classrooms', in W. Harlen (ed.), *ASE Guide to Primary Science Education*, Hatfield: Association for Science Education.
- Dawes, L. (2008) *The Essential Speaking and Listening: Talk for Learning at Key Stage 2*, London: Routledge.
- Dawes, L. (2008) 'Encouraging students' contributions to dialogue during science', *School Science Review*, 90 (331): 1–7.
- Mercer, N. and Hodgkinson, S. (eds) (2008) *Exploring Talk in School*, London: Sage.

CHAPTER 5
SCIENTIFIC ENQUIRY AND THE PASSIONATELY CURIOUS

I have no special talents; I am only passionately curious.

(Albert Einstein)

Enquiry is at the heart of scientific activity. Very young children begin by using their senses to examine the world around them. Experience and observation give rise to questions as language skills develop. Finding out answers and generating new questions can help children to link what they already know to new experiences. Children are naturally curious – maybe even passionately curious – and we foster this in science. We can use practical activity, reasoning and narrative to help children develop their scientific understanding.

Topics discussed in this chapter:

- Science and discovery: what can we expect of children?
- The outcomes of scientific enquiry
- Scientific enquiry and its link to narrative

- Scientific skills and attitudes
- Types of scientific enquiry
- Choosing contexts for scientific enquiry

Science and discovery: what can we expect of children?

Questioning and learning

Children's questions may challenge our ability to provide explanations. Questions such as 'Why is the sky blue?', or 'Why do rabbits have such big white tails?' require some thinking through. Children like to be taken seriously and benefit from straightforward explanations using clear language. But when children ask more speculative questions, 'What would happen if we left my ice lolly in the Sun?' or 'Which coat should I wear now it's raining?', they are asking questions that can be explored through scientific enquiry. Enquiry activities can provide contexts for learning which are both real and familiar to children. Enquiry can provide a resolution to some problem or puzzling observation. It is this resolution which offers the child greater scientific understanding.

As the story 'Children exploring ice balloons' illustrates, scientific enquiries based on simple resources can catch children's imagination and enable them to see familiar events in new and exciting ways.

Example   Children exploring ice balloons

A class of 7- and 8-year-olds spent time exploring ice balloons, taking part in careful observational drawing, touching and listening. 'Why can I hear it crackle?' they asked. 'Why isn't it the same all the way through?' 'Will it melt?' 'Will a big ice balloon melt faster than lots of small ice cubes?' 'What does it weigh?' 'Why do my fingers stick to it?' Alistair wanted to know if the ice balloon would float. He suggested that although ice cubes float in fizzy drinks, the large ice balloon might be too heavy. A classmate remembered that icebergs float – was this the same thing? The children discussed what they knew about icebergs then tested their ideas by putting the ice balloon in a tank of water, where it floated. Watching this inspired Alistair to deeper thought. He noted that when he put the ice balloon in the water, the water level rose in the tank. His next question intrigued everyone. 'What will happen to the level of the water as the ice balloon melts?'

Comment

Alistair's engagement and need to know motivated him to spend the rest of the day exploring this puzzle. At intervals throughout the day he marked the level of water in the tank as the balloon melted and as he did so he became more and more puzzled. More investigation would be needed to answer his new questions. Alistair was passionately curious.

Exploring ice balloons
Source: Peter Loxley

Enquiries such as this provide opportunities to personalise children's learning. Raising their own questions increases children's engagement and stimulates curiosity. Children may not be able to discover the answers to every question from first-hand experience, but because the questions 'belong' to them they are likely to be keen to search for answers using enquiry and information sources.

Can we expect children to discover scientific ideas for themselves?

Research suggests that experience and practical work cannot always lead children towards accepted scientific views (Asoko, 2002). But it is evident that learning through enquiry is greatly enhanced when children have a chance to talk about what is happening. Children talking together have the chance to work out a valid explanation for a puzzling observation. Sometimes, no amount of practical exploration and exploratory talk will resolve a dilemma or answer the question, '*Why* does this happen?' Resolution of the problem may require teacher-led discussion, research using all the resources to hand, or even questioning an expert scientist.

The outcomes of scientific enquiry

The main purpose of scientific activity is to provide reliable knowledge about how the world works. As Feynman points out, the source of scientific knowledge is the interaction of experiment and the imagination of the experimenter.

> The principle of science, the definition, almost, is the following: The test of all knowledge is experiment. Experiment is the sole judge of scientific 'truth.' But what is the source of knowledge? Where do the laws that are to be tested come from? Experiment, itself, helps to produce these laws, in the sense that it gives us hints. But also needed is imagination to create from these hints the great generalizations, to guess at the wonderful, simple, but very strange patterns beneath them all, and then to experiment to check again whether we have made the right guess.
> (Feynman, 1964)

That is, theories about how the world works can be tested by investigation, to which individual scientists (including children) contribute their own unique perspective and ideas. Children's conclusions based on the findings of an enquiry are likely to contain elements of their first-hand experience. Some everyday ideas are firmly held. However, some ideas are correspondingly rather woolly and if children undertake a convincing enquiry they may be very willing to 'change their mind'. The outcomes of scientific enquiry should move children towards a more robust scientific point of view which holds water when tested and applied.

By involving children in scientific enquiry, we can provide them with an understanding of the nature of science. Scientific enquiry enables children to think and behave like scientists. They seek out reliable knowledge by employing first-hand experience, discussion, secondary sources and above all imagination. Imagination helps children to create tentative explanations (hypotheses) and devise enquiries to test their ideas. If an explanation proves inconsistent, they can explore alternatives until they arrive at a more reliable account.

Outcomes of scientific enquiry should enable children to understand and talk about familiar objects and events in new and more reliable ways. As the story 'Paper clips' illustrates, children's curiosity can lead them to create imaginative explanations.

Example   Paper clips

Year 2 were finding out which objects floated and which sank. The teacher asked Ria if she could explain why some things sank and others floated. Ria thought carefully and said that heavy things sank. The teacher asked Ria to think about why a paper clip had sunk although it wasn't heavy. Ria spent some time observing and considering the objects on the bottom of the tank of water. After a little thought she explained that there were scissors at the bottom of the tank and they were magnetic; paper clips were also magnetic so the scissors must have attracted the paper clip and pulled it to the bottom.

Comment

Ria's explanation for why a paper clip sank was highly imaginative and she was making sense of what she saw by drawing on prior learning. When encouraged to test her theory she found that paper clips are not normally attracted to scissors. The evidence showed that Ria's explanation was unreliable and that she needed to look for other reasons why the paper clip sank. It was the teacher's pertinent question, and the chance to discuss it, that provoked her to think about what she knew in order to try to explain what she saw. Without this dialogue, it is likely that Ria would have persisted with her misconception. The teacher had gained insight into what experience of floating and sinking Ria would need to help develop her ideas.

Scientific enquiry and its link to narrative

It is useful when teaching through scientific enquiry to think of a hypothesis as a kind of narrative created by the children. Such tentative descriptions, or personal narratives, are rooted in the child's existing experience and draw on personal stories about how the world works. For example, the story 'Honey bees' illustrates the type of personal narrative or hypothesis children can construct to explain an event which is very familiar to them.

Example   Honey bees

A class of 5-year-olds watched bees visiting a lavender bush in the school grounds. When talking with her teacher about this, Sarah described bees collecting honey from flowers and taking it back to their hive. She explained that when people wanted honey they could open the hive and scoop it out with a spoon to put in jars.

Children draw on their everyday experience and their imagination to suggest what a bee does with nectar. This story made perfect sense to Sarah and matched her experience of the natural world as designed to meet the needs of humans. Subsequent discussion and teaching could focus attention on other insects that visit flowers but do not produce honey. The children could be asked to tell their own story about what the bee actually collects, and what it does once it leaves a flower. Their enquiry can be enriched by video, web resources and picture story books such as Eric Carle's *The Honeybee and the Robber* (1981) to challenge the reliability of the children's own stories. Research and carefully supported discussion can enable children to modify their 'everyday' stories towards a more scientific point of view: in this case, to offer a better understanding of the crucial role insects play in the life cycle of the plant and how plants attract pollinators.

A teacher sets the scene for a science narrative by focusing children's attention on a topic, encouraging close observation and inviting them to offer their thoughts and ideas. The teacher may offer a challenge or a puzzle, or help the children to do so. The way children respond with ideas and explanations of what they observe will reflect their familiarity with how stories work. Younger children may suggest that things happen *because they do* ('that's the way things are'). More experienced children may devise a more complex storyline, either alone or through discussion following practical activity.

Children need to reach an understanding that they find believable but which also matches accepted scientific ideas. This achievement depends on activities and conversations that address the children's existing thinking and move the story on. It is the role of the teacher to provide new information, activities and guidance from which children can begin to build their own understanding. Children can usefully be encouraged to compare understanding by telling each other their stories before and after science activities.

Something to think about

Story books offer the chance to speculate, question and follow a narrative line of thinking, from puzzle to resolution. Can children identify these aspects of the science topic they are studying? Do they enjoy speculating about how things work or asking 'What if – ?' or 'What might happen?' Do they want to think, talk and puzzle it out? Or are they more inclined to 'get it over with' and try to rush to a conclusion? Can we teach the capacity to be curious or is it something children bring along – and that we must foster?

Scientific skills and attitudes

What really makes scientists special is less their knowledge than their method of acquiring it.
(Dawkins, 1998)

Like Kipling's mongoose, Rikki Tikki Tavi, children are 'eaten up from nose to tail with curiosity' but this does not necessarily make them scientists. In order to behave like scientists, children must develop the enquiry skills that will enable them to collect reliable evidence to test the validity of their ideas. Children also need to recognise and manage any hazards associated with their practical work.

As the skills needed to carry out scientific enquiry are mastered, the child becomes more independent in their learning. A scientific approach to enquiry relies on creative thinking to raise questions and form hypotheses, to make predictions and plan how to gather evidence using a range of techniques. Once evidence has been collected, it needs to be interpreted and conclusions drawn with reference to the original hypothesis. Finally, scientists must communicate their findings to a wider audience and be prepared to defend their assertions through careful evaluation of the reliability and validity of their enquiry process.

The development of positive scientific attitudes is also a crucial part of a child's science education. Attitudes that teachers can usefully foster include independence, perseverance, cooperation, respect for evidence, creativity and inventiveness, open-mindedness and respect for living things (de Boo, 2006). Attitudes are much more difficult to teach than skills: for example, a learning objective that says 'Today we are going to learn to persevere' may be somewhat optimistic. Teachers can model positive scientific attitudes, thinking aloud with the children and sharing enthusiasm for the work. Attitudes displayed by the teacher are crucial in shaping the quality of the learning experience for the children. Encouragingly, attitudes are flexible attributes, open to influence and dependent on experience and context. In science, we can create classroom contexts which help children experience strongly positive and socially useful attitudes.

Developing respect for evidence may be a particular challenge as children will arrive at school with a range of preconceptions about scientific concepts, e.g. 'Heavy things sink'. They also bring with them their own culture and experiences. In the story 'Child science investigators' a child exhibits an expectation of adult behaviour, based on her experience which underpins, and might interfere with, the interpretation of scientific data.

Example   Child science investigators

Year 5 children spent a day in their local University Science Education Department 'helping the police to solve a crime'. In the scenario, a lecturer had left her laptop containing her secret research on her desk, and it had been stolen. The investigators urgently needed to find the culprit. Clues left at the scene of the crime included fingerprints, a footprint, a shopping list, fibres and some soil from the criminal's shoes.

Five suspects had been identified, three women and two men, and the children were supplied with samples of their fingerprint; pens which might have been used to write the list; fibres, etc. The children tested the samples, matching findings against the clues and using their results as evidence to decide who was guilty of the crime.

 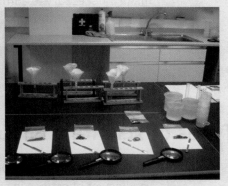

Crime scene investigations: (left) getting ready to match footprints found in the soil with types of shoe; (right) testing the type of soil found in the criminal's shoes
Source: Peter Loxley

> At the end of the day, the investigators gathered to present their evidence. Several children identified the criminal and explained how the evidence supported their conclusion. Then Melanie began her presentation. 'Well, I knew straight away it couldn't be one of the men,' she said, 'because one of the clues was a shopping list and men don't do the shopping.'

When children try to make sense of a situation, they bring their own culturally specific experience with them. In this scenario the 'criminal' actually was one of the women. It would have been interesting if it had been a man; how difficult would it have been for Melanie to acknowledge the evidence before her? Would this be a good chance to discuss attitudes, or perhaps better to discuss the importance of using research evidence?

What do I need to know to teach scientific enquiry?

The basis of a good enquiry is a testable question, one which the children can answer by planning and carrying out an enquiry. For some children, asking the question is the most difficult part of the process. Questions sometimes arise through child-initiated activities but often they are the result of thoughtful teacher-planned explorations. The ice-balloons story offers a good example of an exploration designed to stimulate questions.

One of the most important roles for the teacher is to manage the way children talk about the subject of their enquiry. Teacher-guided talk can help them to generate testable questions, create hypotheses, design investigations, interpret their observations and become active participants in the enquiry. Learning becomes more meaningful if children have opportunities to share what they have learnt with others and to use their new knowledge in other situations.

Good subject knowledge can enable teachers to feel confident in dealing with the unexpected when children are doing enquiries. Sometimes children ask things which make it necessary to admit defeat; we all have limits to understanding! Why is the sky pink sometimes; how do seahorses have babies; what are the blue bits in washing powder; why does a mobile phone pick up some coins but not others? Good questions cannot always be immediately answered. But such valuable learning opportunities can be encouraged and supported, with curiosity fostered by setting up joint enquiry and research involving collaborative discussion amongst the class.

Types of scientific enquiry

The AKSIS project (Goldsworthy et al., 2000) identified six different forms of enquiry that can answer questions in classroom settings. These are: exploring; fair testing; pattern seeking; classifying and identifying; investigating models; technological enquiry.

The project reported that 'fair testing' was perhaps overused in primary schools, and encouraged the use of a wider range of enquiry strategies.

Exploring phenomena and seeking explanations

Exploration enquiries offer the opportunity to observe the behaviour of objects or natural events. Observations can ignite children's curiosity and give rise to questions that can be answered by further planned enquiries as in the story 'The colour of bubbles'.

Example	The colour of bubbles

Children at a science fair were given the opportunity to play with bubbles. They put on gloves and caught the bubbles on their hands but when they took the gloves off and tried to catch them, the bubbles burst. They shone lights through the bubbles and were fascinated by the different colours they could see. The children asked a range of questions: 'Where did the colours come from?' 'Why do the colours seem to slide down the bubbles?' 'Why do the bubbles burst?' They tried to predict the point at which the bubbles would burst. The answers to these puzzles needed further investigation and scientific explanations.

Investigating bubbles
Source: Peter Loxley

A fair-test enquiry

Fair testing relies on observing and exploring relationships between variables. This involves changing one variable (the independent variable) and observing or measuring the effect it has on another (the dependent variable), whilst keeping all other factors the same (Goldsworthy et al., 2000). An example of a question suitable for a fair test is: When I change the height of the ramp what will happen to the time it takes for a car to go down it?

Learning the process of fair testing takes time and needs careful support. With younger children fair-test enquiries may be initiated by the teacher with structured recording formats to guide the children's work. Later, children can be encouraged to generate their own questions and to take increasing responsibility for demonstrating ways of working that characterise fair testing. The skills involved in questioning, setting up an enquiry, collecting and interpreting data, and communicating conclusions require reinforcement and practice over some years.

Enquiries are sometimes labelled fair-test enquiries when they are not. For example, children might question if the length of a child's legs determines how far they can jump from a standing start. Whatever they do to ensure that all jumps are taken from the same point and the resulting distance accurately measured, it is impossible to control some variables which may have a direct impact on the outcomes – such as the strength of each child's muscles or an individual child's willingness to participate to their best ability. In this case a pattern-seeking enquiry would produce more reliable results.

The nature of a pattern-seeking enquiry

These investigations involve children making observations and measurements and looking for patterns in their data. For example, if you did the jumping investigation described above with a class of 30 children, what sort of patterns would you expect if 'length of legs' did influence how far they could jump? This is the sort of investigation where the reliability of the result increases as you increase the size of the sample used. Pattern-seeking investigations provide opportunities for children to apply their measuring and mathematical skills and to critically defend their point of view in light of evidence. The story 'The baby's shape' is an example of how such enquiries can encourage children to use simple data to investigate an interesting question.

Example   **The baby's shape**

Baby Tom arrived to visit a Year 2 class with his mother. Sam noticed how big Tom's head looked in relation to his body and wondered if the same applied to himself and his classmates. Carefully measuring the baby, the children found that his head accounted for about a third of his body length. They then made measurements of their own heads and bodies and found that the same relationship (proportion) did

---

not apply. They began to wonder when the proportions of their bodies had changed. Later the class undertook a teacher-guided whole-school enquiry looking for patterns in the relationship between the two variables, height and length of head. This enquiry became wider and eventually involved all their families. The children discovered that this proportion altered for people aged 0 to 7 years, but after that became fairly constant.

Classifying and identifying

Classifying the world around us helps us impose order on what might otherwise seem to be chaos. Classifying involves children in carefully and systematically collecting and grouping things based on observational data. Their close observations can be used to encourage them to talk about and describe the similarities and differences in materials or objects. The resulting information may well provoke further questions that can be investigated in other ways. For example, a sorting activity looking at different types of paper might result in a fair-test investigation to explore which type of paper is best to wrap a parcel for sending in the post.

Example   The school wildlife pond

The school's wildlife pond offered opportunities to investigate the range of creatures that colonise its varied habitats at different points in the year. Children dipped the pond and each year group developed its own way of classifying and then identifying the animals discovered. Recording ranged from simple picture keys to branching databases. Digital photos and video recording enabled them to study physical characteristics and movement. Careful observation revealed how plants and animals were adapted to survive and thrive in the pond: for example, the pond-skater's ability to glide across the surface and the way the caddis fly larva builds itself a cocoon of stones and twigs to camouflage it from its prey.

The study of wildlife habitats, such as ponds, not only provides opportunities for classifying and identifying animals and plants, but also children can undertake pattern-seeking enquiries concerning populations. As a result of their observations at this pond, the children made models to find out how it was possible for pond-skaters to 'walk on water'.

Testing ideas by modelling

Models are used in science to simulate real-life conditions, in a way that helps to try out ideas and explanations to see if they make sense. For example, children may think that the phases of the Moon are caused by shadows of the Earth cast on the Moon's surface. Using torches and relevant sized balls, children can model the phases of the Moon in a way that matches their hypothesis. In this case modelling is likely to show that the children's view is not reliable when tested against experience and that they need to rethink their ideas.

Example   Emperor penguins

A class of 10- and 11-year-olds were fascinated by a film showing colonies of emperor penguins huddling together to protect their chicks as they endured months of bitterly cold Antarctic weather. One group of children decided to find a way to investigate why penguins huddled in this way. They wondered about how to recreate Antarctic conditions until one child suggested they could make a model to simulate the penguins' behaviour. A simple model emerged; a large beaker was packed with successive rings of plastic test tubes each containing a thermometer. The test tubes were then filled with hot water and the whole apparatus left in the fridge for an hour. An hour later the thermometer readings confirmed that cooling was greatest in the outermost ring of test tubes.

The evidence the children collected helped them to think about what affects how quickly things cool. They concluded that temperature of the water fell more rapidly in the outermost test tubes because here the difference between the temperature of the water and the temperature in the fridge was greater than between the inner test tubes and the ones next to them.

Modelling how huddling together helps keep penguins warm
Source: Peter Loxley

Technological enquiry

Technological design may rely on the application of scientific skills and ideas. For example, the design of a sunhat depends on understanding the properties of the materials from which it is made. Children can test different fabrics to develop an understanding of their properties and then use this knowledge to inform the design. Another example is that of electric circuits. Once children understand that a circuit is needed for electrical current to flow, they can begin to explore the role of switches in interrupting the flow of electricity. They might then be set a challenge to design an intruder alarm that will sound when a door is opened, or a circuit that will turn off the light when the fridge door is shut. This gives the children an opportunity to test their system and evaluate its fitness for purpose as well as demonstrating the strength of their understanding of the underlying concept.

Choosing contexts for scientific enquiry

The context in which an enquiry is carried out gives it purpose and meaning. Effective contexts are those which are already familiar to the children and make their enquiries personally significant. When enquiries are presented with little relevant context (for example: Which is the best insulator? Which is the most absorbent paper? Which sole has the best grip?), children's motivation may be decreased and their engagement diminished. If contexts for learning can be offered that make the children want to find out answers because they are interested and they can see the point of what they are doing, then motivation becomes intrinsic: 'When learning occurs for intrinsic reasons it has been shown time and again to be highly effective learning' (Falk and Dierking, 2000).

Genuine contexts make enquiry more real for the child. For example, 'My coffee keeps going cold when I am on break duty; how do you think I could keep it warm?' or 'We need to make a raincoat to keep teddy dry if it rains on our teddy bear's picnic. Which of these fabrics do you think will be best?'

Engaging cross-curricular contexts

The creative arts provide rich contexts to promote the development of process skills and conceptual understanding. Poetry, narrative, drama and art can all be used to engage children's interest and make them want to find out more. A short poem like Roger McGough's 'Snowman' haiku invites discussion about what the poet is saying, before the class move on to considering the science of materials and change of state. It offers the potential for enquiry: Why do raindrops make the snowman melt? How could we stop him melting?

Snowman

Snowman in a field
listening to the raindrops
wishing him farewell

Roger McGough (1983)

Using fictional narrative can engage children's interest. A well-illustrated picture book or intriguing adventure can provide a range of contexts for investigation. For example, the story of Goldilocks sets the scene for children to learn about cooling and insulation. Children can investigate the reasons why the different bowls of porridge were different temperatures, and explore materials which can be used to keep the porridge warm. Work on forces and structures could be stimulated by the Three Pigs story and an exploration enquiry into life cycles and healthy eating could be inspired by *The Very Hungry Caterpillar* (Carle, 1994).

Making science into a drama and role-play can have a memorable effect

Drama can be motivating and can encourage creative approaches to communicating science ideas. For example, whilst studying invertebrates in the school grounds, children acted out their representation of an ant colony. They dressed as ants which brought food to the 'nest', attended the queen as she laid her eggs and relocated the nest when flood waters threatened. Such dramatisations are memorable and bring learning to life.

Children can also become active participants in creating models that explain a scientific concept; for example, a group of children can role-play the different components in an electrical circuit and show how electricity passes around the circuit. This could then lead into a practical enquiry of what happens when different components in the circuit are changed.

Art and science – a powerful combination

Art, like science, encourages children to observe closely. Collecting objects to draw, paint or to make into collages improves observational skills and at the same time encourages creativity in the representation of the objects. Painting flowers in the style of, for example, Aboriginal art can be a powerful way for children to interpret shape and colour and enable them to create personal representations of the structure of the flower. Studying the work of landscape artists such as Andy Goldsworthy can help children to look at familiar objects in a new way.

Observing the natural world can lead to questions that can be the basis of an enquiry. For example, when observing and drawing leaves, a Year 4 child noticed that when the veins on a leaf were opposite each other, the leaves on the twig were arranged alternately. But when the veins were arranged alternately, the leaves were opposite each other on the twig. This observation led into an enquiry to see if this rule applied more generally. Art offers the opportunity to take the children outside the classroom to learn about the natural world.

Learning outside the classroom

Although the majority of science lessons will take place in the classroom, there is much to be gained from learning outside the classroom. The phrase 'outside the classroom'

Examples of children's art
Source: Peter Loxley

covers both the nearby outdoors and visiting places of interest further away from the school at, for example, a sewage works, a power station, a museum or an interactive science centre. Such visits can create a lifelong interest in a subject. However, such visits might provide only limited opportunities for science enquiry. Using the school playground or a neighbourhood site has a number of advantages and can encourage enquiry which goes on over several years. Carrying out enquiries that can be developed over a number of weeks or even months will help the children to see patterns in nature and to understand seasonal cycles. Observations on the school field throughout the year will help children to see the different stages of the life cycles of plants: for example, the yellow flower and the feathery 'clock' of the dandelion appear so unconnected that children may think they are different plants rather than different stages in the life cycle of the same plant. In learning about local plants and animals, children gain a basis for wider understanding.

A local church and churchyard can be a wonderful resource. As well as learning about plants and animals living in the churchyard, children can learn about materials, their properties and uses. Questions might be: Are all headstones the same? Why have some of the inscriptions on the headstones disappeared? Why is wood used to make the pews in church? How is stained glass made? Why are the carvings on one side of the church door more weathered than on the other side? Such queries necessitate several visits, each with a different focus, to enable children to take full advantage of the resources available. There are also many opportunities for cross-curricular learning.

Similarly, the local park and playground can provide opportunities to explore forces and motion. Children can start with questions such as, 'How can you make yourself go down the slide more slowly?' 'How can you make the swing go higher?' These contexts have real relevance for the children and can lead into more scientific understanding.

If children become familiar with their local area, recognising its unique nature, they are more likely to value and to care for it. They will want to find out more about it and motivation to learn will become intrinsic; they become involved with their learning because they want to learn. This can promote citizenship and education for sustainable development. It can help to begin or confirm an interest in science which lasts a lifetime.

Summary

Science enquiry is by its very nature creative. Enquiry offers children the opportunity to find answers to their own questions; to discover and think about new ideas for themselves for the very first time. Teachers have to be prepared for the unexpected. They act as models for a range of invaluable scientific attitudes, and can enable children to rethink everyday experience in new and exciting ways. Teachers may feel that their own science understanding is tested to its limits by the questions children raise; such an effect holds no fears for the teacher who is aware that it is the process of thinking scientifically that is the most profound learning taking place. The chance to enquire, collect information and think with others to come up with answers to one another's questions is a powerful cycle in which every child can be involved. Teachers can offer stimulating and creative starting points, enabling children to remain, or even become, passionately curious about the natural world.

Further reading

Books

- Feasey, R. (2006) *Scientific investigations in the context of enquiry* in: W. Harlen (ed.) 'ASE Guide to Primary Science Education', Hatfield: Association for Science Education.
- Goldsworthy, A., Watson, R. and Wood-Robinson, V. (2000) *Developing understanding in scientific enquiry,* Hatfield: Association of Science Education.
- Oliver, A. (2006) *Creative Teaching Science*, Chapter 4: Inspiring inquiry, London: David Fulton.
- Warwick, P., Wilson, E. and Winterbottom, M. (2006) *Teaching and Learning Primary Science with ICT*, Maidenhead: Open University Press.

Primary science review articles (Association of Science Education)

- PSR 106 (January/February 2009), 'Science Enquiry'.
  This issue is focused on scientific enquiry skills.
- PSR 91 (January/February 2006), 'Beyond the classroom'.
  This issue is focused on scientific enquiry outside the classroom.
- PSR 90 (November/December 2005), 'The baker did it' by Ian Richardson.
- PSR 85 (November/December 2004), 'Using interactive whiteboard to improve science specific skills' by Sarah Earle.

CHAPTER 6
PLANNING AND ASSESSING CHILDREN'S SCIENCE LEARNING

Well-planned science lessons provide engaging learning opportunities. Planning involves deciding which strategies will best develop children's understanding. The ideas that children bring to the classroom are the basis for learning, and can be assessed to inform planning. This chapter examines approaches to planning and assessment which can be integrated into the three-stage framework for organising science learning.

Topics discussed in this chapter:

- The nature of formative assessment
- The nature of summative assessment
- First steps when planning
- Planning the exploratory stage
- Planning the re-describing stage
- Planning the application stage
- Class management issues

The nature of formative assessment

There are two purposes for assessment. The first is to check children's progress towards a learning goal and to evaluate what needs to be done to promote learning. This is assessment *for* learning or formative assessment. The second purpose of assessment is to create a snapshot or summary of children's progress at the end of a topic or over a period of time. This is assessment *of* learning, or summative assessment, used for formally reporting children's progress to parents and others.

The key characteristics of formative assessment are that it is ongoing, dynamic and progressive (Bell and Cowie, 2001). It also has to be responsive – something has to happen as a result of it. The following teacher's comment highlights the progressive and responsive nature of formative assessment.

> If you do something to find out where they (children) are at, and then you do something from that to change your teaching or what you are doing, then it is formative (assessment).
> (Bell and Cowie, 2001: 544)

Formative assessment may be informal, without written records being made, and can be used to inform teaching and learning in all stages of a lesson. In practice it is often opportunistic, taking place as teachers listen to children's conversations and respond to their queries and comments. When planned, assessment activities may be carried out at the beginning of a lesson and again at the end to measure changes in understanding. Information can be used to inform what is taught in subsequent sessions.

Teachers and children can collaborate to ensure effective formative assessment. From the child's perspective, formative assessment can help them to understand what learning is possible and how it can be achieved. It should also clarify what they have done well and what they need to do to improve (Black and Harrison, 2000). Teachers often share their learning intentions with classes of children, usually towards the start of a lesson. By sharing learning intentions and deciding on indicators of children's progress (success criteria or 'steps to success'), children are better aware of the aims and purposes of their classroom activity (Clarke, 2008).

Although formative assessment can be carried out through different activities, it is by nature dialogic because it requires children to communicate their ideas. Questions – such as: What do you imagine is going on here? What do you think? What do you mean by that? Can you say a bit about . . . ? Can you explain more about . . . ? Why do you think that? What words would you use to explain . . . ? – provide tools to mediate assessment activities and to probe more deeply into children's thinking. Having discovered what the child already knows, we can use the information to respond appropriately.

Something to think about

Is it always possible to plan for formative assessment? What formative assessment opportunities provide the sort of information that can be used to support planning?

Aspects of effective formative assessment

Learning need: Essentially, the purpose of formative assessment is to gather information about children's ideas and to use this to help create new and appropriate learning opportunities. In science classrooms, conceptual development is dependent on finding out, and addressing, the difference between a child's existing ideas and a more scientific point of view. This difference between the children's ideas and the scientific ideas can be defined as the 'learning needs' of the children (Leach and Scott, 2002). The concept of learning need helps us to target teaching strategies for different children, to identify next steps and to hold focused discussions with classes and individuals.

Teachers' questions: Teachers ask questions to stimulate discussion and help children to articulate their current ideas. Teachers' questions are meant to engage children by appealing to their personal memories and their willingness to contribute. They are used to ensure that all children are attending and to generate common knowledge. But some questions are more useful than others. Teachers may slip into asking questions to which children have to guess the right answer – that is, find out what the teacher wants them to say, for example:

T: OK, who can tell me what magnets do? Katy?

K: Stick to the fridge.

T: Um, yes, fridge magnets – but if you have two magnets, what happens?

And so on for many more turns, until the class have come up with the required phrases, 'Like poles repel; unlike poles attract'. Teachers' questions require a lot of hand-waving on the part of the children, and the teacher may have to manage some off-task behaviour created by boredom. This sort of interaction is the source of such phrases as: 'Listening ears on, everyone!' 'Let me see, who is sitting beautifully?' 'I can't ask you because you haven't got your hand up', 'Can you repeat that Josh, I couldn't hear because some people are just not listening' – and so on. Episodes of interminable questions leave the class and the teacher quite baffled by one another, and do not help children to understand anything. Beginning teachers may copy this style from those who have had years of practice at handling children this way. Children, having little choice, rapidly learn the rules and then spend much of their time finding ways to subvert them.

In the story 'What seeds need' the teacher is starting a topic on growing plants with Year 5. Here the deadening impact of 'teachers' questions' is evident.

Example	**What seeds need**

T: Right. Now. What do seeds need to grow? *(hands go up)* Alice?
Alice.   Sunlight and [. . .] water.
T: Hmm, sunlight and water, you think. What else? *(fewer hands)* Bryce?
Bryce: Earth.
Kieran: Compost.

T:	Put your hand up. You might be chosen to talk if you put your hand up. *(Kieran puts up his hand.)* Hmmm, come on, someone different. Muj?
Muj:	Something to grow in.
T:	Yes, something to grow in, but what else? To grow?
Chloe:	Blue pellets to keep away slugs.
T:	That's not vital. What else does it have to have? What other vital things? We've got sunlight, water and soil.
Denes:	Can worms help them grow? On my Gran's allotment, right, she has worms, they [. . .]
T:	*(dismissively)* Worms!
Denes:	*(nodding)* Yes, she lets me pick them up, I can pick up worms.
Alice:	Yes in the soil, they make holes in the soil.
T:	Um, yes, help the soil. Absolutely. Worms. Right, now I want you to put together a role-play for me . . .

Comment

The teacher had not decided whether to stick to talking about germination (seeds usually need water, air and some warmth) or to talk about plant growth (plants usually need light, water, air and some warmth and sometimes a growing medium such as soil). She asks six 'teachers' questions'. She accepts the children's suggestions, sunlight, water and soil – although not sounding too confident about it – but has another idea in mind, and prompts the children to keep guessing what it is: possibly warmth, or air. The interesting idea of slug pellets reminds Denes of soil creatures and he asks a question about worms, which is dismissed as nonsensical by the teacher but picked up by his classmate Alice. Alice's idea that worms make holes reminds the teacher that worms do help plants – which is what she asked – by aerating soil. But this is slightly too complex an idea to fit in the simpler narrative that plants need sun, water, soil and . . . air? warmth? She covers up the slight muddle by rapidly moving on. This cannot happen to teachers who are asking genuine questions, which by their very nature indicate a quest for information or understanding. Teachers do better when they make it clear what they do not know, or what is new to them, clarifying their role as part of the enquiry rather than the complete solution.

The children have no chance to share what they genuinely know or understand. It is evident that Alice seems to understand what plants require; Denes has experience of allotments; Chloe has learned about keeping slugs at bay; Kieran offers the suggestion of compost as a different medium than soil; Muj may be summing up what soil and compost are, or is aware that plants need a habitat, even if it's simply a plant pot. These ideas are not what the teacher wants. Each suggestion is taken as a slightly wrong end point, rather than an opener to a wider discussion. But what is she trying to teach? The learning intention for this session was 'to be able to say what seeds need to grow into plants.' It would be more productive to hand out some seeds and ask the children to tell each other everything they can think of about how to help the seed grow into a big plant. The teacher can then invite children to share what they have heard, or nominate a classmate who they think has something interesting to offer. Having established conditions for germination, and growth, the teacher can then point out or explain the difference, and then summarise the conditions as a list and move on to organising the role-play.

The responses we get from children depend on the types of question we ask. From a question such as 'What will happen to the plant if we stop watering it?' the teacher may be expecting a factual answer: 'It will die'. The teacher is only interested in one answer. But if we show the children an unhealthy looking plant and ask what they think is wrong with it, we are more likely to hear a range of views. To engage children in learning conversation, we need to ask questions which show an interest in their experience or require them to express a point of view, giving their reasons. In the three-stage framework, interesting questions or puzzles are introduced in the exploratory stage and this sets the scene for children's learning in the re-describing stage. Children's responses to puzzles and questions provide us with insight into their existing understanding. Planning questions and puzzles is crucial if we are to determine and subsequently address learning needs.

The 'Blue Earth puzzle' provides an example of formative assessment in practice, in a class of 8-year-old children.

Example   Blue Earth puzzle

Joe's class was shown a picture on the interactive whiteboard of the Earth taken from space. The children were asked to think about why the Earth looked blue from space.

Joe was convinced that the Earth looked blue because the sky was blue. He held firm views about the reasons for the colour and he was not ready to change them. He asserted that the picture from space was taken through the sky so it had to look blue.

When another child suggested that the Earth looked blue because of the seas and oceans that covered it, Joe became quite agitated. He walked up to the whiteboard and said that he was worried about this idea. He used his hands to explain that if the blue was water then the water on the sides and bottom of the Earth would run off and we would have no seas left. He knew that we have seas and oceans; he insisted that the only possible explanation was that the blue had to be the colour of the sky.

Comment

Joe's response revealed learning needs which the teacher had not expected. Here on Earth we constantly live with the effects of gravity, so that intuitively it makes sense that water would fall down and off the sides and bottom of the earth. We need to recognise the explanatory power of Joe's reasoning. He has seen water running downwards. As teachers, we have to make the decision: in what way do we want Joe to change his understanding of the Earth and gravity? Once we decide this, we can plan and organise teaching strategies to help him to understand a more scientific point of view.

Something to think about

Read the 'Blue Earth puzzle' and assess Joe's learning needs. Think about how you might address them.

Self-assessment and peer assessment

Children can be involved in assessing their own progress. To do so, they need to be clear about what they should be able to do as a result of their learning, which they could not do before. Setting children a puzzle to solve provides them with an insight into what they are trying to achieve. Finding solutions to puzzling events brings not only measurable intellectual rewards, but can also provide emotional satisfaction which can positively influence children's attitudes to further learning (Chapter 1).

Just as children need to be taught to talk and think together in scientific ways (Chapter 4), children need to be taught the assessment skills to monitor and manage their own learning. Children may need input in the language of judgement and assessment: for example, 'understanding' can mean being able to explain an idea clearly to someone else, or being able to put an idea into practice, or help solve a puzzle. Simple systems to record self-assessment include the use of 'traffic light' icons to signify whether children perceive they have achieved the learning goals, putting thumbs up or drawing smiley faces on work to show how confident individuals are in their learning.

Whatever strategies are used to promote self-assessment, children need to learn to question and reflect on their learning. Asking themselves particular questions can help shape children's thinking and understanding: *What needs to be done next? How can I best find an answer to that question? Is there any other way to find an answer to that problem? Is there another way of looking at the problem or puzzle? Are there any other words I can use to explain my view more clearly? What reasons do I have for my belief? Do I really understand the meaning of that word?*

These types of question require children to reflect on the nature of their own learning and understanding. Children should be encouraged to communicate and justify their judgements to their peers and teacher, and make suggestions about how to proceed with their learning.

Peer assessment can usefully support self-assessment (Black et al., 2002). Strategies for peer assessment may not be immediately obvious to children. Asked to look at one another's work, they may take the stance of a very harsh and unyielding teacher! Effective ways to assess work and communicate helpful ideas really need to be made explicit. Exploratory talk (Chapter 4) between children has an important role to play in peer assessment. Learning takes place as children listen and respond to each other's ideas, and discussion can focus on how to achieve their learning goals collaboratively. Children need to be taught to offer supportive formative comments and suggestions, to query ideas and note what they have found new or interesting, and that it is not their role to make summative judgements about whether their classmates' ideas are right or wrong, 'good' or 'bad'.

In summary, a key purpose of formative assessment is to provide information for planning. It is also important for children's awareness of their own developing ideas, helping them to be better motivated. For teachers, the chance to talk to children about their understanding is always a source of interest, and one of the profoundly satisfying aspects of our role.

The nature of summative assessment

The purpose of summative assessment is to provide a summary of achievement over a period of time.

Summative assessment requires the systematic collection of data. The data usually reflects what the child can achieve unaided in pencil-and-paper tests. Such data may be for the teacher's use, for discussion with parents, or to match against national criteria as a comparative measure of the success of one child or one set of children against another.

Formative approaches to preparing for summative assessment

Some formative assessment strategies can be used to help children prepare for summative assessment tasks.

1. *Revision*

   When planning their revision, children can traffic-light key words and topics on which the test will be set. The purpose is to reflect on the body of knowledge which they need to understand and to identify the key concepts and areas on which they need to concentrate. The areas identified as red and amber provide the focus for their revision plan. They can then concentrate their efforts on areas of weakness. This will also allow them to focus on questions from past papers which test their 'red' areas and to spend time addressing them rather than doing the whole of the paper. This may motivate children, if they feel that they have control over their own learning.

2. *Peer marking*

   Peer marking practice tests can be a useful strategy to help children develop understanding, because it requires them to construct or, at least, interpret the marking criteria.

3. *Setting their own questions*

   In addition to answering past paper questions, children can set their own questions on particular topics to demonstrate their understanding and to test their peers. The process of setting questions requires children to reflect on their own understanding of a topic, especially if they have to justify why their question is appropriate.

4. *Focused scientific enquiry*

   Children can plan and carry out a range of scientific enquiries on key areas of the curriculum. This enables them to revise the concepts and skills required while still enabling them to think creatively and to be actively engaged in their own learning. This is more meaningful than repeatedly going over key ideas and previous test questions.

   (Strategies adapted from Black et al., 2002)

5. *Collaborative answering*

   Questions from the type of test papers children will be expected to answer alone can be collaborative puzzles. Allocate a question to each group of children and ask them to discuss all their ideas about it. Ensure that children understand that this talk is part of their learning; that they are aware that there is time to think and ask questions, rather than come to hasty conclusions or shut the discussion down. They must respect one another's contributions. After discussion time, they can decide on possible answers. Each group can then explain their question and their thinking on the answer to the class. This strategy ensures that children have support in reading and interpreting questions, and that individuals learn to consider and reason through alternative answers. It helps them to recognise strategies for dealing with the sort of questions they will be asked in tests. Such discussion enables children to internalise ways of thinking (What do I know about this? What do I think? Why do I think that? What other ideas might help?) which will help them to approach further questions with some confidence.

Something to think about

How do you think summative testing could influence children's attitudes to science learning? How did it affect your own attitude? Which formative approaches would you find useful when preparing children for summative tests?

Planning children's science learning

Teachers manage the learning of large numbers of children with a diverse range of ethnic backgrounds, social behaviours, talents and interests. Sometimes, general teaching and learning theories do not easily translate into effective classroom practice (Lijnse, 2000; 2004). It can prove difficult for teachers to apply the outcomes of science education research in their classrooms.

In this book educational theory is translated into classroom practice. The theory chapters in Part 1 provide examples of how research-based ideas can be applied in the classroom. These ideas are brought together into the three-stage framework which can help to organise science learning, and which provides a structure for planning. In Part 2, 'Ideas for practice' exemplify how the three-stage framework can be used to teach specific concepts and skills.

Establishing learning needs

The first step when planning to teach science involves establishing the children's learning needs during the exploratory stage. Children's learning needs are defined by the differences between children's existing ideas and a more scientific point of view. The role of the teacher in addressing learning needs is to organise classroom activities which enable children to modify their existing understanding towards the scientific view. This is the re-describing stage. To help children make sense of the scientific ideas, their thinking needs to be communicated so that the differences between their ideas and the scientific ones can be made explicit.

Because learning needs of different groups and individuals will vary, teachers need to plan strategies to establish and address every child's need. In the exploratory stage, activities should be planned to provide opportunities for children of different abilities to communicate their ideas through appropriate means such as talking, drawing, modelling and writing. Bearing in mind the ideas and experience the children already have, decisions can then be made about what needs to happen in the children's minds to move their thinking towards the scientific view (Asoko, 2002).

Clarifying the scientific point of view

To help establish what the children need to learn, it is useful to express a scientific point of view as a set of meaningful, relevant ideas rather than as a list of facts and definitions. For example, on the topic of light, the National Curriculum for Key Stage 2 states that children should be taught:

- that light travels from a source;
- that light cannot pass through some materials, creating shadows;
- that light is reflected from surfaces.

Individually these decontextualised statements have little meaning and no explanatory power. For example, the proposition that 'light travels from a source' makes little sense on its own. It only has meaning for those of us who can decode it, because we already understand the behaviour of light. We can make sense of it if we are able to link ideas from previous experience and 'translate' new vocabulary (travel, source) into meaningful images in our minds.

To help children make sense of the statement that 'light travels from a source' we need to begin by relating the ideas it contains to children's everyday experience. For example, ideas which contribute towards a scientific way of thinking about light sources might be stated as:

> We need light to see and recognise things. Without light we wouldn't be able to see anything and the world would be completely dark. Light comes from the Sun; the Sun is a source of light. Sources of light give out light. Other sources of light are computer screens, candles, electric lamps, torches, televisions and fires. Light moves or travels out in all directions from a light source. Light has to travel to reach us, and it travels incredibly fast. Some animals can be sources of light; fireflies give out light and can be seen in the dark. Some bright things such as the Moon or shiny paper are not sources of light but are reflecting or bouncing back light from a source.

This exercise – teasing out the 'smaller' ideas that help to make up the 'big idea' that 'light comes from a source' – helps us to clarify just what it is that children need to know in order to make sense of key scientific ideas. Some children will know some of these things. Some will be aware of some of the ideas but may never have heard them put into words, or may never have considered experience in this way, and thought the idea. If we can expand science ideas into accessible, everyday language, we can introduce children to new ways of thinking about their experiences which can change the way that they perceive the world. This creates meaningful, deep learning instead of putting children in the position of having to remember that 'light travels from a source' when they do not know what that means. 'Ideas for practice' in Part 2 of the book provides a wide range of examples of how to present the scientific view in a meaningful narrative.

When constructing a scientific point of view, we should think carefully about how we want to influence children's understanding of the world. The ideas which we teach children can enable them to begin to see some of science's big ideas. For example, a topic on the feeding relationships in a garden, starting with a study of snails, can provide a way into grappling with big ideas such as interdependence and adaptation. Similarly, topics on light and sound provide opportunities not only to explore how we sense the world, but also to find out how different animals and plants sense the world, providing a window on diversity and adaptation.

Something to think about

Reinterpret and expand the statement that 'light is reflected from surfaces' into a set of ideas accessible to children. What experiences could help children to think through the ideas?

Planning the exploratory stage: choosing strategies to elicit children's ideas

Asking the right questions is the key to finding out what is going on inside children's minds. A 'big question' or 'puzzle' sets the scene for the children's learning and helps to stimulate curiosity and discussion. Children's responses to the puzzle, and the information and questions which emerge from their discussion provide feedback on children's existing understanding. So, the design of the puzzle is really crucial to probe understanding and scaffold children's conceptual development. Examples of puzzles and other strategies for exploring children's ideas can be found in the 'Ideas for practice' outlined in Part 2 of the book.

Examples of useful strategies are:

1. *Talking points*
   Talking points (Chapter 4) provide a focused stimulus for children to talk together and to raise their own questions. Talking points are statements relevant to the topic and the puzzle that provoke thinking and the exchange of ideas. Listening to others and offering their own ideas help children to establish their current

thinking and to reflect on alternative ideas (Dawes, 2009). For example, we might offer children the following puzzle: 'What do you think of this idea? "An acorn has an oak tree inside it." Talk to your partner to decide whether this is true or false and why . . .'

This is likely to bring out more ideas than holding up an acorn and asking teachers' questions (to which we already know the answer): 'Who can tell me what this is? What has it got inside? What will it grow into?' Naylor and Keogh (2000) have produced a series of concept cartoons on a range of topics which can provide useful talking points.

2. *Children's drawings*
   Annotated drawings can help to externalise what is going on inside children's minds. For example, we can ask them to draw how they think light enables them to see an object, or what they think electricity looks like inside a wire. The diagram and, crucially, the child's written annotations, are a resource for assessment.

   The following example illustrates this. Thinking about the movement of particles of a gas, a Year 4 class were asked to sit very still. A perfume bottle was opened in a corner of the room. The class were asked to raise their hands when they could smell the perfume. After this activity they were asked to draw a picture of the classroom, annotating it to show the movement of the scent and saying how they think that this movement happened.

3. *Scientific enquiry*
   Scientific enquiry can be organised for the purpose of developing the skills and understanding of how to collect reliable evidence. But such enquiry may raise questions about the behaviour of an object or phenomenon which still require explanation. It is difficult to help children to discover the reasons or causes of physical phenomena for themselves. For example, children may discover that hot water dissolves a larger quantity of salt than cold water, but the reasons why cannot be explained by the data which they collect. The enquiry then produces a puzzle for children to talk about. Scientific enquiries which support children's conceptual development need to be planned carefully so that they generate a need for a scientific explanation which is consistent with the intended learning goals. Chapter 5 (pp. 52–7) discusses how different types of scientific enquiry can be planned to raise questions and promote classroom talk. Enquiry contexts which have the potential for effective conceptual development are those which are familiar enough for children to talk about from their own experience, but which also promote the value of the scientific ideas (Chapter 3).

Something to think about

What strategies have you seen or used in school to elicit children's ideas? Can you think of any strategies which are appropriate for particular science topics you may be planning to teach?

Planning the re-describing stage: choosing strategies to help children make sense of the scientific view

Scientific concepts are ideas which have been created over time by many people. Scientific ideas may be abstract, and can be represented and communicated through words, symbols, gestures, actions, pictures, diagrams, physical models and mathematical formulae (Asoko and de Boo, 2001). They are often counter-intuitive, and to make sense of them children need to be able to construct clear and useful mental models of them (Chapter 3). Below we provide some examples of strategies which teachers can use to help children visualise scientific concepts. Contextualised examples of these strategies can be found in 'Ideas for practice' in Part 2.

1. *Analogies*

   Analogies can help children make sense of scientific ideas because they make the unfamiliar familiar (Treagust et al., 1992). Analogies work because they enable children to use familiar experience and existing knowledge to construct useful mental representations of the scientific concept. For example, when we ask children to imagine electricity in wires to be like water flowing through a pipe, we are helping them turn an abstract idea into something which they can visualise. Because electricity and water are not the same things, and wires are not the same as pipes, this analogy has limitations and, pushed too far, will break down. All analogies have limited explanatory power. However, they can provide useful ways of seeing and talking about concepts which we want the children to learn. Asoko and de Boo (2001) is a good source of analogies for different topics. Part 2 also provides examples of some useful analogies.

2. *Role modelling*

   Children can model a concept through role-play. For example, when teaching how simple electric circuits work, children can play the part of the current which transports the energy from the battery to the bulb. If they understand the model of the current as a transport system for energy, they can model what happens to the energy as the current travels through the filament in the bulb. They can role-play how difficult it is for current to pass through a filament wire. Role-play is based on analogy and hence has similar explanatory limitations.

3. *Physical models*

   Physical models can be useful because they enable children to visualise a concept and to talk about how it works. Models provide children with something concrete to talk about. For example, when teaching about how we digest our food, it is not possible to have a real digestive system to explore. Physical models encourage children to hypothesise about what each part does. This is a form of scientific enquiry. The same applies to the use of models to make sense of more abstract concepts. For example, thinking of the Lottery machine as a model of a gas is both a three-dimensional model and an analogy.

4. *Electronic models and simulations*

Electronic simulations can be used to help children to investigate and make sense of scientific concepts. Simulations can be found on the Internet or purchased on CD-ROM for most scientific concepts. Popular ones include models for electric current, change of state, germination, photosynthesis and the solar system. We need to be aware that children can interpret these models in ways which are different from what we may expect (Sutherland et al., 2004), and to make sense of the scientific ideas involved, children will need to talk about the simulations with each other and the teacher. Simulations that allow the children to alter variables, such as changing the shape or size of a parachute to see the effect on how it falls, can help children to explore possibilities and design investigations. Others can be used to speed up the impact of changing conditions, such as growth in plants, to support hypothesising. However, these virtual investigations are no substitute for hands-on practical work whenever possible.

5. *Use of information sources*

ICT in schools is used most often as an information source. Online illustrated texts, animations and videos can provide a rich source of information on scientific topics. Children enjoy finding things out for themselves and as a result it can change the way that they perceive the world (Chapter 1). However, finding suitable websites can be difficult. Searching the Internet for information can be frustrating for children when most of the information has been written for an adult audience. Even websites designed for children can present ideas in ways which are complex and uninteresting for the intended age group. Time is well spent by teachers in building up a catalogue of the most interesting and useful websites for particular topics. Two examples of successful websites are 'Arkive Education' for wildlife projects and 'The Space Place' which is a NASA website for children. Both have remarkable videos and images for the children to enjoy and to talk about. The Association of Science Education provides appraisals of a large number of websites on their 'Web Search' CD-ROM.

A good science library stocked with both electronic and hard-copy resources can play a vital part in children's learning. Multimedia CD-ROMs provide rich learning experiences for children. David Attenborough's 'Wildlife Collection', for example, provides inspirational footage of both animals and plants which can breathe life into concepts such as adaptation, interdependency and diversity. Dorling Kindersley provides a wide range of science-based CD-ROMs and illustrated books for all ages. For young children there are a series of big books covering science topics – which can be read by teachers and children together.

URLs for the websites mentioned above can be found at the end of the chapter.

How would you decide which is the best way to represent a particular concept? Are there some criteria which you can use to help you? For example, would the Lottery machine model be useful when teaching 7- or 8-year-old children about evaporation? What model would you use to help them visualise what is happening? If we can't think of a suitable model, does this suggest that the ideas are too complex for the children?

Planning the application stage: choosing strategies to promote the usefulness of the scientific view

Our ability to talk about and explain an event or phenomenon depends on the model of it we hold in our minds (Chapter 3). If the model is powerful and reliable it can be used in a wide range of contexts and may even help us explain events we may not have previously experienced. Children need to experience the explanatory power of their newly acquired scientific ideas. In making purposeful use of a scientific point of view they can appreciate its value and may be persuaded to assimilate it into their thinking (Chapter 3). Below we provide examples of strategies which enable children to make use of scientific ideas. Contextualised examples can be found in 'Ideas for practice' in Part 2.

1. *Redesigning nature*
   'Redesigning nature' is a creative activity which involves the application of scientific knowledge for a specific purpose. For example, after learning about pollination children could design an imaginary flowering plant which lives in a place where there is little wind and no insects. Alternatively, after teaching about photosynthesis, children could design an imaginary plant which is able to thrive without roots. It is important that children explain how their design has been informed by their knowledge of the topic.

Something to think about

Imagine that you have just taught 6- and 7-year-old children about habitats. What redesigning nature task could you give them?

2. *Designing and making physical systems*
   Design technology contexts need to be planned carefully so that they help to promote the value of the scientific view. Scientific ideas may not necessarily be useful for informing children's designing and decision-making. Research shows that if

ideas are to be useful they must be taught in ways which relate specifically to the D&T project (Layton, 1993).

Examples of contexts in which children could use their scientific understanding:

- *electrical circuits*, to design a circuit for a model lighthouse, car or house;
- *shadows*, to design and stage a shadow-puppet performance;
- *food groups*, to plan a healthy meal for a picnic or special occasion;
- *properties of materials*, to design a sunhat, rain hat, winter coat or carrier bag.

Something to think about

Which of the design technology projects do you think children could carry out without being taught the relevant science? How would the science improve their design?

3. *Drama and debate*

   Children can play a part in a performance which involves the use of scientific ideas to inform a debate. For example, an environmental theme could be developed around a scenario where a company are seeking planning permission to build houses on a local wildlife area. Children can take on different roles to debate the relevant issues. Examples of other subjects for debate which can be informed by scientific knowledge include waste management, pollution and excessive global warming.

4. *Creative writing*

   Creative writing can provide children with opportunities to make use of their scientific knowledge in enjoyable and satisfying ways. Examples of creative writing contexts include:

   - science fiction stories based on contemporary science;
   - children take on the role of famous scientists, past or present, writing a theme-based article for a local newspaper;
   - poems based on a scientific theme: scientific views provide opportunities for a wide range of poetry including haiku, acrostic or shape poems.

5. *Painting and 3-D modelling*

   Children can depict scientific themes in painting, collage and by constructing 3-D models. For example, having learnt about the phases of the Moon, children can paint what they think the Earth looks like from the Moon. They can paint pictures of camouflaged animals in different settings and design markings for animals to scare off particular predators. Animal colours and markings could inspire the design of fabric patterns for a D&T project. As part of D&T or art projects, children can design and make moving models of imaginary or real animals which are adapted to a specific habitat.

6. *Scientific enquiry*

   Children can use their scientific understanding to raise questions and to make predictions about the behaviour of living or non-living things. They can plan an enquiry to collect evidence or test the reliability of their ideas. For example, children can apply their understanding of thermal insulation to predict which material will best keep ice frozen, or a hot drink warm. They can use their knowledge to design a container to carry ice to a picnic or a hot drink on a long walk.

Some class management issues

1. *Safety*

   The ASE publication *Be Safe* (2001) is a useful source of information to help assess risks associated with primary science activities.

2. *Organising talk*

   Since effective learning is linked to the ability to think and talk about the relevant ideas, we must provide children with opportunities to discuss and express their thoughts. Meaningful discussion can take place during small-group work or whole-class contexts. Children require clear guidelines to work collaboratively in both small-group and whole-class situations (Chapter 4). They need to be aware that their talk together is an important part of their work, and they need to be taught the strategies and skills which will help every child take an active part in exploratory talk.

3. *Worksheets*

   The choice of resources can have a profound effect on the quality of the children's learning and their attitudes to the topic. The disheartening phrase 'death by worksheet' describes the dull nature of the learning experiences which such resources may provide! But well-designed worksheets can be a very useful way of organising some activities. Worksheets should not be overused to the point where children's activity is just focused on 'filling them in'. Whatever resources are used, practical or otherwise, they need to provide the children with something interesting to talk about.

Summary

Assessment is used to inform planning, and planning should outline how assessment will be carried out. Lesson plans should include key questions that can help children to articulate their knowledge and understanding. Questions should help children to think and share experience, and should not simply require children to guess facts. Children should be actively involved in the assessment process. Knowing the learning objectives and knowing the steps needed to achieve them can help children to engage with their learning; but the main motivating drive is children's curiosity. By helping children to ask their own questions and by ensuring that they realise that there is something interesting to discover, we can foster children's natural inquisitiveness and satisfy their wish to learn.

Further reading and useful resources

Books

- Asoko, H. and de Boo, M. (2001) *Analogies and Illustrations: Presenting Ideas in Primary Science*, Hatfield: ASE Publications.
- Clarke, S. (2008) *Unlocking Formative Assessment*, London: Hodder & Stoughton.
- DfES (2004) *Planning and Assessment for Learning, Assessment for Learning. Primary National Strategy: Excellence and Enjoyment: Learning and Teaching in the Primary Years*.
- DfES (2004) *Planning and Assessment for Learning, Designing Opportunities for Learning. Primary National Strategy: Excellence and Enjoyment: Learning and Teaching in the Primary Years*.
- Mitchell, R. (2006) 'Using ICT in teaching and learning science', in W. Harlen (ed.), *ASE Guide to Primary Science Education*, Hatfield: Association for Science Education.
- Naylor, S. and Keogh, B. (2000) *Concept Cartoons in Science Education*, Sandbach: Millgate House Publishers. (Concept cartoons are also available on CD ROM.)
- Naylor, S., Keogh, B. and Goldworthy, A. (2004) *Active Assessment*, London: David Fulton.
- Oliver, A. (2006) *Creative Teaching Science*, London: David Fulton, Chapter 3: Planning for a creative approach.

Websites with information, ideas and resources for teaching a wide range of topics

- Duck Builder Game: www.cgpbooks.co.uk/online_rev/duck/duck.htm
- Arkive Education: www.arkiveeducation.org/
- Web Search published by ASE: www.sycd.co.uk/primary/managing-science/web-search.htm
- NASA website for children: http://spaceplace.nasa.gov/en/kids/
- Science resources for children, young people, teachers and parents: www.planet-science.com/home.html
- Planning resources for teachers: www.primaryresources.co.uk/science/science.htm
- BBC schools home page: www.bbc.co.uk/schools/websites/4_11/site/science.shtml
- Science-based film clips which can be used to set the scene for children's learning: www.planet-scicast.com/films.cfm
- ASE teaching resources website: www.schoolscience.co.uk/

CHAPTER 7
THE ORIGINS OF SCIENTIFIC KNOWLEDGE

This chapter looks at the origins of science to show how it has changed the way we understand and feel about the natural world. We focus on the development of science from the time of the ancient Greeks. It may be argued that science was going on before this time and in other parts of the world, but it is widely accepted that what we call science today can be clearly traced back to the work of the ancient Greek philosophers.

We have included this chapter to help teachers recognise the unique nature of scientific knowledge. In Chapter 1, Richard Feynman describes scientific knowledge as 'wonderful pieces of gold' which can change the way we think and feel about the world. In his best-selling book *Unweaving the Rainbow*, Richard Dawkins compares the feelings of awe and wonder which science can inspire to the aesthetic passion stirred by the finest music and poetry. How we feel about science will influence how we teach it. If we believe it to be an amazing human achievement comparable with the greatest works of art, we are likely to inspire those same feelings in our children.

Topics discussed in this chapter:

- The nature of scientific knowledge
- Early scientific theories
- Christianity's influence on the development of science
- Galileo's influence on the development of science
- The new age of science

The nature of scientific knowledge

> Scientific knowledge is knowledge, not fact – a gallery of pictures painted by scientists to portray in some simplified, comprehensible way the (seemingly) infinite complexity of nature. The pictures are put up and taken down, cleaned, replaced, and destroyed. Any account of scientific knowledge is therefore . . . an account of unfinished business.
>
> (Holden, cited in Rogers and Wenham, 1980)

The purpose of a scientific theory is to enable us to picture how nature works. For example, Sir Isaac Newton's theory of gravitation enables us to construct the most remarkable images (mental and physical) of how our solar system works. Not only that, the same theory enables us to visualise how the whole universe was formed (Chapter 8). Some scientific theories, like Newton's, are masterpieces of science in the same way as great paintings or poems are thought of as masterpieces of art.

Science masterpieces, however, are never completely finished. Whereas works of art are often unique and subjective visions of the world, works of science are mainly collaborative and objective representations. When one generation of scientists stops working on a theory, the following generation continues the work. Scientific theories are therefore unfinished pictures of the natural world which scientists constantly struggle to improve. New generations of scientists evaluate, investigate and apply their own imaginations to the representations of their predecessors.

Something to think about

Why do the authors compare scientific theories to pictures? What point are they trying to make about the nature of scientific knowledge?

Behind every scientific idea there is a fascinating story which often involves exceptional people challenging the conventional wisdom of their time. The history of science involves stories about the lives of real people, with human frailties as well as exceptional abilities. Many scientists in the past endured hardship and sacrifice in their pursuit of scientific knowledge. In this respect science and art are very similar. Both of these cultures owe a debt to the tenacity and genius of a relatively small number of extraordinary people.

Why is scientific knowledge unique?

To understand the unique nature of scientific thinking, we must first reflect on the way people explained their world before the emergence of science. Traditionally, different civilisations have developed their own mythological stories to explain where they came from, to interpret the origins of natural phenomena and to underpin their social customs. These forms of knowledge integrate everyday experiences and metaphysical imaginings into a coherent and powerful belief system which satisfies intellectual, social and psychological needs. All mythologies have in common accounts of how the actions of supernatural powers cause things to happen in the natural world.

For example, Australian Aboriginals developed a vast body of oral literature. Prior to colonisation by the Europeans in 1788, there were about 300,000 Aboriginals living in small tribes throughout Australia. Each tribe had its own traditional 'dreamtime' stories which gave the tribe both its spiritual identity and an understanding of the nature of the world in which they lived.

Dreamtime stories relate to the time of the Dreaming, before humans populated the land. The Dreaming is a time of creation when the eternal ancestors wandered the Earth creating new life forms and sculpting the landscape. *The Dreamtime* represents an aboriginal account of how life was created.

The Dreamtime

An Australian Aboriginal creation myth

In the beginning the Earth was a bare plain. All was dark. There was no life, no death. The Sun, the Moon, and the stars slept beneath the Earth. All the eternal ancestors slept there, too. But at last the eternal ancestors woke themselves out of their eternity and broke through to the surface of the Earth. This was Dreamtime. Now the ancestors arose and they wandered the Earth. Some were in animal form, as kangaroos, or emus, or lizards. Some were in human shape. And some were part animal, part human, part plant. Two of the ancestors were Ungambikula. As they wandered across the world, they found half-made human beings. These beings were made of animals and plants, but they were shapeless, bundled up, vague and unfinished. With their great stone knives, the Ungambikula carved heads, bodies, legs and arms out of the bundles. They made the faces, hands and feet. At last the human beings were finished. So every person was created from nature, and owes allegiance to the animal or plant that made the bundle from which it was created; such as the plum tree, the grass seed, the lizard, the parakeet, or the rat. When this work was done the ancestors went back to sleep. Some returned underground, while others became rocks and trees. The trails they walked in Dreamtime are holy trails. Everywhere they went they left sacred

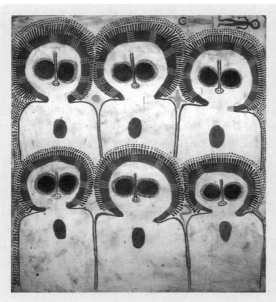

Charlie Allungoy (Numbulmoore), *Wanalirri Wanjina*, 1970 Natural pigments on bark, Australia.

Wanalirri is the ancestral Wanjina central to Ngarinyin law; the people were drowned by the Wanjina Wanalirri's ability to evoke floods to create justice to punish people for disobeying the law. Governed by a commitment to repaint the Wanjina's impression on the rock, repainting insures rejuvenation keeping nature 'alive' whilst continuing to honour the eternal ancestors' presence.

Source: Copyright to the Ngarinyin clan estate Biyarrngongo of the artist Charlie Allungoy (Numbulmoore), Ngarinyin and Wilinggin Aboriginal Corporations and Mamaa The Untouchable Ones from Cave to Canvas art projects (explanation given by family member Yvonne Burgu as translated by Heather Winter). Picture supplied by the National Museum of Australia.

traces of their presence – a rock, a waterhole, a tree. And so the Dreamtime does not just lie in the distant past, the Dreamtime is the eternal Now. Between heartbeat and heartbeat the Dreamtime can come again.
(Livesey Museum for Children)

Every Aboriginal tribe had it own ceremonies in which their Laws of the time of the Dreaming were told and interpreted in ways which informed the life of the people.

"For the Ngarinyin language group their Law was governed by the Wanjina who is the creator spirit who formed the land, the animals and the people. Creating the Law for Aboriginal people in Australia to live by their image is found in the rock art sites to remind people of how the law started. The Wanjina spirit of the Ngarinyin creates all life; the babies, water, green grass, bush food, yams all our food, they are all governed by the Wanjina's law. Senior Law people today still live their lives and teach their younger generations these laws."
(Interview with Mr Paddy Neowarra, Chairman of Ngarinyin and Wilinggin Aboriginal Corporations. Interview and translation by Heather Winter (Melbourne University) on the 2 November 2009 in Derby, Western Australia.)

The Laws for Aboriginal people have traditionally had a profound spiritual and psychological influence on the Aboriginal people, and have underpinned their cultural knowledge and customs for many thousands of years. Dreamtime stories informed every aspect of aboriginal life, from the time of conception to the moment of death. Underpinning Aboriginal culture is the belief that the eternal ancestors live amongst them in numerous forms including parts of the landscape such as rocks, hills and mountains. The belief that these spiritual ancestors exist as features in the landscape has created a powerful spiritual bond between the Aboriginal people and the land on which they live. For Aboriginal tribes different features in the landscape provide iconic representations of their spiritual beliefs. Aboriginal people think of themselves as custodians of the spiritual landscape in which they live.

Something to think about

Pandora's Box is one of the ancient Greeks' most well-known and powerful myths. It is a story of desire and deceit which depicts some of our worst traits and fears. Research the story on the Web. Why are stories like this so memorable? Can they influence the way people think and behave? Can science have a similar impact on people?

Most cultures have their own traditional ways of understanding the world. Great civilisations of the past such as those of the ancient Greeks, Romans and Aztecs believed that phenomena such as thunder and lightning, droughts, earthquakes and pestilence were caused by the actions of malevolent gods. As a result, sacrifices were offered to persuade the gods not to wreak havoc on the world. Today, people's religious beliefs are based on the interpretation of ancient texts such as the Jewish Torah, the Christian Bible and the Muslim Qur'an (Koran).

How is scientific knowledge different from religious knowledge?

Science began when people first imagined that phenomena such as thunder and lightning may not have anything to do with the action of gods. Underpinning scientific knowledge is the belief that there are natural explanations for how the world works, which people can discover for themselves.

Scientific ways of understanding the world can be traced back to the time of the ancient Greeks. Like most other civilisations, the ancient Greeks explained the behaviour of their world in terms of the actions of supernatural beings. Explanations for phenomena such as rain, thunder, lightning and disease were attributed to the action of capricious gods. Human fallibilities were imposed on these gods, so at times they might be happy and content, but at other times angry or jealous. It was believed that their moods affected their behaviour in ways which had consequences for the people. For example, angry gods could cause earthquakes or storms, while in a more benevolent mood the gods could prevent famine and disease.

Greek society at this time was affluent enough for some privileged people to have the time and confidence to challenge contemporary beliefs. There was tolerance of a wide range of religious views and, as a result, there emerged a group of radical thinkers who found pleasure and intellectual satisfaction in challenging the authority and even the existence of the gods.

The theologian Xenophanes (520 BCE) was one of the earliest philosophers to challenge the validity of the traditional myths. He claimed that the gods as described in the traditional tales were not real but a fabric of people's imagination. He argued that it was no coincidence that in every culture the gods took on the appearance and behaviours of the local people.

Homer and Hesiod have ascribed to the gods all those things which are shameful and reproachful among men: theft, adultery and deceiving each other . . . Mortals believe that the gods are born, and that they have clothes, speech and bodies similar to their own . . . If cattle, horses and lions had hands, and could draw with those hands and accomplish the works of men, horses would draw the forms of gods as like horses, and cattle like cattle, and each would make their bodies as each had themselves . . . The Ethiopians claim their gods are snub-nosed and black, while the Thracians claim theirs have blue eyes and red hair.
(Gregory, 2003: 11)

Something to think about

The philosopher-scientists of ancient Greece did not as a rule do experiments to help them discover knowledge. Most of their time was spent in thinking, reading, reasoning and arguing. They were mainly concerned with persuading each other that their views made most sense. Do you think we should do more reasoning, arguing and persuading in our science lessons?

Who were the first scientists?

The term 'scientist' is relatively modern and first used in the nineteenth century. However, to avoid confusion we use the term in this chapter to describe those ancient philosophers who sought out natural explanations for the behaviour of the physical world.

Many of the first scientists came from Miletus in Asia Minor which is now part of Turkey. This was an important cosmopolitan trading centre which had strong links with eastern cultures. Exposure to these other cultures and their mythologies caused philosophers like Xenophanes to reflect on the nature of their own knowledge. For example, if other cultures had their own creation stories which differ in essential ways from the Greeks', which accounts are to be believed? After all, how many different ways can the Sun and stars be created? Surely only one account could be true. It seems that once sown, these seeds of doubt grew into radically new ways of thinking. The rejection of mythological explanations was a liberating act which enabled the Greeks to search for new ways to understand the world.

Around 600 BCE philosophers started to develop the first scientific theories. They considered the world to be an ordered system in which events such as rain and earthquakes had natural causes. The word *cosmos* is a Greek word which means a sense of good order or a well-ordered place (an ordered, harmonious whole). The scientists believed that everything that happened within the *cosmos* could be explained by the way it was structured. Therefore, phenomena such as drought, lightning and disease were not caused by the whim of unpredictable gods, but for natural and predictable reasons which were the result of the way the physical world was organised. The origins of scientific thinking can be traced back to the philosophers such as Thales of Miletus

(624–565 BCE) who thought all the materials on the Earth were made of water and Anaximenes of Miletus (c. 570 BCE) who thought everything was made of air. Heraclitus of Ephesus (535–475 BCE) believed that the causes of events in the natural world would be comprehensible to humans once they had discovered its fundamental structure, which clearly demonstrates the ancient Greeks' commitment to natural, rather than supernatural explanations. This type of thinking led to the development of the first scientific models of the universe.

Early scientific theories

Believing that everything in the physical world was part of a well-ordered system, the first scientists put their minds to creating representations of the universe which would help them explain how it worked. Thales was one of the first to provide a systematic way of explaining the world. He thought the Earth was a big flat island surrounded by sea. He imagined the planets, stars, Sun and Moon to be fixed to a bowl spinning around the stationary sea and Earth every twenty-four hours. This model of the universe enabled him to explain day and night and to provide reasons for the movement of the objects in the heavens. However, if we observe the Moon and planets on different nights we find that they have moved their position relative to the stars that surround them. The Moon and the planets seem to wander amongst the stars as well as rotate around the Earth. How could this be possible if they were all firmly fixed to the same spinning sphere? What does this tell us about the reliability of Thales' model?

Flat Earth model of the universe

In later years Thales' simple model was replaced by more complex models. Observations of ships disappearing and reappearing over the horizon convinced the ancient Greeks that the Earth must be round. The separate motions of the Moon and planets were accounted for by adding extra spheres. After much modification the models started to become very complex. Some had over fifty spheres moving in different ways and still could not precisely account for the movement of the planets. Aristotle's (384–322 BCE) model shows a simplified version of the multi-spheres model.

Something to think about

Scientists today describe the best theories or models as beautiful and elegant. Do you think this description applies to Thales' and Aristotle's models of the universe? Explain why.

According to Aristotle the universe consisted of a terrestrial region which was subject to change, and a celestial region which was unchanging. This division was convenient because it allowed Aristotle to provide different types of explanation for the movement of objects in the different regions. In the celestial region, the Moon, Sun, planets and stars were all attached to solid, transparent spheres and moved in perfect circles around the Earth. Aristotle considered circular motion to be superior to other forms of motion and the heavens to be perfect and unchanging.

The terrestrial region was far from perfect and things in it were subject to change. According to Aristotle, everything in this region was made from a combination of four

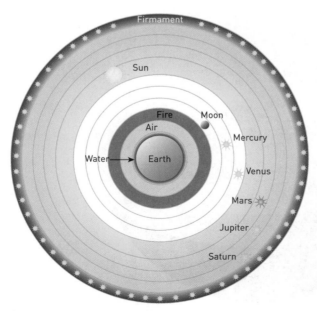

Aristotle's model of the universe

elements: earth, water, air and fire. Each element had its natural place in the *cosmos* and always strove to return to it. Therefore, a rock when released would fall to the ground because it was made of earth and wanted to return to its natural place. The concept of the four elements was a very powerful scientific model and could be used to explain why things in the terrestrial world were able to change their form. For example, phenomena such as burning could be explained by the separation of wood into its basic elements. If we believe wood to be made from earth, water, air and fire, then burning can be explained as a process through which these elements are released. When wood burns we see fire being released along with the other three elements.

Was the geocentric theory ever challenged?

The geocentric (Earth-centred) model of the universe continued to be accepted for over two thousand years. Ironically, the heliocentric (Sun-centred) model which later

School of Athens by Raphael (1483–1520). Painted between 1510 and 1511, this picture depicts the great Greek philosophers and other ancient scientists. Plato and Aristotle are the two central figures

Source: De Agostini Editore Picture Library/DK Images

replaced it in the seventeenth century had been suggested by an ancient Greek called Aristarchus in the third century BCE. Aristarchus audaciously proposed that rather than the Sun moving around the Earth, the Earth may in fact be moving around the Sun. He suggested that the movement of the heavens was an illusion caused by the rotation of the Earth. To persuade other scholars to believe in his model, he had to persuade them that the Earth was moving. This is not an easy thing to prove because we do not sense its movement.

Aristarchus could not prove that the Earth was spinning and the Sun was stationary. Other philosopher-scientists argued against him. If the Earth was moving then it would create a continuous wind as it moved through the air. (Why don't we feel this wind?) With the physical evidence pointing against a moving Earth, it was not possible for Aristarchus and his supporters to persuade the early scientists to reject the geocentric model.

In the development of the early theories we can see how the philosopher-scientists used their imaginations to create representations of the world and tested them against observable evidence. The ancient Greeks observed that the Sun, Moon, planets and stars revolve day and night around what seemed to be a stationary Earth. The model of a geocentric universe was the obvious explanation, yet they were aware that it did not properly fit with all their observations. For this reason the ancient Greeks were never firmly convinced that the geocentric model truly represented the physical world. They realised that their conceptual portrait was unfinished and more work was required.

Christianity's influence on the development of science

The ancient Greeks were never able to complete their scientific masterpiece of the structure of the universe. By 200 BCE the Greek empire was on the wane as the Romans became the dominant military and political force around the Mediterranean. Under the influence of the Romans science began to languish. The Romans were more interested in the social implications and practical application of Greek scientific knowledge than continuing with its development.

With the emergence of Christianity and the fragmentation of the Roman Empire, people started to look once again towards the spiritual rather than the physical to help them understand their world. As the power and influence of the Christian Church grew, scientific thinking was discouraged and scholars were expected to look instead to religious texts as the only true source of knowledge.

In 390 CE, Augustine wrote:

What has Athens to do with Jerusalem, the Academy to do with the Church, the heretic to do with the Christian? . . . We have no need for curiosity after Jesus Christ, and no need of investigation after the gospel. Firstly we believe this, that there is nothing else that we need to believe.
(Gregory, 2003: 154)

From Augustine, we get a sense of the antagonism that the early Christian Church held to the development of scientific thinking. As far as the Church was concerned people should be more concerned with understanding their relationship to God than seeking new knowledge about the physical world. Understanding God was the way to attaining salvation in the spiritual world after death. Science had no part to play in the saving of souls.

How science was kept alive in the Muslim world

During the seventh to the thirteenth centuries the ideas of the Greek philosophers were kept alive in the Muslim world. The works of Plato, Aristotle, Euclid, Archimedes, Hero, Ptolemy, Galen and Hippocrates were translated into Arabic and stored in great libraries. These works were studied by Islamic scholars who produced critiques of them and commentaries which presented the ideas in ways which non-specialists could understand. In this way Greek science continued to flourish at the heart of Islamic intellectual life.

Something to think about

Find out how Arabic/Islamic culture has contributed to the development of science.

For a thousand years there was virtually no science studied in Western Europe. During this time learning focused on the interpretation of religious texts and, hence, monasteries developed into the main centres of education. It wasn't until the eleventh century, when universities began to be established, that Western Europe's interest in science was reignited. By 1200 CE universities were flourishing in Bologna, Paris and Oxford.

With the advent of universities Western scholars began to take an interest in the classical works of the ancient Greeks. Key works were translated from Arabic or Greek into Latin. Demand fuelled supply and soon translations of ancient Greek texts and especially commentaries by Islamic and Greek scholars were being distributed throughout Europe. The most popular works were those of Aristotle and Galen. Aristotle's works on natural philosophy, interpreted by Islamic commentators, formed the framework on which medieval science came to be constructed.

Science plays a subservient role in the Christian world

Medieval scholars spent much time interpreting Aristotle's manuscripts and comparing them with religious texts. Where there were inconsistencies, the Greek teachings were regarded as erroneous. The Church demanded that such 'errors' be amended. Perhaps the biggest clash concerned the origins of the physical world. Christian belief was based on the biblical account in The Book of Genesis, in which God created the world. But according to Aristotle the world was eternal and had no beginning. This was a difficult dilemma and led to much debate between the followers of Aristotle and the theologians. Theologians maintained that *revelation* was superior to all other

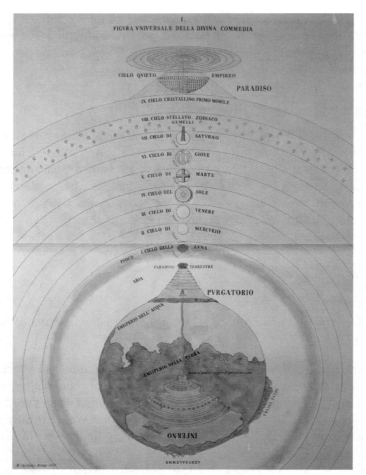

Dante's model of the medieval universe (historical image)
Source: © British Library Board / Bridgeman Art Library Ltd

forms of knowledge. Natural philosophy – science – was built on reason, not revelation, and so was considered to be less reliable than theology.

Science was subservient to theology until the sixteenth century. Aristotle's natural philosophy was useful to Christianity because, on the whole, it was consistent with scripture and consequently enhanced doctrine. Dante Alighieri's (1265–1321) model of the medieval universe demonstrates how the Church integrated Greek cosmology into its doctrine.

All the celestial objects (Sun, Moon, planets and stars) above the Earth were thought to be perfect and unchanging. Each was attached to a solid translucent sphere which rotated through the love of God around the Earth. Beyond the ninth outer sphere is the tenth Heaven. This is the eternal and infinite realm of God, of which people can have no knowledge. In contrast, earthly things within the terrestrial region were within the realm of human understanding. Within the terrestrial region the Church was happy to adopt Aristotle's natural (scientific) explanations. When clashes between science and doctrine arose, such conflict was attributed to errors in the interpretation of Aristotle's works. For medieval scholars in Western civilisation, an understanding of how the world works was a mixture of theology and ancient Greek science. This provided a coherent and acceptable way of thinking in which scientific knowledge and religious belief combined to serve useful social and spiritual purposes for many centuries.

Something to think about

Do you think religious and scientific views can be compatible? Compare examples of religious thinking and scientific thinking to justify your answer.

Galileo's influence on the development of science

There are periods in history when the time is right to challenge the established world-view. For example, it became possible for Greek philosopher-scientists to challenge the mythological beliefs of their society and develop a natural way of explaining their world. This once new and radical natural philosophy endured for over two thousand years and eventually became established knowledge throughout the Western world. Once the powerful Christian Church integrated Greek cosmology into its own teachings, the authority of Greek philosophers such as Aristotle became as absolute as the doctrine derived from the holy texts. Scholars who dared to challenge Aristotle could be accused of heresy as they were in effect challenging the teachings of the Church. This was the situation in 1543 when a Polish monk, Nicholas Copernicus, published his book *On the Revolution of the Heavens* in which he argued for a Sun-centred model of the universe.

The importance of Copernicus' book was that he was able to show that a Sun-centric universe was a possibility. His model was too complex to be popular at the time and for 50 years it was regarded as little more than a moderately useful academic text. However, Copernicus had sown seeds of doubt in Aristotle's natural philosophy. Other scientists were starting to question its infallibility. The astronomer Tycho Brahe published a detailed account of an unusual star which first appeared in the sky in 1572; it shone brightly for about two years then disappeared again. This was evidence that change could occur in the heavens, contrary to the teachings of both Aristotle and the Church. In 1577 Brahe observed the great comet pass through the sky and argued that it must have been travelling beyond the Moon and hence through the celestial spheres. According to Aristotle's cosmology the spheres were solid; nothing could travel through them. Both Brahe and Aristotle could not be right.

The time was right to begin new work on Aristotle's masterpiece. What was needed was a powerful advocate who was prepared to argue and publicise the case against Aristotle and to persuade the Church that it was time to think again about the Earth's place in the cosmos.

Galileo challenges accepted beliefs

That powerful advocate was Galileo Galilei (1564–1642) who, with the help of the newly invented telescope, set out to prove that Aristotle's cosmology was wrong. When Galileo turned his telescope towards the heavens he was able to observe things that were impossible to see with the naked eye. For example, he observed the moons of Jupiter orbiting around the planet. He also used his telescope to show that the Sun had spots which moved across its surface and that the Moon's surface seemed mountainous. He discovered that the planet Venus had phases which were very similar to the phases of the Moon. The world seen through Galileo's telescope was a very different world from the unblemished, unchanging one described by Aristotle. Galileo published his observations in easy-to-read books which became very popular with the educated elite all over Europe. The books sparked people's interest in science and awakened them to the possibility that there was more to know about the world than was contained in ancient Greek texts.

Something to think about

The telescope is an example of how new technologies have played a crucial role in the advancement of science. What is the difference between science and technology? Provide an example of how science has aided the development of a new technology.

Galileo

Type of telescope used by Galileo

Sources: © Bettmann / Corbis (left); DK images (right)

Galileo's popularity made him less sensitive to the views of other scholars. At times he could be scornful and arrogant. His often rude dismissal of other people's views made him unpopular with some of his fellow academics, especially those who remained firm believers in Aristotle's science. His arrogance and contempt for some of his peers can be witnessed in his letter to Joannes Kepler (1571 to 1630):

> I wish, my dear Kepler that we could have a good laugh together at the extra-ordinary stupidity of the mob. What do you think of the foremost philosophers of this University? In spite of my oft-repeated efforts and invitations, they have refused, with the obstinacy of a glutted adder, to look at the planets or Moon or my telescope.
> (University of St Andrews)

At the time Galileo wrote his letter to Kepler he was determined to publicly refute Aristotle's Earth-centred theory in favour of Copernicus' Sun-centric model. The response of the Church was to try to reason with Galileo and they asked him not to directly promote the Copernican model until he had conclusive proof. After all, they had the proof of their own senses that the Earth was stationary. The same old arguments that were used in ancient times for believing in a stationary Earth were used against Galileo. They had endured so long because they were very difficult to dispute. We cannot feel the motion of the Earth, so how can we ever really know whether it is moving? Followers of Aristotle preferred to be led by their common sense, rather than by the arrogant Galileo.

The Church runs out of patience with Galileo

For some years theologians were very patient with Galileo and allowed him to speak his mind in public as long as he did not say anything that was explicitly contrary to the teachings of the Church. Church doctrine recognised Copernicus' model as a mathematical theory which could be useful for calculating the motion of the planets; they did not accept that it described the physical reality. The notion that we lived on a moving Earth which rotated and at the same time orbited the Sun was considered by the Church to be both philosophically incredulous and theologically heretical. A Church report on the possibility of a Sun-centred cosmos concluded it to be:

> foolish and absurd, philosophically and formally heretical inasmuch as it expressly contradicts the doctrine of Holy Scripture in many passages, both in their literal meaning and according to the general interpretation of the Fathers and Doctors.
> (Poole, 1990: 44)

Galileo was eventually warned to abandon his support for the doctrine of Copernicus. Threatened by imprisonment, Galileo reluctantly agreed, but later published a book called *Dialogue Concerning the Two Chief World Systems*, which was designed to refute and even ridicule Aristotle's ideas, and at the same time to promote the Copernican theory.

Some influential theologians saw his book as a direct attack on the teachings of the Church. This was the last straw and Galileo was arrested and put on trial for heresy. It was no ordinary trial. Galileo had been a friend of the Pope for many years and was a popular public figure. Although the Pope felt humiliated and betrayed by Galileo he still dealt with him leniently. Galileo was guilty of heresy and could have been executed. As it was, he was sentenced to house arrest; he was 70 years old and lived another nine years.

Something to think about

Galileo's scientific beliefs steered him onto a collision course with the Christian Church. Their different beliefs predictably led to conflict. A similar situation arose between Charles Darwin and the Church in the twentieth century. Do you think conflicts between religious and scientific beliefs are inevitable? Does one always contradict the other or is it possible to reconcile both world-views?

Although the theologians managed to silence Galileo, interest in science had been rapidly growing throughout Europe. Scientists no longer had to rely solely on their senses to collect data; they now had access to a range of powerful instruments. Telescopes, microscopes, thermometers, prisms, pendulum clocks and barometers were becoming widely available. Galileo and his contemporaries had seriously discredited some of the old science of ancient Greece and had started to replace it. This sparked a renaissance in scientific thinking which spread throughout Europe.

The new age of science

By the time Galileo died in 1642, some scholars were still holding on to the ancient cosmology because they lacked alternative explanations. What made the Sun, Moon and Earth move? What held them in orbit? These were questions which scientific scholars in the middle of the seventeenth century could not answer. The British scientist Robert Hooke thought there must be some force of attraction between the heavenly objects which keep them in orbit. The French philosopher-scientist Descartes imagined that objects could naturally move without being pushed along by a force. Therefore, the planets did not require a divine driving force to keep them moving. These ideas represent the type of thinking of the scientific community at the time. There were many ideas, but no one had managed to put them together in a way which would explain how a heliocentric *cosmos* would work. That is, until Isaac Newton published the *Principia* in 1687 which explained how the force of gravity could control the movement of the heavens. Newton's great achievement was to realise that gravitation is a universal force which not only applies to objects on the Earth such as apples falling from trees, but also to objects in the heavens such as the movement of the Moon, Sun and planets. Newton's theory of universal gravitation turned the Copernican model into a physical possibility by explaining how the natural force of **gravity** could control the movement of objects in the heavens.

Newton's model of the universe held together by a force so powerful that it controls not only the movement of the Moon but all the distant planets that move around the Sun is one of the most enduring masterpieces of scientific thinking. It is an awe-inspiring vision which owed as much to the power of his imagination as it did to the power of his reason and his dogged determination to once and for all solve the problem of the spheres. After 1,500 years of scholars exploring ancient texts for scientific explanations, Newton had firmly established the possibility of progressing beyond the conventional knowledge of the ancient Greeks.

In more recent times, the work of scientists has enabled more complex conceptual portraits of the universe to be constructed. Science has now produced a truly awe-inspiring theory called the **Big Bang**, which not only explains how the universe could have been formed but also completely transforms how we visualise its nature. Newton's theory of universal gravitation is so powerful that it remains an important part of this latest masterpiece.

Women in science

Social conditions until the late 1960s meant that women found it either impossible or very difficult to work in investigative science; their achievements until recently were necessarily informal or simply went unrecorded. Women now have better opportunities to work as scientists. We need to discuss such issues with children. They should be aware that, despite changing times, stereotypes are doggedly persistent. A 'scientist' in the print media is often a male with bewildered hair and a wild grin, wearing a white coat and flourishing a foaming test tube, or a whiskery Victorian gentleman. We need to talk about the history of science and the reasons why we see no women contributing. We need to provide inspiring examples of role models for all children.

Something to think about

Find out about the lives and work of scientists such as Marie Curie (1867–1934), Rosalind Franklin (1920–58), Dorothy Hodgkin (1910–94), Barbara McClintock (1902–92) and Christiane Nüsslein-Volhard (1942–present day).

Summary

The origins of science can be traced back to the time of the ancient Greeks when a small number of radical thinking people began to seek natural, rather than supernatural, explanations for how the physical world works. These first scientists developed new knowledge from experience and reasoned argumentation. The theories developed by the ancient Greeks endured for 2,000 years until many of them proved to be unreliable when rigorously tested in the sixteenth century. Out of this period emerged a new scientific age, with more rigorous methodology and greater freedom for people to express their ideas. From that time onwards our understanding of how the natural world works has developed at an ever increasing rate.

Further reading

Books

- Crump, T. (2002) *Science: As Seen Through the Development of Scientific Instruments*, London: Constable and Robinson Ltd.
- Brown, H. (1994) *The Wisdom of Science: Its Relevance to Culture and Religion*, Cambridge: Cambridge University Press.
- Fara, P. (2009) *Science: A Four Thousand Year History*, Oxford: Oxford University Press.
- Fortey, J. (2007) *Eyewitness Great Scientists*, London: Dorling Kindersley Ltd.
- Gregory, A. (2003) *Eureka: The Birth of Science*, Cambridge: Icon Books.
- Reed, A. W. (1993) *Aboriginal Myths, Legends and Fables* [compiled by A. W. Reed], Chatswood: N.S.W.
- Sobel, D. (1999) *Galileo's Daughter: A Drama of Science, Faith and Love*, London: Fourth Estate.

Primary science review articles (Association of Science Education)

- PSR 96 (January/February 2007), 'Earth, air, fire and water, in our elements' by Tara Lievesley.

PART 2
SUBJECT KNOWLEDGE AND IDEAS FOR PRACTICE

Overview

This part provides 'Subject knowledge' and 'Ideas for practice' for the following themes:

- The Earth and beyond
- Energy and the well-being of the planet
- Interdependence
- Diversity
- Adaptation and evolution
- Health and well-being

- Particle nature of materials
- Changing materials
- Electricity and magnetism
- Forces and motion
- Light
- Sound

'Subject knowledge' sections begin with a brief historical context to introduce some of the key scientists who contributed to the development of the knowledge presented in the chapter. We would encourage you to find out more about the lives and work of these great scientists. Within each theme are 'Something to think about' scenarios for reflection and personal learning. These are designed to make you think creatively about key ideas in a different context or to encourage you to extend and develop your understanding.

'Ideas for practice' sections are based on the three-stage framework for science learning introduced in Chapter 2. Separate parts deal with ideas for teaching science in the Lower (ages 5–8 years) and Upper (ages 8–11) Primary phases. The 'Ideas for practice' are not lesson plans but suggestions to illustrate how the teaching of particular topics can be organised using the three-stage framework. They will need to be modified to meet the needs of a specific age group.

'Ideas for practice' sections are based on the following outline structure:

- *Scientific view*: Represents the view of the world which we want the children to value and adopt as their own.
- *Scientific enquiry skills*: Skills children will need to explore the topic and to make sense of the scientific view.
- *Exploration stage*: Presents a range of teaching and learning strategies to set the scene for the children's learning and to explore their ideas about the topic.
- *Re-describing stage*: Presents a range of teaching and learning strategies which can be used to help children make sense of the scientific view.
- *Application stage*: Presents opportunities for children to make use of their newly acquired scientific knowledge in different contexts. The application of scientific ideas in techno-logical contexts feature prominently, but other contexts are also used including art, drama, poetry and creative writing.

In each stage terms such as 'talk together' or 'work collaboratively' are written in italics to emphasise the key role that classroom talk plays in children's science learning. These terms refer to teaching and learning strategies discussed in Chapter 4. Detailed discussion of the other strategies used in the 'Ideas for practice' sections can be found in Chapter 6.

The role of information and communication technology

The book does not have a chapter dedicated to the use of ICT. This is because we see the use of ICT tools as integral to science lessons. When planning a science lesson ICT resources are required for gaining information, modelling ideas, recording data and presenting findings.

'Ideas for practice' sections include ICT in use:

- as sources of information;
- to simulate and model ideas;
- for recording information both inside and outside the classroom (digital cameras);
- for measuring and recording changing levels of sound, light and temperature (data loggers);
- for detailed observation and recording (digital microscopes);
- to present data and outcomes of enquiries.

CHAPTER 8
THE EARTH AND BEYOND

Over the past few decades scientists have sent many missions out into the solar system to discover its secrets. Space probes have sent back pictures and made discoveries which have enabled us to understand the structure of our solar system in great detail. In addition to the information gained by spacecraft, new and more powerful telescopes have enabled scientists to see beyond our solar system to gain understanding of the faraway objects which populate the universe.

This chapter presents a scientific view of how the universe was first created and how the solar system was formed. It explains the causes of common phenomena such as day and night, the seasons and the phases of the Moon.

Topics discussed in this chapter:

- Historical context
- A close-up view of the stars
- How the universe was created
- The structure of the solar system
- Experiences related to the Earth, Moon and Sun

Part 1: Subject knowledge

Historical context

Our present-day understanding of the structure of the solar system dates back to the sixteenth century when a Polish monk called Nicholas Copernicus (1473–1543) suggested that the Earth may revolve around the Sun. Before this time it was generally accepted that the Earth was at the centre of the universe with the Sun, Moon, planets, and stars orbiting around it. Copernicus challenged this view and presented a radically new model which placed the Sun at the centre of the cosmos. For many people the idea of a heliocentric universe contradicted Christian doctrine. However, by the start of the seventeenth century a small but influential number of scientists believed Copernicus was probably right.

The most significant of these scientists was Galileo Galilei (1564–1642). With the help of the newly invented telescope, Galileo was able to provide a persuasive argument against the established view and in favour of Copernicus' heliocentric universe. Galileo established the possibility of challenging and improving traditional views. This was the birth of modern science (see Chapter 7).

A close-up view of the stars

Viewed from Earth the stars appear to be specks of light hanging in the sky. They create interesting patterns, but don't seem to be doing anything spectacular. However, close-up things are very different. We need to take a closer look to find out what makes them shine.

Something to think about

What would you expect to see if you could get closer to a star? What would it look like? Are all stars the same? What do you imagine they are made from?

Our nearest star

From Earth, our nearest star is the Sun. The Sun is a relatively small star, but enormous compared to the Earth. A total of 109 Earths would be required to fit across the Sun's disk, and its interior could hold over 1.3 million Earths. Of course it looks quite small in the sky because it is 150 million kilometres away. The Sun's outer visible layer is called the **photosphere** and has a temperature of 6,000°C. Although the Sun appears

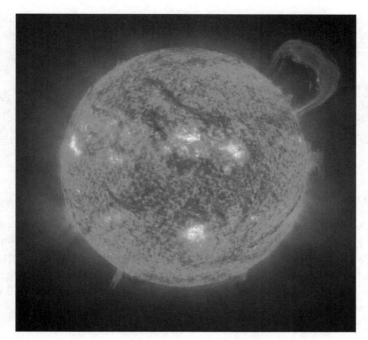

Solar flares
Source: Courtesy of NASA

to be calm and unchanging, it is in fact a raging nuclear furnace. **Solar energy** is created deep within its core where the temperature is 15,000,000°C. Every second the Sun releases 5 million tons of pure energy. If you visited the Sun you might be amazed by the spectacular solar flares which dance across its surface.

Scientists think the Sun has been burning for 4.6 billion years. At the end of its life it will begin to swell up, ultimately growing so large that it will swallow the Earth. Fortunately, the Sun has enough fuel for another five billion years or so.

Out into the Milky Way and beyond

The universe is full of stars like the Sun. All the stars we see in the night sky are nuclear furnaces emitting vast amounts of energy. Many of them are much bigger than the Sun, but appear so small because they are much further away. Most of the stars we see from Earth belong to the Milky Way **galaxy** in which the solar system is situated. More than 200 billion stars make up the galaxy. With the naked eye we can only see approximately 2,000 stars at any one time.

A galaxy is a huge collection of stars, dust and gas. The Milky Way is a spiral galaxy. If viewed from the 'top' it would look like a slowly spinning pinwheel. The Sun is located on one of the spiral arms. The Milky Way gets its name from a Greek myth about the goddess Hera who sprayed milk across the sky. In China the band of stars across the night sky is called the *Silver River* and in the Kalahari Desert in Southern Africa it is described as the *Backbone of Night*. Even if we could travel at the speed of light (300,000 km per second), the galaxy is so immense it would take about 25,000 years to reach the middle. Since time travel is not yet possible, scientists rely on very powerful telescopes to explore the Milky Way.

Something to think about

What would the sky look like if we could see all the stars in the Milky Way from Earth?

Stargazing through the Hubble Telescope

Four hundred years ago Galileo was the first scientist to use a telescope to explore the night sky. Through the telescope he observed that Saturn had rings and Jupiter had moons. He also saw that the hazy patch across the centre of the sky called the Milky Way was not a cloud but an assortment of innumerable stars. The telescope changed forever our understanding of the nature of the universe and has enabled scientists to take some amazing images of the stars.

Something to think about

What can we find out about the universe by looking at pictures taken by telescopes such as Hubble? What do these remarkable images tell us about the nature of the universe? You can view pictures taken by the Hubble Telescope at http://hubblesite.org/gallery/.

Hubble Telescope
Source: © Dorling Kindersley / DK Images

We now have telescopes which can see into the depths of the known universe. The Hubble Telescope is the most powerful optical telescope ever made. It was launched into orbit around the Earth in 1990 to provide an unobstructed view of the universe. Hubble is so powerful that it enables us to see objects in space which are 1.5 billion times fainter than can be seen with the naked eye. Since its launch the Hubble Telescope has taken the most astonishing photographs, which show the universe to be a dynamic and beautiful place in which new stars are constantly being born in stunning stellar nurseries and old stars meet their end in spectacular explosions.

Outside the Milky Way galaxy, the universe may contain over 100 billion galaxies, each of which on average contains 100 billion stars. A universe which contains over 10,000 billion, billion stars is unimaginable; we can only be in awe of the magnitude of the universe around us.

How the universe was created

The biggest question of all

The big question for scientists is where all these galaxies and stars came from. Have they always been there, or have they developed from something else? The ancient Greek scientists believed that the heavens were unchanging and had always existed as we see them today. In the seventeenth century the Christian Church calculated

An impression of the Big Bang leading to the formation of the universe
Source: © Mark A. Garlick (www.space-art.co.uk)

4004 BCE to be the date of the creation of the universe. Apparently this figure was worked out by adding up the ages of the people in the Old Testament.

Big Bang theory

The debate about whether or not the universe had a beginning was only resolved relatively recently. Discoveries by Edwin Hubble in 1929 and by Arno Penzias and Robert Wilson in 1964 provided evidence for an expanding universe and the possibility that something happened which caused the universe to be formed. The event which caused the creation of the universe is commonly known as the *Big Bang*.

Understanding what happened in the Big Bang continues to be a major challenge for the scientific community. What seems to be agreed is that an indescribably large explosion sent subatomic particles of matter hurtling out into space. Over the first 300,000 years these particles combined to form **atoms** of hydrogen and helium. Over the next billion years hydrogen and helium gas were drawn together by the force of gravity into huge dense clouds, from which the first stars and galaxies were formed.

The structure of the solar system

How was the solar system created?

The universe was already over 11 billion years old when our solar system was created from the embers of dead stars. As stars get older they manufacture a range of different materials within their nuclear furnace. In addition to helium, they produce other materials such as iron, silicon, oxygen and carbon. Towards the end of their lives very large stars become unstable and can explode, throwing out all these materials into space. These exploding stars are called **supernovas**. The different materials created from supernova explosions form clouds of dusty and gaseous debris called nebulae.

Nebulae are places in which solar systems are created. Our solar system was constructed within a gaseous and dusty nebula about 4.6 billion years ago. The Sun was formed from lighter materials such as hydrogen and helium. The planets were created from tiny particles of rock, metal and ice. These heavier materials smashed into each other as they spun around the Sun, merging into pebbles. Under the force of gravity these pebbles fused to form rocks, then boulders. After about 100 million years the planets had formed.

Planets: celestial wanderers

People have been studying the movement of the planets since before the time of the ancient Greeks. The planets are things of interest and fascination because they do not appear to behave like the myriad other 'stars' in the sky. When viewed from Earth, they do not maintain a fixed position within the star patterns: they seem to wander about from one **constellation** to another. The planets are named after Roman Gods.

Steps in the formation of the solar system
Source: © Mark A. Garlick (www.space-art.co.uk)

The structure of the solar system (not to scale)
Source: DK Images

For example, Venus is the Roman name for the goddess of love. The Romans thought Venus to be the brightest and most beautiful object in the heavens.

The planets are not stars because they do not emit their own light. Planets orbit a sun and can be seen because they reflect the Sun's light. The four inner planets in our solar system (Mercury, Venus, Earth and Mars) are quite different from the outer

Table 8.1 Information about the major planets

Planet	Structure	Size (diameter)	No. of moons	Icy/rocky rings
Mercury	rock and metal	4,878 km	0	0
Venus	rock and metal	12,103 km	0	0
Earth	rock and metal	12,756 km	1	0
Mars	rock and metal	6,786 km	2	0
Jupiter	gas	142,984 km	16	3
Saturn	gas	120,536 km	18	7
Uranus	gas	51,118 km	17	10
Neptune	gas	49,528 km	8	6

planets (Jupiter, Saturn, Uranus and Neptune). The inner planets are relatively small and made mostly of rock, whereas the outer planets are quite enormous and mostly gaseous. All the planets are held in their orbits by the gravitational force of the Sun.

Caught in space

A moon is an object which orbits a planet. The force of gravity of the planet pulls the moon around in its orbit as if it were attached by an invisible string. The small inner planets have few or no moons orbiting them, while the bigger outer planets which have far more gravity have captured lots of moons. Some also have rings of ice and rock orbiting around them.

Something to think about

Gravity controls the movement of all the planets in the solar system. How does it do it? What would happen if gravity could be turned off?

Why is Pluto no longer a major planet?

There used to be nine designated planets in our solar system. However, in 2003 a new object in the depth of our solar system was discovered, using a powerful telescope based at the Palomar Observatory in the USA. The object was at first considered to be a tenth planet and was named Eris after the Greek goddess of conflict. This was an apt name as its discovery caused a heated debate amongst the scientists about whether or not it was big enough to be a planet. Eris is one of the most distant objects that scientists have discovered in the solar system, being more than three times farther from the Sun than Pluto. It is also bigger than Pluto, which is why there was so much debate about whether or not it should be classified as a planet. With the prospect of other small planets being discovered in the future, the International

Astronomical Union designated Eris as a dwarf planet. This meant Pluto had to be downgraded to a dwarf planet, and hence we consider that there are now only eight major planets.

Space debris: meteors, asteroids and comets

There are huge amounts of rock and ice speeding around the solar system. This space debris ranges in size from specks of dust to massive chunks of rock hundreds of kilometres wide. We can observe the fiery trail of small fragments of space rocks when they plunge into the Earth's atmosphere and burn up. We see them as shooting stars or **meteors**. Sometimes the Earth passes through areas of space which have a high concentration of ice and dust which can create a spectacular shower of meteors. Each year, between 13 and 21 November, large numbers of meteors rain down on the Earth. This is the Leonid meteor shower first discovered in 1833. In that year it was estimated that up to a thousand meteors per minute lit up the sky. Astonishingly, over 4.5 million tonnes of space rock bombard the Earth every year. Most of these rocks (meteoroids) are very small and burn up in the Earth's atmosphere; however, larger rocks have crashed into the Earth's surface creating craters.

What do we know about the asteroid belt?

Asteroids are the name we give to the space debris which orbits the Sun in a region between Mars and Jupiter. This region is called the asteroid belt. Asteroids are irregularly shaped rocky objects which vary in size from tiny pebbles to about 930 km in diameter. The biggest asteroid (Ceres) has recently been classified as a dwarf planet. Sixteen of the 3,000 known asteroids are over 240 km in diameter and some even have orbiting moons. Scientists think that Jupiter's strong gravity may have prevented the asteroids from building up into a planet-sized body. Another explanation could be that all the rocky debris in this part of the solar system may have once been a planet that was destroyed by a collision with a large **comet**. There is enough material in the asteroid belt to form a planet about half the size of our Moon.

Even if Jupiter prevented the creation of another planet billions of years ago, we need to be grateful that its strong gravitational force prevents the asteroids from soaring towards the inner planets. Many objects have struck our Earth in the past. It is thought that an impact with a huge piece of space debris about 65 million years ago caused mass extinction of life, including the loss of the dinosaurs. Other theories suggest that the building blocks of life and much of the water we have on Earth arrived on the multitude of asteroids and comets that bombarded our planet in its

An impression of the asteroid belt
Source: © Mark A. Garlick (www.space-art.co.uk)

infancy. We have good reason to fear another collision with even a relatively small asteroid. On 30 June 1908 an asteroid about 100 m in diameter struck the Earth and devastated more than half a million acres of forest in the remote region of Tunguska in Siberia.

Imagine the effect if it had landed on one of the Earth's largest cities. The scariest event of recent times happened on 23 March 1989, when an asteroid 400 m wide very nearly struck the Earth. Scientists estimated that Earth and the 50-million-ton asteroid had been in the same position in space but, fortunately, a vital six hours apart.

Where do comets come from?

Comets are huge dusty snowballs which normally reside in the freezing outer regions of the solar system. The dark, cold area of the solar system where comets can be found is called the Oort cloud, which is 100,000 times further away from the Sun than is the Earth. The cloud is made up of about six trillion comets which surround the solar system. Just like the planets and the asteroids, the comets are held in orbit around the Sun by its powerful gravitational force. Sometimes a comet drifts away from the Oort cloud and travels through the inner solar system. When this happens the comet starts to warm up as it gets closer to the Sun. The energy from the Sun causes some of the ice to thaw and to change into a gas which streams out to form a long tail. This gives the comet the distinctive shape which we see from Earth. Lit by the Sun, the comet glows as brightly as a planet.

A comet with its distinctive tail
Source: Courtesy of NASA

Throughout history, comets have been perceived as omens heralding disaster or great events. Records of comets exist before the time of the ancient Greeks. The following account of a comet was found in an ancient text in 1140 BCE:

> a star arose whose body was bright like the day, while from its luminous body a tail extended, like the tail of a scorpion.
> (Brady, J., 1982)

It is possible that this comet could be the same one which was named after the English astronomer Edmond Halley. Halley's Comet was recorded many times in history before Halley predicted its return in 1705. Many people, both ancient and modern, have seen this comet. It is very bright and a regular visitor orbiting the Sun every 76 years. It was last seen in 1986, and is predicted to return in 2061. Halley will never return to its original home in the Oort cloud. It is now trapped by the Sun's gravity in a smaller orbit which takes it just beyond Neptune before heading back towards the Sun.

Experiences related to the Earth, Moon and Sun

The spinning Earth

From Earth the most easily recognisable objects in our solar system are the Sun and the Moon. By watching the movement of the Sun it is easy to think that it travels

The Earth viewed from the Moon
Source: Jamie Marshall / digitaleye / DK Images

around the Earth. In fact, the movement of the Sun is an illusion caused by the spin of the Earth. When we watch the Sun rising in the morning and setting in the evening we rarely imagine how these events are caused by the rotation of the Earth.

Something to think about

Have you ever thought how fast we are moving on the surface of the Earth as it spins around on its axis? Standing on the equator you would be speeding along at about 1000 mph. Why don't we sense this movement? Shouldn't we expect the movement of the Earth to create gale-force winds as it cuts through the air?

What do we know about the Moon?

At 384,400 km away the Moon is our closest neighbour in space. This may seem a long way away compared to the distances we travel on Earth but, compared to the overall size of the solar system, the Moon is very close. Some scientists think that the Moon may have been created when an object the size of Mars smashed into the Earth billions of years ago, throwing huge amounts of rocky material into space. Over a long time gravity fashioned this material into the Moon we see today. If we look at the Moon with binoculars we can see that its surface is covered with craters caused by impacts with space debris.

Phases of the Moon

As we move through a month in time – a twelfth of our journey around the Sun – the Moon appears to change shape. A full moon happens when the whole surface of the moon facing us is lit up by the Sun. As the Moon orbits the Earth the proportion of its surface facing us which is lit by the Sun decreases (wanes) and, consequently, we see reducing fractions or phases of the moon. The Moon appears to change shape progressively until we can see no part of it at all. At this stage the side of the Moon facing away from us is fully lit by the Sun, leaving our side in darkness. As the Moon continues its orbit around the Earth the proportion of its surface reflecting sunlight towards the Earth steadily increases (waxes) until once again the side facing us is fully lit.

Model of shadows on the side of the Earth and Moon facing away from the Sun
Source: Mike Dunning / © Dorling Kindersley / DK Images

Something to think about

The illustration on page 111 shows both the Earth and Moon partially lit by the Sun. If you were standing on the Earth, what phase of the Moon would you see? On the other hand, what would the Earth look like when viewed from the Moon? How long would day and night be on the Moon, considering that it takes about a month to rotate on its axis?

Why do we have seasons?

Owing to the **tilt of the Earth's** axis, the intensity of sunlight received by the northern and southern hemispheres changes throughout the year. Different areas of the Earth receive different amounts of sunlight, depending on the Earth's position around the Sun. When the northern hemisphere is angled towards the Sun, rays of sunlight shine directly onto this part of the world, creating a hot summer climate. As the Earth continues around the Sun the situation changes until the northern hemisphere is angled away from the Sun. This creates cooler, winter conditions in the north because of the reduced amount of sunlight it receives. Because the direction of the Earth's tilt always remains the same, the southern hemisphere experiences opposite seasons to the north.

Something to think about

Find out about the equinoxes and solstices. Use a globe (Earth) and a torch (Sun) to model the spring equinox and the winter solstice.

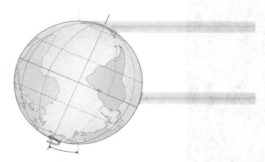

Intensity of light varies due to tilt of Earth
Source: Peter Bull / © Dorling Kindersley / DK Images

Solar eclipse

The ancient Chinese thought that during an **eclipse** the Sun was being eaten by a dragon or demon. They would yell and shout, and bang on pots and drums to frighten it way. The Incas had similar beliefs. The ancient Greeks thought that an eclipse was

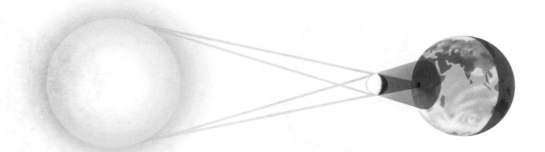

Solar eclipse
Source: Janos Marffy / © Dorling Kindersley / DK Images

a sign that the Sun, which they considered to be a god, was abandoning them. The word 'eclipse' comes from the Greek word meaning 'abandonment'.

Today, eclipses still fascinate and maybe frighten us. During a solar eclipse the Moon moves between the Earth and the Sun, and for a few minutes the Sun seems to disappear, which can be an alarming experience. The stage of an eclipse when the Moon completely covers and blocks out the Sun is called *totality*. During this time the glow of the Sun's outer atmosphere with its spectacular solar flares becomes visible. Although total solar eclipses are quite frequent, about two every three years, relatively few people witness them because the shadow cast by the Moon onto the Earth is very narrow. It is often less that 100 km across. Only people who view the eclipse from within the shadow will see its totality.

Something to think about

What would an eclipse of the Sun look like if the Moon was either bigger or smaller? What would we see if the Moon was further away from the Earth? Would a solar eclipse still be such a spectacular event if the relative sizes and distances of the Moon and the Sun from the Earth were different?

Why lunar eclipses are more common

Lunar eclipses are more commonly observed because at any one time they can be seen from a huge area of the Earth. Lunar eclipses occur when the Moon travels into the shadow cast by the Earth. The Earth casts a huge shadow which can take up to four hours to cross the face of the Moon. Anyone standing on the night side of the Earth can witness the lunar eclipse. Surprisingly, the Moon often turns red when it is eclipsed. This is because the Earth's atmosphere acts like a prism and separates the sunlight into its different colours. Of the colours of the **spectrum**, red light is refracted the most and becomes directed onto the face of the Moon. The Moon reflects this red light back to the Earth.

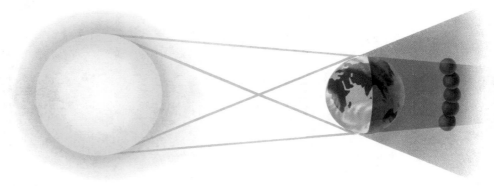

Lunar eclipse
Source: Janos Marffy / © Dorling Kindersley / DK Images

Summary

The solar system was formed by the force of gravity from the remains of dead stars more than 11 billion years ago. The largest objects in the solar system are the Sun and the eight major planets. The Sun is a fiery nuclear furnace which releases huge amounts of energy into the solar system. The four planets closest to the Sun are mainly made from rocks and metal; the other planets mainly consist of gas. Large amounts of rocky and icy debris litter the solar system. These objects include rocky asteroids, icy comets and a vast number of meteors, which often plunge through the Earth's atmosphere creating the effect of 'shooting stars'.

The Moon is our nearest neighbour in space. It is the only part of the solar system that we have physically visited. Unmanned spaceships have been sent to photograph many parts of the solar system, but the Moon is the only place that we have been able to send people to explore. The Moon orbits around the Earth once each month and over that time appears to change shape progressively. The phases we observe from the Earth are caused by the way sunlight is reflected from the surface of the Moon.

At any one time the Sun's light shines on one side of the Earth, leaving the other side in darkness. As the Earth spins around on its axis, different parts of the Earth move from light into shadow causing the phenomena we call day and night. The seasons are caused by the angle of tilt of the Earth.

Further information and teaching resources can be found at the end of the 'Ideas for practice' section.

Part 2: Ideas for practice

Topic: Moon craters

Age group: Lower primary

Scientific view

The Moon is a barren and lifeless place. Unlike the Earth it has no air to breathe, no rivers or seas to swim in and there are no sounds to listen to. Its mountainous surface is silent desert peppered with craters created by meteoroids (space rocks) smashing into its surface.

Scientific enquiry skills

In these activities children will:

- raise and try to find answers to questions;
- think creatively to explain links between cause and effects;
- test ideas using evidence from observation and measurement;
- compare what they saw happen with what they expected would happen;
- use first-hand experience and information sources to answer questions.

Exploration stage

Children's talk involves trying out their own ideas

Setting the scene

Read this poem with the class.

The Moon
The Moon out
There.
The Sun out
There.

The whole galaxy out

There

and me stuck in my bedroom

Ki Ellwood-Friery, aged 8 years old (1996)

Talk about children's responses to the poem. What do they think about when they look up at the Moon? Do they think the Moon is special? What do they think it is made from? Would they like to visit the Moon? If they could see it close up, what would it look like? Find out if any of the children have viewed the Moon through binoculars and ask them to describe what they could see. There are lots of interesting websites which provide photographs of the Moon, such as the NASA website for children www.nasa.gov/audience/forkids/kidsclub/flash/index.html

Scientific enquiry

Working in small groups children can discuss images of the Moon. Talk to the children about the nature of the lunar landscape and encourage them to interpret the images in their own words. Compare the surface of the Moon to a desert. Make children aware that the Moon is more barren than any desert on Earth because there is no air to breathe and hence there is no life. Children could record their observations by producing a painting of the lunar landscape. They could also write a poem describing how they would feel when walking on the Moon. Children's work could be used to create a display. *Talk together* about their pictures and poems. Focus the talk on their representations of the Moon's craters. What other words would they use to describe them?

Puzzle

What are craters? How were the ones on the Moon created?

In groups children discuss how they think the craters could have been formed. Encourage the children to *work collaboratively*. Provide each group with an opportunity to present their ideas to the rest of the class and see if any consensus emerges.

Formative assessment

Use the children's poems, paintings and their responses to the puzzle to assess what they know and what they need to learn in the next stage.

Re-describing stage

Children's talk involves making sense of scientific ideas

The purpose of this stage is to model how the space rocks which speed around the solar system could have caused the Moon craters.

Provide children with pictures of asteroids, meteoroids and comets, and talk about how these space rocks can be found speeding around the solar system. Could space rocks like these have created the craters on the Moon? Are there any other possible causes? Children can *work collaboratively* to provide an agreed response.

Scientific enquiry and modelling

Children can test the space rock hypothesis by dropping a variety of rocks into trays filled with sand or flour. Flour is best but messy. They can use digital cameras to record the size and shape of the craters produced.

Encourage the children to hypothesise about questions such as:

- Will bigger space rocks make bigger craters?
- Does the shape of the crater depend on the shape of the space rock?
- Does the size of the crater depend on how fast the space rock is travelling?

Talk together about the reasons for the children's hypotheses and use the sand tray to test them out. Provide opportunities for the children to compare their photographs with photographs of craters on the Moon and to talk about the similarities and differences. Do their photographs support the scientific explanation that space rocks caused the craters on the Moon?

Assessment and further learning

Encourage children to justify their conclusions and assess their progress. What else would they like to find out? Children can raise their own questions for further learning.

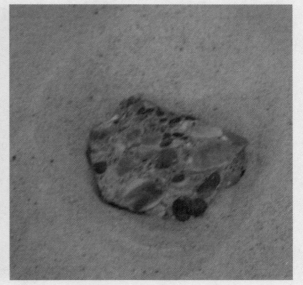

Exploring craters
Source: Peter Loxley

Application stage

Children's talk involves trying out scientific ideas

Scientific enquiry

We probably know more about Mars than any other planet in the solar system (except the Earth). Like the Moon, its surface is covered by craters created by collisions with space rocks. Children can use a range of sources to compare the surface of Mars with that of the Moon.

Link to creative writing

An imaginary journey to the Moon or Mars can provide a stimulating and creative context for children to apply and enrich their developing understanding of our neighbours in space and to develop their creative writing skills.

Assessment

Listen to the children's stories and discuss the results of their scientific enquiry to assess their understanding of the topic.

Topic: Phases of the Moon

Age group: Upper primary

Scientific view

The Moon is our closest neighbour and the brightest object in the night sky. Although it shines so brightly it has no light of its own. We can see the Moon because it is lit up by the light of the Sun. It appears to change shape because as it moves around the Earth we see different proportions of light and shadow.

Scientific enquiry skills

In these activities children will:

- raise and try to find answers to questions;
- think creatively to explain the phases of the Moon and to establish links between cause and effects;

- ask questions and decide how to answer them;
- consider what sources of information they will use to answer questions;
- review their work and the work of others and describe its significance and limitations.

Exploration stage

Children's talk involves trying out their own ideas

Setting the scene

Read this poem with the children

The Moon
The Moon is just a big potato floating in the sky
And little men from outer space are often passing by.
If they're feeling hungry they eat just a bit for dinner,
That's why the Moon is sometimes fat,
But at other times it's thinner.

Poskitt, K. (1991)

Discuss children's responses to the poem. Have they noticed the phases of the Moon, that is, its changing shape? Do they have a better explanation for why the Moon seems to change its shape? Children can *work collaboratively* to draw pictures of its different phases. Each group should explain why they think the Moon changes shape.

Modelling

In groups the children can use globes (Earth), tennis balls (Moon) and torches (Sun) to try to model the phases of the Moon. Encourage *collaborative* ways of working in which ideas are shared and reasons for their views given.

Puzzle

Children can make a list of questions that *puzzle* them about the phases of the Moon.

Formative assessment

The outcome of this stage should be a record of what children think they know for certain and what they need to find out. A common misconception is that the phases of the Moon are caused by shadows of the Earth. At this stage children's misconceptions should be challenged by asking them to develop a reasoned argument for why their ideas make sense. Inconsistencies in their arguments can become the focus of discussion.

Children modelling the phases of the Moon
Source: Peter Loxley

Re-describing stage

Children's talk involves making sense of scientific ideas

The purpose of this stage is to address children's misconceptions and to provide them with a reliable model to explain the phases of the Moon.

Scientific enquiry

In small groups children can research answers to their puzzling questions, using a range of information sources including books and the Internet sites. Help the children to make sense of the information from different sources. Each group could present their findings to the rest of the class using pictures and web-links in a PowerPoint presentation. *Talk together* about issues which arise from the presentations. Establish the premise that we see the Moon because it reflects sunlight down to the Earth.

Modelling

Armed with new knowledge, ask the children to review the way they modelled the phases of the Moon. Each group can present and explain their models which can then be compared. Children need to persuade each other that their models best explain what we actually observe happening to the shape of the Moon. Encourage them to use language such as: waxing and waning, full Moon, new Moon, crescent Moon and gibbous Moon.

Organise a whole-class model with a group of children standing holding hands in a circle, facing out to represent the Earth. Use a big white ball to represent the Moon and a powerful torch for the Sun. Make the room as dark as possible. Turn out the lights and ask the children in the circle to explain what they can see. Shine the torch on to the Earth. Which children are in the dark and which are lit up by the Sun's light? Relate to day and night. The circle of children (Earth) now rotate so that each moves from night to day and back again. Now introduce the Moon and demonstrate how its movement around the Earth creates the phases. Compare with the children's models. Reinforce the point that the phases of the Moon are caused by the way sunlight is reflected off its surface.

Assessment and further learning

Question the children during modelling to assess their levels of understanding and their progress. What else would they like to find out? Children can raise their own questions for further learning.

Children practise modelling the phases of the Moon for the camera. The activity is best done in a darkened room
Source: Peter Loxley

Application stage

Children's talk involves trying out scientific ideas

Thought experiment

Challenge the children to imagine what the Earth looks like when viewed from the Moon. How would it change with time? To help them, they could model how the Earth would change in the same way they modelled the phases of the Moon. Would we expect the Earth to have similar phases? Encourage the children to use their knowledge of the phases of the Moon to develop a reasoned argument to answer this question. Children can also apply their understanding of how the rotation of the Earth causes day and night to hypothesise about the length of day and night on the Moon.

Links to art and creative writing

Children can paint portraits of the Earth as they imagine it would look when viewed from the Moon. They can also write poems inspired by the topic.

Assessment

Listen to group conversations and children's explanations for the phases of the Earth to assess their understanding of the topic.

Earth rising as viewed from the Moon
Source: Courtesy of NASA

Information and teaching resources

Books

- Bond, P. (1999) *Space*, London: Dorling Kindersley.
- Howe, A., Davies, D., McMahon, K., Towler, L. and Scott, T. (2005) *Science 5–11: A Guide for Teachers*, London: David Fulton, Chapter 7: The Earth and beyond.

Primary science review articles (Association of Science Education)

- PSR 108 (May/June 2009) 'Journeys into Space'
  This issue is dedicated to topics related to the Earth and beyond.
- PSR 88 (May/June 2005) 'Watching the moon from Tenerife' by Baruch, Machell and Norris.
- PSR 72 (March/April 2002) 'Earth and space'
  This issue is dedicated to topics related to the Earth and beyond.

Useful information and interactive websites

- Pictures taken by the Hubble Telescope: http://hubblesite.org/gallery/
- The NASA website: www.nasa.gov
- This is NASA's kids website: www.nasa.gov/audience/forkids/kidsclub/flash/index.html
- Mars Express Mission which is a European Space Agency project: www.esa.int/esaMI/Mars_Express/SEMMTFNFGLE_0.html
- Animations of phases of the moon: www.childrensuniversity.manchester.ac.uk/interactives/science/earthandbeyond/phases.asp
- Science stories about outer space: www.highlightskids.com/Science/Stories/h13sciStoryArch_OuterSpace.asp

CHAPTER 9
ENERGY AND THE WELL-BEING OF THE PLANET

Energy makes things happen. It is used every day to heat and light our houses, to run our cars and to make electronic gadgets work. It is used for transport and today we travel in ways that previous generations would never have thought possible. Industry uses large amounts of energy in manufacturing processes. However, concerns about the amount of energy we use and the depletion of fossil fuels feature regularly in the news and on television.

Topics discussed in this chapter:

- Historical context
- Understanding energy
- Types of energy
- Energy sources

Part 1: Subject knowledge

Historical context

Gottfried Leibnitz, a seventeenth-century German scientist, was one of the first people to study energy. In the late seventeenth century, he proposed the theory of *vis viva*, which means 'living force'. Leibnitz believed that moving objects needed this 'living force' to move and he developed a mathematical formula to calculate it. He thought that *vis viva* could not be lost or destroyed.

Lavoisier (1743–94) had explained heat in terms of the 'caloric theory', which suggested that heat consisted of a fluid called caloric which could be transferred from one body to another to warm it. Count Rumford (1753–1814) proposed a different theory. He observed that when cannons were being bored the metal became hot and he suggested that mechanical *vis viva* was converted to heat *vis viva*. Rumford's views were not accepted for a number of years. Thomas Young (1773–1829), a British physician and physicist, introduced the term 'energy' instead of *vis viva*.

Throughout the nineteenth century scientists continued to develop their understanding of the nature of **energy**. James Joule (1818–89), who gave his name to the unit of energy, suggested that there was a relationship between electricity, heat and mechanical work. He thought the energy needed to do work was contained in **molecules**. Lord Kelvin (1824–1907) together with William Rankine (1820–72) developed the first two laws of **thermodynamics**. In Greek *thermo* means heat and *dynamics* means power. These laws state that energy cannot be created or destroyed and that it is converted from one form to another.

Understanding energy

Technology enables us to use energy purposefully

Throughout history people have exploited energy through the use of technology. They have used the heat and light energy that the Sun has always provided. Once people had learnt how to make fires with wood, they had an energy source that enabled them to heat and light their homes and to cook. Some 5,000 years ago the ancient Egyptians harnessed the energy from the wind to make their sailing boats travel faster, and they may have even used kites to help lift the heavy stones they used to make their temples and pyramids. The ancient Greeks built their homes to take advantage of the natural light and heat from the Sun. Hot water from natural **geothermal** springs was used by ancient Romans for bathing, and at the same period the Chinese burnt oil in lamps to heat and light their homes. The Persians built the first windmills which were used to grind grain, and in the Middle Ages windmills and watermills were used widely in Europe to grind corn and to pump water.

What is energy?

Energy can be defined as the ability to do work or to make things happen. We cannot see energy but whenever something moves, heats or cools energy is involved. When sound or light is produced energy is involved. In everyday language, the word 'energy' is often applied only to living things and relates to enthusiasm or motivation, for example, 'The politician spoke with energy', 'I haven't got the energy to go to the gym'. In science the word is used differently and it is not confined to living things. Matter is the 'stuff' that everything is made of, and all matter has energy in the bonds between the particles in its atoms and between atoms and molecules. The unit of energy is the joule.

All the energy which we use today was released billions of years ago as the result of the 'Big Bang' which is considered to be the origin of our universe. Since then no energy has been created and none has been destroyed. All the energy that existed at that time still exists.

Much of the energy we use on Earth comes directly or indirectly from the Sun. Plants store the Sun's energy by the process of **photosynthesis**. Animals, including ourselves, gain access to this energy by eating plants or eating other animals which have eaten plants. We can then make use of the Sun's energy to move, make sounds and to heat our bodies. **Fossil fuels** such as coal and oil are made from dead plants and animals and provide us with other ways to harness the Sun's energy. We use machines to transfer the energy stored in fossil fuels into other types of energy which we can use to do work and make things happen. For example, we manufacture petrol from oil and use it to run our cars and other vehicles. We burn fossil fuels in power stations to produce electricity and burn natural gas in our homes to keep us warm and cook our food.

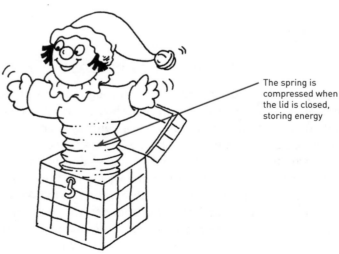

The spring is compressed when the lid is closed, storing energy

Jack-in-the-box
Source: © Dorling Kindersley / DK Images

Toys such as a jack-in-the-box also indirectly depend on energy from the Sun to work. To push 'jack' into the box we need to do some work in order to compress the spring. The energy to do this work comes from the energy stored in our food – the Sun's energy. This energy is then stored in the compressed spring. When the box is opened the spring releases and it pushes 'jack' upwards creating movement. As a result the stored energy is transferred into movement or kinetic energy of the puppet.

Something to think about

Can other sources of energy be traced back to the Sun? Does wind get its energy from the Sun?

Types of energy

It can be useful to categorise energy as **kinetic (movement) energy** and **potential (stored) energy**. Potential energy is stored energy which can be transferred into other forms of energy when the conditions are appropriate. The chemical energy in petrol is stored until the car is started. It is then transferred by the engine into kinetic energy and sound energy. A boulder balanced at the top of a hill has potential energy because of its position. When released the force of gravity causes it to move downhill and its stored energy is transferred into movement energy.

Although energy is described as having different forms, it can be helpful to think of it as the same energy behaving differently. For example, in an electric circuit the

Table 9.1 Types of energy

Kinetic or movement energy	Potential or stored energy
Moving objects have **kinetic energy (KE)** which is dependent on their mass and their speed. The larger the mass and the greater the speed, the more KE they have.	**Elastic or spring energy** is energy stored because of tension or strain forces acting on an object: for example, in a compressed or stretched spring or a stretched rubber band.
Heat energy is internal energy associated with the movement of atoms and molecules in matter.	**Chemical energy** is energy stored in the spring-like bonds between atoms and molecules, which hold the particles together.
Electrical energy is associated with the movement of charged particles in an electrical circuit.	**Gravitational energy** is associated with the position of an object: the higher above the ground it has been raised, the more energy is stored.
Light energy is an example of electromagnetic energy that travels in waves.	
Sound energy is associated with the movement of vibrating objects.	

chemical energy in the battery is transferred to electrical energy in the circuit. This is the same energy behaving in two different ways.

Something to think about

Think about a woman and the multiple roles she has in her life. She might be a daughter, a mother, a wife, a voter, a washer of kitchen floors or a university professor. In all roles she is the same woman but in each role she takes part in different types of activities; she behaves differently and her impact is seen differently. Can you make useful comparisons with energy?

The transfer of energy can make things happen

When energy is transferred something happens. In a candle chemical energy is stored in the wax but it is of no practical use until the candle is lit and the wax starts to melt and burn. Burning results in the chemical energy in the wax being transferred to heat energy and light energy, which can be useful.

Here are two everyday examples of how energy transfers make things happen.

1. A battery-operated toy works when the chemical energy stored in the battery is transferred into electrical energy and then into movement and sound energy.

2. A cyclist needs to do work to turn the bicycle's pedals and to make it move. The energy to do the work comes from the cyclist's food and it is transferred into movement energy.

In both cases energy has been transferred and something has happened.

Something to think about

A lottery winner wins a large amount of money. It can be saved under the mattress until the winner is ready to spend it and at this point a lot of things can happen. Can you make useful comparisons with the transfer of energy?

Can energy be used up?

Energy cannot be created or destroyed but it can be transferred in ways that means that some of it is no longer useful. Consider a small room being heated by a coal fire; the room is warm and cosy. If the door to the hall is opened, the fire is now heating a much larger area of the house and the room becomes less warm. If we open the windows and the fire is heating air outside the house, the room is even less warm. The heat has not disappeared but it is now so spread out it is no longer useful. The energy has been dissipated.

Whenever there are transfers of energy, some of the transfers will not be useful. When mowing the lawn, unwanted sound energy will spread into the surrounding air and may well irritate the neighbours. Unwanted heat energy that results from the friction of moving parts in the mower will transfer to air particles and warm them slightly. Neither of these transfers is useful.

Something to think about

Imagine that you are using an electrical vacuum cleaner. Think of all the energy transfers that are taking place. Which of these are useful transfers? Which transfers are not useful?

Energy sources

What is the difference between energy and energy sources?

The news media sometimes suggest that we are running out of energy when in fact we are running out of sources of energy. Energy cannot be created or destroyed. Some energy sources, on the other hand, can be destroyed. Fuels are sources of energy and fossil fuels are examples of **non-renewable energy** sources. There are concerns that supplies of fuels are running out. Before this happens it is important that we find alternative means of heating and lighting houses and alternative energy sources for running our cars.

Which energy sources are non-renewable?

Much of the energy we use comes from the fossil fuels: coal, oil and natural gas. Millions of years ago, plants used light energy from the Sun to make their **biomass** through the process of photosynthesis (see Chapter 10). When plants died many decayed, but some did not. Instead they were preserved in shallow marshes and lagoons. Similarly, when tiny marine plants and animals died their remains were covered by sediments and preserved on the seabed. The energy from the sunlight was locked up in the cells of these plants and animals. Over hundreds of millions of years, as a result of heat and pressure, the plant remains were fossilised and converted to coal, and the animal remains were fossilised and converted to oil and gas – hence the term 'fossil fuels'.

Fossil fuels are burnt to generate electricity and to heat our buildings. Oil is also used to make fuels for vehicles and to make plastics and other chemicals. Although fossil fuels took millions of years to create, they can be burnt in a matter of minutes. They are still a major source of energy but the supply is running out.

Greenhouse effect: human activity adds to greenhouse gases such as carbon dioxide, methane and water vapour, which trap the Sun's energy
Source: Richard Ward / © Dorling Kindersley / DK Images

Problems with fossil fuels

There are relatively small amounts of carbon dioxide in the atmosphere. However, when fossil fuels are burnt, carbon which has been locked inside the fuels for millions of years is released in the form of carbon dioxide, causing the amount of this gas in the atmosphere to increase significantly. Carbon dioxide is described as a **greenhouse gas** because it can absorb large amounts of heat and it acts like a blanket surrounding the Earth. Although the Sun's rays are able to pass through it to reach the Earth the heat becomes trapped. This is thought to be one of the causes of excessive **global warming** and the resultant changes in our climate.

The Earth has always benefited from the 'greenhouse effect' of its atmosphere and this is what has created the conditions for life on the planet. It is *excessive* global warming due to high concentrations of gases such as carbon dioxide that is causing problems for life on Earth.

The need to turn to renewable energy sources

As the Earth's fossil fuels continue to be depleted much attention is being given to using **nuclear energy** and **renewable energy** sources for generating electricity, for heating and for producing fuels. Using renewable energy sources may reduce the amount of greenhouse gases being released into the atmosphere. Governments have met in a series of World Summits to discuss ways of reducing consumption of energy sources and of making more use of renewable energy sources. Renewable energy sources have two major advantages over fossil fuels: they cannot be used up and most do not produce greenhouse gases. At the moment, the technology associated with some of these energy sources is expensive and this can be a barrier to their more widespread use.

What are the advantages of solar energy?

Solar energy provides both heat and light energy to the Earth. It can be used to heat water in pipes and tanks directly. It can shine directly into houses to heat them. This is called passive heating. Light energy from the sun can be transferred to electricity in a **photovoltaic cell**. These cells have been available for many years and we are familiar with their use as an alternative to batteries in, for example, calculators. Groups of photovoltaic cells, solar panels, have been used on houses to supply domestic electricity since the middle of the twentieth century, but until now these panels have been very expensive and their use has been limited. As the technology improves, it is hoped that solar panels will become more economically viable.

Solar energy in action

It is easy to understand the potential of using solar energy to produce electricity in hot countries but even in temperate countries light energy can be useful. Builders of a new ecohousing development in England are installing photovoltaic tiles (solar panels) on the roofs of the houses. As well as providing electricity to individual households, excess electricity can be sold to the National Grid. Some houses are also able to heat their water by installing solar water heaters on roofs. In addition to this, all houses have thick layers of insulation to minimise heat loss, thus reducing the consumption of electricity and gas for heating the house.

Recent research has led to the production of very thin photovoltaic tiles, which can be manufactured at half the cost of traditional units. It is hoped that in future this will make the installation of such tiles economically possible for many more people.

The rooftops of energy-saving houses – two sides of the same rooftop: the green roof slows down the run-off of rain water and reduces the potential for localised flooding. The solar water heaters at the top of the roof provide some of the hot water for the houses, and the photovoltaic tiles and wind turbine generate electricity

Source: Linda Nicholls

A wind farm: as the wind causes the blades to rotate they turn a turbine, which generates electricity
Source: Dave King / © Dorling Kindersley / DK Images

Is wind energy a feasible option?

When the Sun heats the atmosphere, air moves and creates winds. Wind turbines use the energy in the wind to generate electricity. The electricity they generate is described as 'clean' because no fossil fuels were burnt in the process. Although they provide clean energy, wind farms are controversial. They may spoil the aesthetic appeal of some of the most beautiful areas of the country; local residents may find them noisy. The current state of technology means that wind turbines can only produce a fraction of the electricity we require.

Wind energy in action

Dabancheng is a six-mile-wide plain between the mountains in Xinjiang Province in eastern China. The plain acts like a natural tunnel for the winds that blow between the mountains. It used to be part of the Silk Road, but now 118 giant wind turbines which generate electricity for the provincial capital, Urumqi, are sited there. China is a rapidly growing industrial economy and the emissions from its factories and power stations are adding significantly to atmospheric pollution. At the same time, some of China's oilfields are starting to become unproductive and coal prices are increasing. There is an urgent need to find alternative energy sources for its population of a thousand million people. Wind energy is becoming increasingly important.

The country's wind generation capacity has increased rapidly and more large wind farms are planned.

Is water the answer to the problem?

The energy in moving water can be exploited in a number of ways.

- *Hydroelectricity*
  The energy from falling water has been used for hundreds of years to turn water-wheels to operate machines such as flour mills. Hydroelectric dams enable people to generate electricity on a large scale. Water is held back by the dam and when it is released into sloping pipes it turns a turbine which generates electricity. Most of Norway's electricity is generated by hydroelectric means.

- *Tidal energy*
  Tidal movement is created by the gravitational pull of the Moon on the oceans. Tidal energy is associated with the rise and fall of the water. Using turbines, the movement energy of the tide can be transferred into electrical energy. This form of energy is little used at the moment because of the cost and the need for a high tidal movement.

  The Severn Estuary, situated between south Wales and the West Country, has the second highest tidal rise and fall in the world and is considered to be a possible site for turbines to generate electricity. This will be a hugely expensive project, and a feasibility study is being carried out.

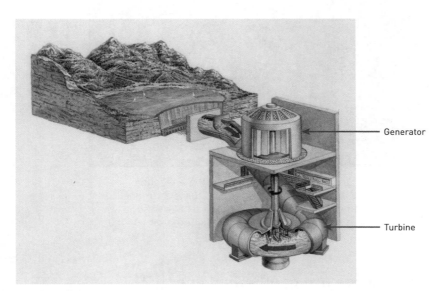

A hydroelectric dam: as the falling water rushes through the pipe the blades of the turbine rotate and this generates electricity
Source: Andrew Beckett / © Dorling Kindersley / DK Images

Supporters of the project say that when using tidal energy there are no greenhouse gases produced, that it is a clean source of energy and it could provide about 5% of the electricity used in the UK. However, there are concerns about the environmental impact of such a project. Conservationists point out that the barrage, which will disrupt the tidal flow, will lead to the disappearance of mudflats and saltwater marshes. This will mean a loss of habitat for numerous plants and animals, including the tens of thousands of wading birds that feed on the invertebrates in the estuary mudflats.

● *Wave energy*
Waves are formed when wind passes over the seas. The movement energy of the waves can be used to generate electricity but, as with other alternative energy sources, it can be expensive.

However, recent advances in technology have resulted in the development of the 'anaconda' generator, a cheap and robust wave-power machine. This device is a long snake-like tube made of fabric and rubber which is filled with water and sealed at both ends. It is tethered to the seabed and sits under the surface of the water facing the waves head-on. The motion of waves causes the water in the tube to travel in pulses towards its tail where there is a turbine. The electricity generated by the movement of the turbine is fed to shore via a cable.

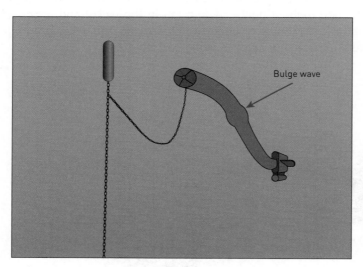

Bulge wave

An 'anaconda' generator – a simulation of the anaconda: the bulge wave moves towards the tail and turns a turbine. It is expected that when fully developed the 'snake' will be 200 m long with a diameter of 7 m. It will be tethered 40–100 m under the sea

How can we use geothermal energy?

Geothermal (from the Greek *geo* = earth; thermal = heat) energy comes from the Earth itself. The temperature of the Earth's core is thousands of degrees Celsius and,

SUMMER

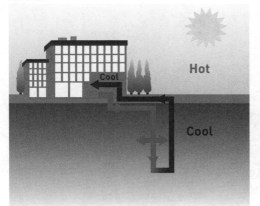

WINTER

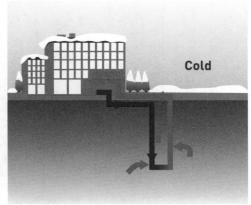

A geothermal pump

throughout the year, the top three metres of the Earth's crust have a temperature between 10 and 16 degrees Celsius. This heat energy can be harnessed to provide domestic heating.

Geothermal pumps work in a similar way to the cooling system in a refrigerator, transferring heat from one area to another. Fluid is pumped through pipes which run either horizontally or vertically down into the ground. The fluid absorbs the ground's heat and transfers it to the house, where it is concentrated by a special pump and used to provide underfloor heating or to heat the domestic water supply. In the summer, when the ground is cooler than the buildings, the pump transfers heat from the house back to the ground, cooling the houses as it does so.

The debate about using biofuels

When considering the debate about the use of **biofuels**, it may be helpful to think about the carbon cycle.

Some carbon is removed from the air for relatively short periods of time. For example, carbon dioxide is used by plants for photosynthesis but when plants and animals respire they return carbon dioxide to the atmosphere. **Decomposers** release carbon from dead plants and animals back into the atmosphere. Some carbon dioxide is absorbed by the seas but this can be released back into the atmosphere. However, some carbon that has been removed from the atmosphere can be locked up for millions of years, as in the case of fossil fuels.

Biofuels are made from living things or, in the case of biogas, from animal waste products; wood is an example of a biofuel. When wood is burnt, it provides heat and light energy and it releases carbon dioxide, a greenhouse gas, into the atmosphere. Burning biofuels is considered by some to be more environmentally friendly than burning fossil fuels, because when fossil fuels are burnt the carbon that was removed from the atmosphere millions of years ago and 'locked' underground in the form of oil, coal and gas is released back into the atmosphere at a much faster rate than it can

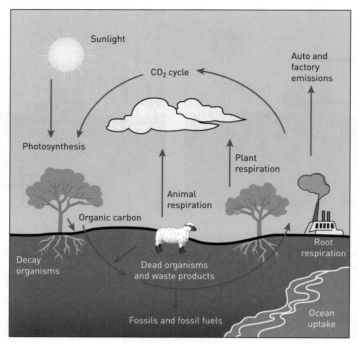

The carbon cycle: some carbon is locked in rocks and fossil fuels for millions of years

be removed. This is adding to the total amount of carbon dioxide in the atmosphere. When trees are burnt they release the amount of carbon dioxide that they have taken from the atmosphere during their growing phase (See Chapter 10). If wood fuels come from a sustainable source, where replanting matches harvesting, there should not be a net increase in carbon dioxide in the atmosphere (Centre for Alternative Technology). Opponents would argue that large areas of woodland would be needed to provide this extra wood and, if they are not managed in a sustainable way, there will be a net increase in atmospheric carbon dioxide. There is also concern that other gases released when wood is burnt can pollute the atmosphere and contribute to global warming.

Plants such as corn and sugar cane are being used to manufacture bio-ethanol and bio-diesel, which are being used as alternatives to petrol and diesel. As with wood, the emission of carbon dioxide from these fuels is less than from fossil fuels, but there are hidden costs. Fuel is needed to produce the fertilisers used on the fields and for the machinery used in farming and processing the crops. This may make biofuels just as polluting as petrol and diesel. In addition to this, people still need to be fed and, to find the extra land needed to grow crops for biofuels, some governments are considering cutting down forests or clearing ancient peat-based land, which contains stored carbon dioxide. This would result in a significant increase in the level of atmospheric carbon dioxide.

To produce biofuels farmers are planting large areas of land with one type of crop. This is known as monoculture. This results in reduction of habitats for animals and native plants, leading to an overall reduction in biodiversity.

Nuclear energy is a controversial option

Nuclear energy can make a significant contribution to meeting people's needs for energy but its use is controversial. A full discussion is outside the scope of this chapter but, briefly, the benefit of this type of energy is that it does not result in the release of greenhouse gases. Increasing provision of nuclear energy will enable governments to meet their targets for fighting global warming. Opponents argue that nuclear plants are hugely expensive to build. There are extreme risks to health because of the possibility of accidental leakage of radioactive particles, and there is also the possible danger of attack by terrorists who want nuclear material to make weapons. Added to this, nuclear waste remains radioactive for many years and safe storage is a very expensive long-term problem.

Something to think about

Governments need policies relating to the provision of energy. How should they be providing electrical and heat energy for domestic and industrial use? Should they introduce transport policies to reduce the amount of oil we are using? Can renewable energy sources provide what we need? Do the benefits of using renewable energy sources outweigh the disadvantages? What about nuclear energy? Do we need to alter our behaviour in the way we use our resources, including reducing the amount of energy we use in our homes and the amount we travel?

Summary

Energy can be explained as the ability to make things happen and it can be described in different ways. Energy becomes useful to humans when it is changed from one form to another. Energy cannot be created or destroyed but it can become dissipated and less useful to us. Most energy transfers can be traced back to the Sun, one of our main sources of energy.

Sources of energy can be classified into two main groups. Non-renewable sources of energy such as oil, coal and gas are used to provide heat, electricity and to power vehicles. When they are burnt, carbon which has been locked up in them for millions of years is released into the atmosphere as carbon dioxide at a faster rate than it can be removed. This causes a net increase in the amount of atmospheric carbon dioxide and this is part of the cause of excessive global warming. Renewable sources of energy are used to provide heat, electricity and to power vehicles. Solar energy, wind energy and water energy are described as clean sources of energy because they release no carbon dioxide into the atmosphere. Biofuels release carbon dioxide but they only return to the atmosphere the amount of carbon dioxide they absorbed during photosynthesis. This may then be used by other plants in the process of photosynthesis. At the moment, alternative energy sources are expensive and cannot provide the energy we need to maintain our present way of life.

The future well-being of our planet will be affected by decisions made by governments around the world and the lifestyle choices made by the people.

Further information and teaching resources can be found at the end of the 'Ideas for practice' section.

Part 2: Ideas for practice

Topic: Wind energy

Age group: Lower primary

Scientific view

Energy makes things happen and gets things moving. We put petrol or diesel energy in our cars to get them moving. People get the energy they need from their food. Wind is another source of energy which can make things move.

Scientific enquiry skills

In these activities children will:

- raise and try to find answers to questions;
- use first-hand experience and information sources to answer questions;
- communicate their findings to an audience;
- make simple comparisons;
- explain their results, drawing on their knowledge and understanding.

Exploration stage

Children's talk involves trying out their own ideas

Setting the scene

Puppets can be used to develop contexts which stimulate children's interest and promote scientific ways of talking (Naylor and Keogh, 2000). In our story the puppet Zak is an alien from a faraway planet. Make up a story about Zak's planet and how it is running out of oil. There is no longer enough petrol to run cars. Zak has heard that people on Earth are very clever and has come to ask for our help.

Puzzle

Is there another way Zak's people can power their cars? Can we help to find a solution?

Children can *talk together* about possible solutions to Zak's problem. Encourage the children to ask questions about the sources of energy that are available on Zak's home planet. Establish what the term 'energy' means to the children. Zak's planet is very windy and perhaps the wind could be used to push the car along. Is wind a source of energy? Could the children design a wind-powered car? Perhaps they could make a working model which Zak can take home.

Scientific enquiry

Children can explore videos and pictures of vehicles which are powered by the wind, including land yachts, sailing boats of all sorts and wind surfers. *Talk together* about how they move. Why do some have more sails than others? Why are some sails of different shapes? Why are some sails bigger than others?

Using Lego construction kits, children can make simple four-wheeled buggies to which a sail can be attached. Children can talk about the best shape for the sail and test their ideas. Each group should consider their results and decide on the best shape and size of sail for harnessing the power of the wind. Use PAT-tested hairdryers supervised by the teacher to create the wind. *Working collaboratively*, each group should try to reach agreement on their best design. They can then present their best design to Zak who is keen to ask them questions about how they work. Zak is especially *puzzled* about how the wind makes the buggies move and why bigger sails seem to work better than smaller ones.

Formative assessment

Explore children's responses to the puzzle and, together with the feedback from subsequent discussions, decide what the children know and what they need to learn in the next stage.

Re-describing stage

Children's talk involves making sense of scientific ideas

The purpose of this stage is to explore the concept of energy and to apply the ideas to Zak's question. Start by focusing children's exploratory talk on what energy can do for them.

Talking points: true, false or not sure?

- Wind energy can be used to make machines work.
- Very strong winds are more useful than gentle breezes.
- Sailing boats can only travel in the same direction as the wind.
- Strong winds have a lot of energy and can be dangerous.
- Running in the wind takes your breath away.

Talk together about the children's responses to the talking points. Children can list all the things that wind energy can be used for. What would happen if there was no wind? What causes winds to blow? How many words can they find to describe the wind? What does it feel like when they run into the wind?

Modelling

How do we know that wind has energy? Do gale-force winds have more energy than a breeze? What about hurricanes? How do we know when the wind has lots of energy? What can gales and hurricanes do? Talk about how wind has energy because it is moving. Strong winds, with lots of energy, can blow things down and do a lot of damage. Use an electric fan to enable children to experience the moving energy of the wind. Help children to visualise the stream of air colliding with them.

In a safe, open space children can role-model being a stream of moving air (wind) created by a giant fan. Children can model different wind strengths. Compare the movement of air in a strong wind with a mild wind. Ask children to model and describe a gale-force wind and perhaps a whirlwind. Ask them to imagine what would happen if there were trees in their path. Show the children video footage of a hurricane and discuss why it is so destructive. Ask the children to describe what it would feel like to be out in such a strong wind.

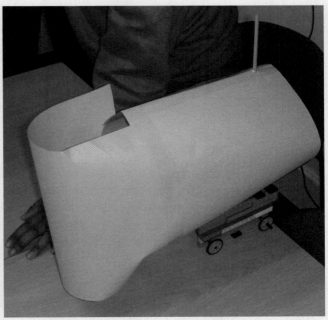

Zak and the wind buggy: Zak ready to fly home with the design of the fastest wind buggy
Source: Linda Nicholls

Solving the puzzle

Ask the children to explain in their own words how the movement of the wind (wind energy) makes the buggy move. The sails catch the energy in the moving wind and it pushes the buggy along. The bigger the sail, the more wind pushes against it and the faster it goes. Different sizes and shape of sails collect different amounts of wind energy. If there is no wind, the buggy cannot move. The buggy moves in the direction the wind blows. If the wind blows in a different direction the buggy will move in a different direction.

Children's drawings

Now the children can draw pictures for Zak to take home, which explain how the wind pushes the buggy along and why bigger sails collect more energy. Encourage the children to explain their pictures using their own and scientific words.

Assessment and further learning

Use the children's drawings and explanations to assess their progress. What else would they like to find out? Children can raise and investigate their own questions.

Application stage

Children's talk involves trying out scientific ideas

The application phase provides opportunities for the children to apply their emerging understanding of the concept of energy more widely. Focus on water as a source of energy. How can we use water energy? Show pictures of surfers; how are they using the energy in the water? Show pictures of hydroelectric dams and discuss how the energy of the falling water is used to generate electricity. Look at the ways in which waterwheels have been used in different periods of history and discuss how they can use the energy of the water.

Links to design technology

The children can design and make a waterwheel. Research plans of simple waterwheels, or use construction kits to create models. Once they have made the wheel they can test it. Ask them to predict what they think will happen when they change the speed of the water. Can they think of how they could improve their design? Finally, ask them to draw plans to show how their waterwheels could be used to lift a weight or turn a wheel.

Assessment

Listen to conversations, and question groups about how their waterwheels work to assess their understanding of energy sources.

Topic: **Global warming**

Age group: **Upper primary**

Scientific view

The sun is a vast and constant source of energy. It provides the Earth with heat and light. As the Earth spins on its axis some parts of the Earth are warmed and lit up by the Sun (day), while other are in darkness (night). The parts which are heated by the Sun during the day release heat and cool down slowly at night. From this perspective the Earth is like a giant radiator which gains heat during the day and loses it during the night. Losing heat during the night prevents the Earth becoming overheated. Gases released from burning fossil fuels can pollute the Earth's atmosphere and reduce the heat lost from the Earth. In recent years average temperatures around the Earth have been increasing. We may be experiencing excessive global warming.

Scientific enquiry skills

In these activities children will:

- raise and try to find answers to questions;
- use information sources to answer a question;
- communicate their findings to an audience;
- make systematic observations and measurements, including the use of ICT for data-logging;
- use their scientific knowledge and understanding to explain observations and measurements.

Exploration stage

Children's talk involves trying out their own ideas

Setting the scene

Ask the children to talk about their favourite holiday destination. Why did they like it? Ask them to describe the weather. For the children who like sunny destinations ask them to describe what it feels like to have the hot Sun shining down on them. What are the dangers? What is the sunniest holiday destination in the world?

Scientific enquiry

Children can use a range of information sources, including holiday brochures, to answer the questions. Children can work in groups and present their findings to the rest of the class. Once they have found the sunniest places, the next thing is to talk about why they are so sunny. Compare the winter and summer temperatures with those in Britain. Which is the coldest place on Earth? Why are some parts of the world sunnier than others?

Talking points: true, false or not sure?

- Spain is hotter than Britain because it is closer to the sun.
- Britain is cold because it is always cloudy.
- The Arctic is cold because it is full of ice.
- The desert is hot because there are no trees to shade under.
- Countries on the equator are hotter than other countries.

Children should decide if they think the statements are true, false or if they are not sure. Discuss children's reasons for their answers. *Talk together* about why some places get more sun than others. Develop patterns from the children's enquires, identifying the areas of the world which on the whole are sunniest. The sunniest places with the highest average temperature are generally closer to the equator.

Modelling

Remind children that the Earth travels around the Sun each year. Talk about the effect that the tilt of the Earth has on the amounts of sunlight that different parts of the Earth receive as it travels around the Sun. Use globes and torches to model how areas nearer the equator get on average more of the Sun's energy.

Puzzle

Ask the children what happens to all the heat energy which the Sun provides for the Earth. The Sun is always shining on some part of the Earth. Why doesn't the Earth just keep getting hotter and hotter? What happens to all the heat?

Formative assessment

Discuss children's responses to the puzzle and decide what the children know and what they need to learn in the next stage.

Re-describing stage

Children's talk involves making sense of scientific ideas

To solve the puzzle children need to be aware that the Earth gives out energy as well as receiving it.

Modelling

Model the Earth as a big radiator constantly emitting heat just like the radiators in our houses. Why do radiators go cold at night when the heating system is turned off? What happens to their heat? Compare this to the behaviour of the Earth. Is it a good thing that the Earth doesn't store up all the energy it gets from the Sun? Does the land or the sea cool down quickest? Children can set up their own fair-test models to answer this question. The safest way of doing it is to put a range of appropriate solids and liquids at room temperature in the cooler section of a fridge. Take temperature reading of the solids and liquids at regular intervals. Discuss reasons for the results. Children can use information sources to find out how differences between land and sea temperatures influence the weather.

Global warming

Talk together about what would happen if the Earth did not act like a radiator. Discuss global warming and its causes. Children can use information sources to find out about the greenhouse effect – what are its benefits for life on Earth? What effects might excessive global warming have?

Scientific enquiry

Children can explore the greenhouse effect using thermometers and small plastic bottles. Each group of children will need one clear plastic bottle and two thermometers. One of the thermometers should be fixed with its bulb inside the bottle. Seal around the neck of the bottle so that air cannot escape. On a warm day lay the bottle on its side in a sunny position. Use the other thermometer to measure the air temperature. At intervals in the day measure the temperature inside the bottle and the corresponding air temperature. With electronic sensors children could continue taking readings well into the evening. Record the results graphically and compare the changes in temperature. Interpret the results to help explain the greenhouse effect. Apply this knowledge to make sense of how layers of greenhouse gases act like the bottle to prevent heat escaping from the Earth into space. As the layers get thicker (denser) less heat escapes and the average temperature of the Earth increases. This can then lead to more research into the origins of the greenhouse gases. Based on their experiments and research, children can present a report on the greenhouse effect and global warming.

Assessment and further learning

Use the children's report to assess their progress. What else would they like to find out about global warming? Children can raise and investigate their own questions.

Application stage

Children's talk involves trying out scientific ideas

One of the causes of global warming is that burning fossil fuels releases carbon dioxide into the atmosphere. This gas acts like a blanket around the Earth slowing down the rate at which it can cool. Using alternative sources of energy can reduce the amount of fossil fuels we use. Encourage children to think about how the heat and light energy from the Sun could be used as an alternative to burning fossil fuels.

Links to design technology

How can we make use of the sun's heat energy and light energy? Can we store it? Children can *work collaboratively* to invent ways of collecting and storing the energy from the Sun. Discuss limitations and problems with their designs.

Solar cells

Let the children explore some familiar objects that use solar energy such as calculators and toys with solar cells. This is best done outside on a sunny day but if this is

Solar toys: solar-powered toys are fitted with small photovoltaic tiles. They work in strong artificial light but they work much more efficiently in sunlight
Source: Peter Loxley

not possible they can work in the classroom using lamps. Encourage the children to explain in their own words how the toys work. What happens to the Sun's energy? What does it enable the machines to do?

Another name for solar cells is photovoltaic cells. 'Photo' means light and the light energy from the Sun is absorbed by the cells and transferred to electrical energy. Discuss the role of the solar cell. What is happening to the sunlight when it shines on the cell? Can photovoltaic cells be used to charge batteries? This is a way of storing the sun's energy. What are the advantages of using solar energy? What are the disadvantages? Children can research this topic using appropriate information sources.

Design-and-make project

Children could design and make a model house powered by a solar cell on the roof. The children's familiarity with conventional electrical circuits will help their understanding. If there are houses in the neighbourhood that have photovoltaic tiles fitted on their roofs, take the children out to see them. Ask a builder to come to talk to the children about the tiles and to take them on a visit to one of the show houses to see the technology in situ. Alternatively, use photos or videos. They can also consider the benefits of using passive solar heating to heat their houses.

Solar toys and photovoltaic cells that can be used to make simple circuits can be purchased from the same sources as other school science supplies.

Assessment

Can children apply their knowledge of solar cells to make simple circuits to light one or more bulbs? Can they explain the benefits of using solar energy?

Information and teaching resources

Books

- Littledyke, M., Ross, K. and Lakin, L. (2000) *Scientific Knowledge and the Environment: A Guide for Students and Teachers in Primary Education*, London: David Fulton Publishers.
- Wenham, M. (2005) *Understanding Primary Science*, London: Paul Chapman Publishing Ltd, Chapter 12: Energy.

Primary science review articles (Association of Science Education)

- PSR 100 (November/December 2007), 'Harnessing wind and Sun: using energy wisely' (editorial).

- PSR 87 (March/April 2005), Issue focuses on energy and sources of energy.
- PSR 75 (November/December 2002), 'Teaching sustainable development: Why? What? How?' by Jenny Mant and Mike Summers.

Useful information and interactive websites

- Up-to-date information from The Royal Society: http://royalsociety.org/climatechange
- Up-to-date information from the BBC: www.bbc.co.uk/climate
- Interactive game: www.carbondetectives.org.uk/content/home/index.html
- Energy and the environment: www.childrensuniversity.manchester.ac.uk/interactives/science/energy/

CHAPTER 10
INTERDEPENDENCE

Plants and animals in the same habitat depend on each other for their mutual benefit and survival. Feeding relationships, showing the transfer of energy through the food chain, is one means of exploring this interdependence. This chapter looks at how plants store the Sun's energy as food, and how animals are able to access a share of this energy. We will look at feeding relationships as cycles, as well as chains and webs, recognising the essential role of the decomposers in this cycle.

Topics discussed in this chapter:

- Historical context
- Growth in green plants
- Feeding relationships
- Decomposers – nature's recyclers

Part 1: Subject knowledge

Historical context

How our understanding of photosynthesis was developed

For many centuries people accepted Aristotle's (384–322 CE) ideas that plants grew in the soil and were fed by soil. It was not until the middle of the seventeenth century that Jan Baptista van Helmont (1580–1644) questioned and rejected this idea. He grew a willow tree in a pot for five years. At the end of this time the mass of the tree had increased by 74 kilograms but the mass of the soil had hardly changed. He thought the increase in mass was due to the water absorbed by the plant over the years.

Puzzling observations

In about 1754 Charles Bonnet (1720–93) observed that a brightly lit leaf under water gave off bubbles of gas. Almost twenty years later, Joseph Priestley (1733–1804) carried out a famous experiment which would now be considered unethical. He put a mouse in a closed jar and timed how long it took before it collapsed. He found that if he added a green plant to the jar, the mouse survived for much longer. In a similar and somewhat more ethical experiment he put a lighted candle in a jar with a plant. It burnt for some time before it went out. Twenty-seven days later, Priestly focused light onto the wick of the candle using a magnifying glass and found that it re-ignited. From this he proposed that plants return to the air whatever it was that the breathing animals and the burning candles remove. We now know that this gas is oxygen.

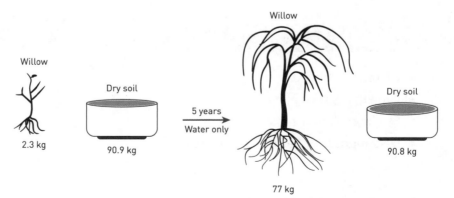

Van Helmont's experiment: Van Helmont had added only water to his plant. There was no change in the weight of the soil after five years so where had the extra weight of the plant come from?

Puzzle solved

Over the next two centuries scientists continued to develop their knowledge of this process. They found that **chlorophyll** is needed for a reaction to occur and that this is contained in chloroplasts, found mainly in leaves. Carbon dioxide is absorbed by the leaves and this reacts with water to produce glucose and oxygen. Sunlight is needed for the reaction to occur. The term 'photosynthesis' (light-making) was introduced in 1893 by Charles Barnes.

Major research was carried out by Melvin Calvin (1911–97) and his team of scientists in the middle of the twentieth century. They discovered that photosynthesis was a two-stage process. In the first stage, the light phase, energy from sunlight is transferred to chlorophyll to fuel the chemical reactions that occur in photosynthesis. In this phase the hydrogen and oxygen in water that had been absorbed by the plant are split and the oxygen is released into the atmosphere. In the second stage, the dark phase, the hydrogen made available in the light phase combines with carbon dioxide to make **glucose**. The energy from the sunlight is transferred to the chemical bonds in the glucose. They also showed that the 'dark reactions' of photosynthesis do not need light. This sequence of reactions is called the Calvin Cycle. Calvin received the Nobel Prize for this work in 1961.

Growth in green plants

Something to think about

Imagine you are standing near a 500-year-old oak tree. How tall is the tree? How many people do you think you would need to make a circle around the trunk? Remembering the proverb 'Great big oaks from little acorns grow', think about the acorn that this giant oak grew from. What was inside it? Where do you think all the wood in this tree came from?

More about photosynthesis

Green plants produce sugars during the process of photosynthesis. Plants do not take in food from the soil. As Calvin explained, the raw materials for photosynthesis are carbon dioxide, which enters the leaves through pores called stomata on the underside of the leaf, and water, which is absorbed by the roots and travels through xylem tubes to get to the leaves. Plants do take water and minerals such as magnesium and sodium from the soil.

Green plants are green because they contain the pigment chlorophyll, which is stored in chloroplasts. This pigment appears green because, when light falls on it, it absorbs the blue and red light and reflects or scatters green light. In the chloroplasts, carbon dioxide and water are converted to glucose, using the energy from the blue and red light. The by-product of photosynthesis is oxygen, which passes out through the pores on the underside of the leaf into the air. This oxygen supports life on Earth.

A person is dwarfed by an oak tree that has been growing for hundreds of years
Source: Linda Nicholls

Photosynthesis can be described using equations:

carbon dioxide + water + light energy ⟶ glucose + oxygen

light energy

$$6CO_2 \quad + \quad 6H_2O \quad \xrightarrow{\hspace{2cm}} \quad C_6H_{12}O_6 + \quad 6O_2$$

Plants cannot store large amounts of glucose and what is not used immediately is changed into other chemicals. Some is converted into other sugars, which are transported from the leaves to all the other parts of the plant through a set of pipe-like structures called the **phloem**. Some is converted into starch, a complex energy-rich **carbohydrate**, which can be stored in different parts of the plant. Some is converted into **cellulose** and used to make the cell walls of the plants. Glucose is also a building block for making proteins and fats.

This means that most of the 'stuff' that a plant is made of comes from carbon dioxide in the air and water. If van Helmont had realised this in 1650, he would have been able to explain why his tree had gained 74 kilograms when there was no change in the mass of the soil.

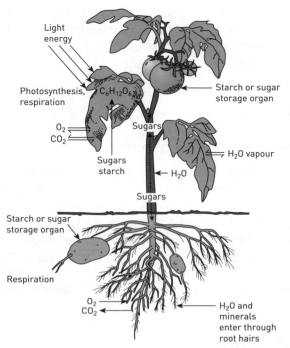

Light
energy

Photosynthesis,
respiration $C_6H_{12}O_6$

Starch or sugar
storage organ

O_2
CO_2

Sugars

Sugars
starch

H_2O vapour

H_2O

Sugars

Starch or sugar
storage organ

Respiration

O_2
CO_2

H_2O and
minerals
enter through
root hairs

Photosynthesis and the storage of sugar and starches

Why do we 'feed' plants?

If plants make their own food why does a Venus flytrap eat insects? And why are there shelves full of 'plant foods' at the garden centre?

The answer to both questions is the same. Flies and 'plant foods' both provide nutrients or minerals. Even though plants make their own food through photosynthesis, they need these nutrients in order to maintain their health. The Venus flytrap is found growing in poor soil conditions which do not provide enough nutrients. It extracts and absorbs the minerals from the fly's body. Soil and plant foods provide plants with minerals such as potassium, magnesium, phosphorus and nitrogen. These minerals can be compared with the minerals and vitamins that animals need to stay healthy. They are not a source of energy but without them we fail to thrive.

Something to think about

Imagine you are standing inside a leaf observing photosynthesis. It is daytime. Can you describe what is happening? What can you see? Can you hear anything? How is the water getting into the leaf? How are the carbon dioxide and oxygen getting in and out? What will happen overnight?

As well as carrying out photosynthesis, plants also need to respire. They use carbon dioxide during photosynthesis and oxygen during **respiration**. Respiration takes place throughout the day and night and any excess carbon dioxide produced during the process escapes through the stomata (See Chapter 13).

Feeding relationships

Animals and plants depend on each other

Living organisms depend on each other in a number of ways for their survival. Animals help plants by acting as **pollinators** or agents of seed dispersal. Some animals and plants have developed very close relationships and provide mutual benefits for each other. For example, African acacia ants live in the base of swollen thorns on acacia trees. They feed on nectar and special **protein** particles found in the tips of the leaves. In return, the ant offers the tree protection by attacking leaf-eating insects and other **herbivores**. The ants do not attack the pollinators which visit the acacia's flowers, allowing the tree to reproduce. Plants can provide both food and shelter for animals.

Something to think about

Think again about the 500-year-old oak tree. What animals and plants live in its branches, on its trunk and in the ground underneath it? What are they getting from the tree? What is the tree getting from them?

How do animals obtain energy?

Plants make their own food during photosynthesis; they are considered to be self-sufficient. They are **producers** or **autotrophs**. Most of the energy they capture through photosynthesis is used for growing and living but some of it is stored in the plant and this becomes an important source of energy for animals. Animals are not self-sufficient as they cannot make their own food. They get their energy by eating plants or other animals which have eaten plants. **Food chains** demonstrate how energy is transferred from one organism to another.

Here is an example of a simple food chain:

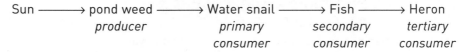

Sun ⟶ pond weed ⟶ Water snail ⟶ Fish ⟶ Heron
producer *primary consumer* *secondary consumer* *tertiary consumer*

The arrows show the direction of energy flow. The pond weed can photosynthesise and is the producer. The **primary consumer** eats the plant. If an animal eats only plants it is called a herbivore; the water snail is a herbivore. Animals that eat only other

Interdependence – an oak tree ecosystem
Source: © Dorling Kindersley / DK Images

animals are **carnivores**. **Secondary** and **tertiary** consumers are usually carnivores. However, a few animals are **omnivores**: they eat both plants and animals. Bears are omnivores because they eat fruit, berries and fish. Some humans choose to be vegan and eat only food that comes from plants, but most humans are omnivores.

Energy transfer in food chain

Animals get their energy from food and they use about 90% of this energy to carry out life processes. Any energy that is not used in this way is stored in their bodies. Similarly, plants use about 90% of the energy from the sugars they make to carry out life processes and they store any unused energy. It is this stored energy that is available to the next animal in the food chain. Let us use the pond food chain as an example. If 100 units of energy from the Sun are used by the pond weed to make sugars, 10 units are available for the snails, 1 unit for the fishes and 0.1 unit for the herons. Only a fraction of the original energy stored in a plant is available to the tertiary consumer, the heron.

Feeding relationships in a pond: can you draw a food web based on the organisms in this pond?
Source: Mick Loates / © Dorling Kindersley / DK Images

The representation of the food chain in a pond offers a very simple model of how energy is transferred. In reality most animals feed on a range of plants and other animals. As well as eating pond weed, snails will eat other plants in the pond. As well as eating snails, the fish will eat other small invertebrates and so on. A **food web** can show the complexity of feeding relationships.

There are usually a large number of plants at the base of the food web. The number of primary consumers is usually fewer than the number of plants. The number of secondary consumers is fewer than the number of primary consumers. At the 'top' of the food chain, the organisms are very small in number compared to the base of the food chain. This can be represented by a pyramid of numbers.

Something to think about

Consider again the 500-year-old oak tree. What do you think happens to all the leaves that fall off it every autumn? What do you think happened to the bodies of the birds and squirrels that lived in its branches when they died? Imagine what the countryside would look like if all the leaves that had fallen off the tree in the past 500 years were still lying around it. Where has all the energy gone?

A woodland pyramid: a pyramid showing the decrease in the numbers of organisms at each level in the food chain. This also reflects the amount of energy available at each level of the food chain

Decomposers – nature's recyclers

Decomposers play a crucial role in food chains and webs and without them **ecosystems** would not function. **Fungi** and bacteria are decomposers. They break down proteins, **starches** and other organic matter in dead and decaying animals and plants by secreting **enzymes** onto them. This decomposes the organic matter into liquids which the **bacteria** and fungi absorb. A group of animals that have a very similar role are the **detritivores**. Detritivores are more complex organisms than fungi and bacteria. They have mouth parts and they eat small amounts of dead and decaying organisms. Earthworms, slugs and snails are detritivores and, although there are some differences, detritivores can be considered to be decomposers.

Decomposers recycle materials

As well as getting the energy they need by breaking down organic matter, decomposers play a vital role in that they recycle nutrients from the dead and decaying organisms back into the soil, making them available to growing plants. Instead of thinking of food webs and chains as linear, we can think of them as part of a food cycle.

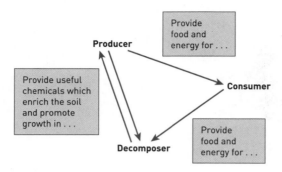

Magnificent maggots

In the natural world, maggots are often found inside the bodies of dead animals, eating the decaying flesh, breaking down the tissues and returning the minerals to the soil. However, they can also be used to help in a different way. In the First World War, an American doctor, William Baer, found that when soldiers were injured on the battlefield and their wounds became infected with maggots, the wounds often healed much more quickly than those of the soldiers who had been cared for using traditional treatments at the military hospital. When he returned to the United States, Dr Baer carried on using maggots to help to heal infected wounds. Antibiotics had not yet been discovered. When antibiotics became available in the 1940s and 1950s, the use of maggots died out because doctors now had a more pleasant way of combating infections.

However, in the last decade there has been a resurgence of interest in the use of maggots for healing infected wounds such as leg ulcers, which are difficult to treat with conventional treatments. The maggots used for this are specially bred and are only about 2 mm long. They clean the wound by eating away the dead tissue. They do this by squirting enzymes onto the tissue. This turns the cells into a liquid which the maggots can then suck up. The maggots are very well adapted to do this because they breathe through tubes that have openings near their bottom end, which means they never have to stop eating to take a breath! The maggots, which do not eat healthy tissue, are left on the wounds for three days, during which time they triple their body size and leave the wounds clean and healthy and able to heal.

Why should children learn about decomposers?

By teaching children about a practical application of decomposers, such as composting or using worm farms to break down organic waste, we are helping them to learn about how they can make an active contribution to their community. We can offer them the opportunity to reflect on the way in which society uses its resources and think about other ways in which their own families can reduce the amount of waste they throw out every week in their wheelie bins or black sacks. Learning about decomposers is therefore very relevant.

Earthworms at work in a composter
Source: Linda Nicholls

Our generation is the first to knowingly degrade the environment at the expense of children now and in the future – a fact that challenges much of our rhetoric about the importance of children in society. The evidence presented here suggests that it may not be possible to deliver ECM (*Every Child Matters*) at all unless the environment becomes one of its leading considerations. Sustainable development is not an optional extra for children's policy and services; it is a necessary part of building a society that cares for its children.
(SDC, 2007: 9)

Summary

Animals and plants in the same **habitat** depend on each other for their survival. Plants provide food and shelter to animals. Plants are self-sufficient and make their own food. Photosynthesis, which takes place in the green parts of the plant, is the process by which plants make this food. They use the light energy from the Sun to convert carbon dioxide from the air and water into glucose. The Sun's energy is locked up in the glucose and this energy enables the plant to carry out all the life processes. Some of the glucose is converted into other carbohydrates, proteins and fats, which are stored in the plant. These are the building blocks of the plants cells and are responsible for the increase in mass of the plant.

Animals are not self-sufficient and they have to eat plants or other animals in order to gain the energy they need. Feeding relationships in a habitat can be described using food chains or food webs. When plants and animals die, their remains are broken down by decomposers or detritivores. This returns important chemicals to the soil. These chemicals promote healthy growth in plants.

Further information and teaching resources can be found at the end of the 'Ideas for practice' section.

Part 2: Ideas for practice

Topic: Food chains

Age group: Lower primary

Scientific view

Plants capture the Sun's energy and use it to help grow their roots, stems, leaves, flowers and fruits. In turn these different parts of a plant provide food for animals to live and grow. Herbivores eat only plants while carnivores obtain energy from eating other animals. Essentially, all animals are dependent on plants to provide food.

Scientific enquiry skills

In these activities children will:

- raise and try to find answers to questions;
- use first-hand experience and simple information sources to answer questions;
- think about what might happen before deciding what to do;
- follow simple instructions to control the risks to themselves and others;
- explore using their senses and record their observations;
- communicate what happened though speech and ICT.

Exploration stage

Children's talk involves trying out their own ideas

Setting the scene

Bring in some snails. Let the children look at them using magnifying glasses; let them watch how they move and how they use their antennae.

Show the children Matisse's picture. Ask them to imagine what it could be. Does it remind them of an animal? Establish that it was Matisse's way of picturing a snail. Do they think it looks like a snail? How is it similar? What are the differences?

The Snail by Matisse
© Succession Henri Matisse / DACS, London 2009.
Photo: Tate Picture Library

Scientific enquiry

Working collaboratively children can draw and paint their own picture of a snail. Once finished the paintings can be discussed and used to establish children's existing understanding. Compare children's pictures with photographs of different types of snails. Encourage the children to observe the live snails and compare them with their pictures. Explore their knowledge and understanding of snails by discussing how the snail sees where it is going and what it might be looking for. Children can *talk together* about what snails like to eat and where they find their food. Do they know of any animals that eat snails? How does the snail keep safe?

The children can explore which types of food snails prefer by setting up an investigation. Snails can be kept safely in tanks in the classroom (See *ASE*, 2001). Foods such as cucumber, apple, soft fruits and different leaves can be put into the tanks and children can observe which the snails prefer.

Puzzle

Show the children an empty snail shell. Tell them you found it in your garden and were wondering why it was empty. Do they know what might have happened to the snail? What animals eat snails?

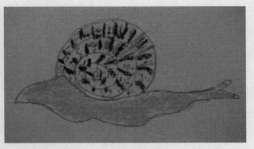

Child looking closely at the snails and children's snail drawings
Source: Babs Dore and Linda Nicholls

Formative assessment

Use feedback from the enquiry and the puzzle to decide what the children know and what they need to learn in the next stage.

Re-describing stage

Children's talk involves making sense of scientific ideas

The purpose of this stage is to introduce the idea of food chains. Discuss children's responses to the puzzle. Information sources can be shared by groups and used to stimulate discussion about which animals eat snails. Discuss the idea of feeding relationships and establish a simple food chain which includes snails.

Sun → plants → snails → thrush

Talk about how some animals depend on plants for their food. What would happen to the birds if there were no plants for the snails to eat? Do other animals eat the birds? Extend the food chain.

Sun → plants → snails → thrush → fox

Start to introduce some scientific vocabulary. Do snails eat only plants? What do we call animals that eat only plants? What other things do birds eat? What do we call animals that eat both plants and other animals? What other things do foxes eat? What do we call animals that eat only other animals? Explore scientific vocabulary such as *herbivore*, *carnivore* and *omnivore*.

Assessment and further learning

Encourage children to construct food chains using a range of plants and animals. Use children's justifications for the structure of their chains to assess their progress. What else would they like to find out? Children can raise their own questions for further learning.

Application stage

Children's talk involves trying out scientific ideas

Outdoor scientific enquiry

Take the children into the school garden or the local park. Examine leaves for damage and look for small animals which may have caused it. Observe animals that visit flowering plants and look under stones and logs for animals which live there. Talk about what the different animals eat and start to create simple food chains. Appropriate information sources will help resolve issues which arise. If you can find a spider's web ask the children to think about why the spider spins its web. Can they see anything caught in the web? Can they create a food chain that includes a spider? You can sometimes encourage a spider to appear by gently spraying water on the web. This mimics the movement of the web that occurs when a small insect is captured.

The children can take photographs of the plants and animals to create food chains back in the classroom. *Talk together* about what would happen if certain animals were missing from the food chain.

Link to music

Teach the children the traditional song 'There was an old woman who swallowed a fly.' Compare real food chains with this imaginary one. Children could make up their own scientific song based on their knowledge of actual food chains. They could also use musical instruments to add sound effects to their song such as the sound of a snail sliding across the ground or the sound of a bird swooping down to catch its prey.

Assessment

Use feedback from the enquiry, food chains and song activities to assess children's understanding of the topic.

Topic: Decomposers

Age group: Upper primary

Scientific view

> The plough is one of the most ancient and most valuable of man's inventions; but long before he existed the land was in fact regularly ploughed, and still continues to be thus ploughed by earthworms.
> Darwin, C. (1881) *The formation of vegetable mould through the actions of worms, with some observations on their habits*, London: John Murray.

Darwin discovered that worms aerate soil and mix in decomposing materials. Worms also break down rotting materials and mix it into the soil. As a consequence they improve the soil for plant growth. Darwin found that worms turn over the top six inches (15 cm) of topsoil every 20 years. Worms and other decomposers such as bacteria and fungi play an important part in the food cycle by returning useful chemicals from dead and decaying animals and plants to the soil.

Scientific enquiry skills

In these activities children will:

- raise and try to find answers to questions;
- use a range of sources of information including first-hand experience and other sources including ICT;
- use simple equipment and materials appropriately and take action to control risks;
- make systematic observations and use drawings and diaries to record in a systematic manner;
- use observations to draw conclusions;
- review the work of others and describe its significance and limitations.

Exploration stage

Children's talk involves trying out their own ideas

Setting the scene

Bring in some earthworms or show video footage of worms. *Talk together* about what the children know about worms. Ask them how they would describe worms. Talk about what they like and don't like about them. *Working collaboratively*, children can imagine they are worms living underground. What would they do all day? What would they eat?

What eats them? How could they see where they are going? What type of soil would be best to live in? What makes worms come to the surface? Could they live in a sandy desert? What danger would they be in when it rained? How would they keep safe?

Scientific enquiry

Children can investigate where earthworms like to live. On an area of lawn or soil they can try to induce worms to rise to the surface using a range of strategies. Look out for worm-casts. They can try stamping on the surface or watering the surface. Soapy water may irritate worms and make them leave their burrows; they must then be rinsed in fresh water if collected in this way. Children can collect some worms and set up a wormery in the classroom. Note that worms must be kept out of ultra-violet light and given food and water.

Puzzle

Charles Darwin was very interested in worms, especially how they produced worm-casts. His work led to worms becoming known as 'Nature's ploughs'. What did he mean by this? Does this name provide a clue to how worm-casts are produced?

Formative assessment

Use feedback from the collaborative work and the children's responses to the puzzle to decide what they know and what they need to learn in the next stage.

Re-describing stage

Children's talk involves making sense of scientific ideas

The purpose of this stage is to help children to picture how worms plough soil in ways which help plants to grow.

Talk together about how farmers use ploughs to break up the soil and to mix organic materials into it. Ploughing breaks up the soil and compost into smaller pieces and mixes them together. It also allows air to mix with the soil and excess water to drain away. Generally, plants grow better in soil which has been ploughed. Show children pictures of farmers ploughing the land.

Scientific enquiry

How do worms plough the soil? Children can use a combination of information sources and practical enquiry to find a solution to this puzzle. Observe the behaviour of worms in a wormery and note what they are doing in each layer of the soil. Observe what is happening to the organic layer.

A wormery: children can observe worms moving through
different types of soil in a wormery. The wormery should be
kept out of sunlight and it should be kept moist
Source: Tim Ridley / © Dorling Kindersley / DK Images

Darwin meticulously recorded his observations and made copious notes to explain them. Children could keep a diary of their observations with diagrams and explanations of the behaviour of the earthworms.

Use of information sources

Children can start to create their own hypotheses about how worms *plough* the soil. They can check their understanding using information sources. Key ideas are that earthworms tunnel through the soil, turning it over and creating passages, which help to aerate the soil and provide drainage for rainwater. The roots of plants use these worm tunnels to spread out and find water. Darwin realised that earthworms dragged decaying plant matter underground to eat. In doing so they also turned the soil over. What were left after digestion were worm-casts, which act as a very rich natural fertiliser for the soil. The earthworm is a decomposer because it helps to break down dead and decaying plants, turning them into compost and returning important minerals to the soil. Without decomposers plant and animal remains would not be recycled.

Assessment and further learning

Question the children about the behaviour of the worms recorded in their diaries. Use the feedback to assess their progress. What else would they like to find out? Children can raise their own questions for further learning.

Application stage

Children's talk involves trying out scientific ideas

Links to design technology and sustainable development

There is currently much interest in the use of worm farms as a means of composting waste food and other plant matter. Some children might have a worm farm at home and they will be able to share what they know. Children can research online how to make a worm farm. Setting up a worm farm in the school garden would be an excellent opportunity for children to become actively involved in making a contribution towards waste management. They can also research how worms are used to clean up soil that is contaminated with industrial waste. These activities would provide purposeful cross-curricular links with citizenship and sustainable development.

Other decomposers

Bacteria and fungi are decomposers but they do not dig tunnels and aerate the soil in the same way as earthworms. Ask children to research how a range of decomposers break down plant material. What conditions are best for fungi? Where and when can we find fungi? What part of a fungus is a 'mushroom'?

Scientific enquiry

Put a clean apple in a clean plastic bag, make some holes in the bag and bury it in the school garden. A second similar apple could be put in a similar bag without holes and buried nearby. The two bags could be compared at regular intervals over the next couple of weeks. The children could apply their developing knowledge of decomposers to explain their observations. (Review health and safety issues in *Be Safe*.)

Debate

The work could be extended to include different forms of waste management. This could lead to a debate about how to reduce waste and what to do with it in the future.

Assessment

Use the outcomes of the children's research into the practical use of decomposers to assess their understanding of the topic.

Information and teaching resources

Books

- Peacock, G., Sharp, J., Johnsey, R. and Wright, D. (2009) *Primary Science: Knowledge and Understanding*, Exeter: Learning Matters, Chapter 5: Ecosystems.
- Wenham, M. (2005) *Understanding Primary Science*, London: Paul Chapman Publishing Ltd, Chapter 5: Variety, adaptation and interdependence.

Primary science review articles (Association of Science Education)

- PSR 101 (January/February 2008), 'More than just mushroom' by Liz Holden.

Useful information and interactive websites:

- Natural History Museum: www.naturalhistorymuseum.org.uk
  Click on 'Nature on Line'.
- Kew Gardens, the great plant hunt: www.greatplanthunt.org/
- Science stories about animals: www.highlightskids.com/Science/Stories/h13sciStoryArch_Animals.asp

CHAPTER 11
DIVERSITY

Evidence suggests that life on Earth has existed for about 3.7 billion years. As far as we know, life is unique to our planet. Why is this so? What is life? There is no absolute reason why we should be able to answer these questions, but we are an inquisitive species and like to get to the bottom of things. Scientists have looked at living things in a systematic way and have provided some answers to these big questions. For example, we now know what living things have in common and what conditions are essential to support life. This chapter looks at life on Earth, from the chemicals needed to build living things to the great diversity of life forms that colonise almost any habitat available on the planet.

Topics discussed in this chapter:

- Historical context
- Characteristics shared by all living things
- Life cycles of plants and animals
- Why there is variation in the same species
- How classification helps make sense of a complex world

Part 1: Subject knowledge

Historical context

Where did life come from? World religions answer this question by designating a god, or gods, who created life. The charming but discredited Theory of Spontaneous Generation says that if you put ears of wheat and an old cloth in a box, after about a month you will miraculously find that the box now contains a nest of mice. People noted that frogs appear from mud and maggots from meat; they reasoned that living things arise from non-living things. But in the 1800s French chemist Louis Pasteur showed that bacteria do not come from nowhere, but exist around us and are introduced into food, water and ourselves in ways we cannot see.

In 1952, American scientist Stanley Miller demonstrated that if you mix basic chemicals such as water, methane (which contains carbon), ammonia (which contains nitrogen) and hydrogen, warm them and run electric currents through them, you can synthesise amino acids. Amino acids are some of the complex chemicals from which living things are built. More recently, scientists and entrepreneurs have deciphered the genetic code which can generate and organise living cells. Scientists can now synthesise sequences of the code. This knowledge potentially gives people the capacity to build a life form from non-living materials. We may see such activity as a Doctor Frankenstein project or a benevolent attempt to help those with genetic problems. How the scientific knowledge is applied, who by and what for, is for societies to consider and decide.

The characteristics shared by all living things

What are living things made from?

All known life on Earth is built around carbon and carbon-based compounds. Living things use energy to organise these chemicals into complex molecules, from which cells, tissues, organs and entire bodies are built. All living things require an energy source – that is, they feed if they are animals, or absorb sunlight if plants. The ability to make complex materials from basic chemicals enables living things to reproduce and grow.

Cells are the most basic units of living things. Organisms such as bacteria and yeast are made from single cells. In more complex organisms such as humans, cells combine to make tissue, organs and organ systems.

How does a living organism behave?

We can decide whether something is living or non-living by examining its behaviour. The key characteristics of living organisms are movement, **reproduction**, sensitivity,

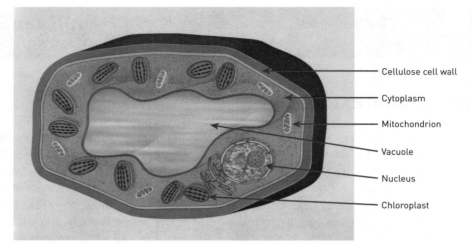

A plant cell
Source: © Dorling Kindersley / DK Images

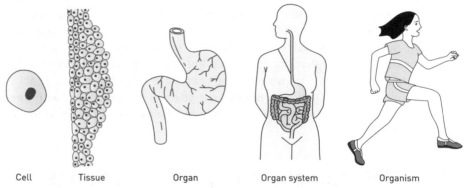

How cells combine to make a human being: the cell is the building block of all organisms

growth, **respiration**, **excretion** and nutrition. Non-living things can share some of the same characteristics but not all them. For example, a car can move, its alarm system can sense vibrations and it excretes waste products such as carbon dioxide and water. However, it cannot grow and reproduce in the way living things do.

Something to think about

Fire moves, grows, and throws off sparks to start new fires; it uses up oxygen, makes waste products carbon dioxide and soot, and is sensitive to water. Does this mean that fire is alive?

Food provides the basic materials to maintain life

Carbon compounds containing hydrogen, oxygen and nitrogen are known as organic chemicals; they are the chemicals of life.

Food that we (and other animals) take in every day provides us with the materials to make the different kinds of organic chemicals our bodies need for energy, growth and repair. For example, starch, found in rice, potatoes, maize and flour, is a long chain of glucose molecules containing carbon, hydrogen and oxygen. The chemical bonds within a glucose molecule contain energy which can be released for use if the bonds are broken. That is what happens in cells during respiration to provide the energy for the processes of life.

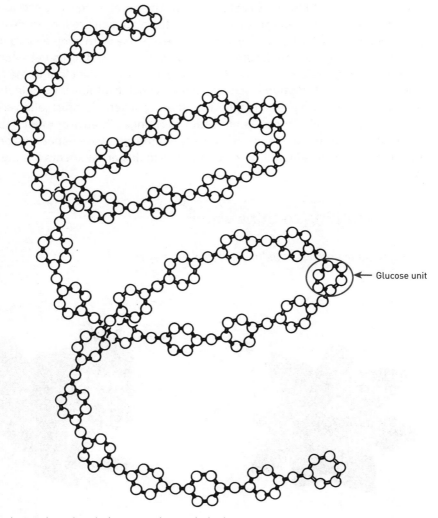

← Glucose unit

A starch molecule is a complex carbohydrate
Source: © Dorling Kindersley / DK Images

Proteins found in milk, fish, meat and eggs are long chains of amino acids. Amino acids always contain nitrogen along with carbon, hydrogen and oxygen. Different amino acids combine to form different proteins. Some proteins act as enzymes, which help reactions to take place in cells.

Life cycles

Plants

A flowering plant is built from organic chemicals. Seeds contain a store of starch to fuel the growth of the embryo plant. When water enters the seed the process of breaking down starch into sugar begins. Sugar molecules release the energy they contain and this is put to use to build the new root and stem. The developing roots provide more water. Once the first leaves emerge above the soil, the plant can produce its own food through photosynthesis (see Chapter 10). It can make glucose from simple inorganic materials, and use this to grow and develop. Insects, mammals and birds help flowering plants reproduce by transferring pollen from the male part of one plant to the female part of another. After **fertilisation** a seed is formed which contains a combination of genetic information from two parent plants. This sharing of genetic information creates greater variety which enables a species to adapt to changes in environmental conditions.

Plants disperse their seeds in a variety of different ways depending on the habitats to which they have adapted. Two common seed dispersal agents are animals and the wind.

Something to think about

Some plants do not have flowers. How do they reproduce?

Seed dispersal
Source: © Kim Taylor and Jane Burton (left); Steve Gorton / © Dorling Kindersley (right) / DK Images

Animals

Animals exchange or transfer genetic material through special cells called gametes. Gametes fuse to form an **embryo** which develops into an immature form and eventually an adult. The young of some animals such as frogs and butterflies undergo complete transformation or **metamorphosis** as they develop. Others, such as spiders, shed their skins and grow into a new and larger version, each stage looking fairly similar to the adult form. Some animals spend much time and care on rearing their young: for example, in the 14 days or so that blue tit chicks are in the nest, the parents will bring at least a thousand caterpillars for them. Even humble creatures like earwigs are ferocious in defence of their eggs. Many mammals will defend their young at all costs. The young are the creature's genetic investment in the future; unless the young survive, the creature's genes will be lost to the gene pool of the **species**. For creatures like elephants and humans, things become even more complicated by the development of emotional bonds. Protective care may well be extended to unrelated young.

Something to think about

Why do you think a herd of elephants will risk their own safety to defend an orphaned calf against a pride of lions?

What influences how animals behave?

Development is associated with physical growth, but also involves the unfolding of the adult body from the juvenile. Generally, adults are able to reproduce whereas juveniles cannot. Maturing over time can enable creatures to learn. Learning influences behaviour; learning over time can help the creature to work out how to behave if it is to have the best chance of survival.

Behaviour is a mix of what the creature does because of its instincts, and the impact of what it has learned throughout its life. Some creatures rely almost entirely on instinct to govern their behaviour. That is, behaviour is 'hard-wired' into their **genetic code**. How such a creature acts is dictated by the interaction of the environment with its genes. For example, the way that magpies build nests is not based on any previous experience: it is instinct. Learning takes place as a result of the experience a creature gains as it goes about its life. Magpies scavenging a rabbit carcase on a busy road quickly learn to time their retreat as traffic goes by. Those that cannot learn do not survive to pass on their genes to the next generation.

Learning has no impact unless it is put to use – that is, unless it influences behaviour, or is communicated in some way. Human learning is powerfully coupled with our ability to use language to communicate. We are not confined to what we know and have learned as individuals, but can draw on the understanding of others, and can make decisions about behaviour with others, to our mutual benefit.

Animals may act as individuals, groups, or colonies. They relate to one another by instinct and can accept retribution if they step out of line. A hungry young wolf will defer to older members of the pack when there is food; if it does not, it will be bitten, and so it will learn. Generally, survival is the strongest driving force for much animal behaviour. If a creature does not survive to breed or does not succeed in raising young, its genes are lost. It can create no future creatures. Learning held within individuals is lost on death, but learning distributed amongst social groups is still available when individuals die. Individuals learn by various mechanisms such as habituation, conditioning, or emulating others. So it is that we as teachers and parents exert a very powerful influence on children and, equally powerfully, children influence one another.

Why there is variation in the same species

Members of an animal species can interbreed, producing young that are capable of reproduction themselves. Animals cannot breed with members of another species. There are some strange 'mixes' created by human intervention, such as mules which have a male donkey and a female horse as parents. However, these are usually sterile and are not a viable species.

Genetic variation

Each animal is a distinct representative of its own species, carrying an individual genetic code. A wide variety of creatures may all belong to the same species. A dog show is a good place to witness variation; the dogs look and behave very differently, but as a species are still capable of interbreeding. This *variation* within a species has great advantages if the species is to survive. A particular habitat might require that a dog has long legs, or a thick coat, or be camouflaged by being brown, or be able to discern scent over a distance; each aspect of variation has its own advantages in survival terms. Some aspects of a variety may be disadvantageous. If we think of the Canadian winter, a variety of dog with a thick coat and the ability to run tirelessly over long distances will be advantaged. If, however, the variety of dog fitting this description also has a weak sense of smell and poor hearing, the balance of its likelihood to survive alters.

Environmental variation

Variation within a species can also be due to environmental conditions. Well-fed wolves with healthy teeth and bones are stronger than malnourished, parasite-ridden individuals and therefore more likely to survive. But this sort of variation is not transmitted through the generations. A wolf can inherit keen eyesight, and can pass this advantage on to its offspring. But a wolf cannot inherit being well fed.

Variation in dogs
Source: Steve Shott (top left); Dave King (bottom left); Tracy Morgan (top and bottom right) / © Dorling Kindersley / DK Images

Variation within a species is important because those creatures which have a combination of attributes which help them do well will survive to breed. They will pass on the distinctive genes which are their variation of the species' blueprint to another generation. Conversely, those variations which disadvantage a creature make it less likely to breed successfully. The creature which best fits its environment will survive – as Charles Darwin recorded (Chapter 12).

Classification helps make sense of a complex world

Classification of living things allows us to group similar species, and distinguish them from others. Living things are classified by identifying similarities and differences between them. Classification puts the huge range of animals and plants on our planet into some sort of order, so that we can make better sense of it. Similarities between creatures indicate that, in the past, they may have been a single species in which variation became just too great to allow breeding. Starting with the features of the creatures themselves, a scientific system of classification helps us to discern genetic relationships and better understand how they, and we, fit into the natural order.

Diversity helps maintain life on Earth

The Earth has always been a changeable place, and the capacity of a particular life form to survive depends on what sort of circumstances it finds itself in. Living things

Classification of living things

Source: Peter Anderson (top left); DK Images (top right); Kim Taylor (bottom left, right) / © Dorling Kindersley / DK Images

have colonised even the most inhospitable of environments on Earth. In the struggle for survival, the small advantages conferred by being a particular *variety* can be the difference between life and death – and between breeding success and failure. Varieties of a species separated by land, food supply or water, may become so different that they can no longer interbreed and go on to become different species. This process, **evolution**, has produced an impressive *diversity* of animals and plants.

Diversity benefits not just a particular species, but life on Earth generally. The great variety of life on Earth makes it much more likely that even if some species are lost, others will remain. We humans have gained much control over our own environment, and we massively affect the environment of everything else on the planet. This does not mean that we are exempt from feeling the adverse effects of such problems as climate chaos, rising sea levels and pollution of air and sea. Like the dinosaurs we are vulnerable to changes in our environment and completely dispensable in cosmic terms. Whatever fate has in store for us, it is likely that the diversity of living things will ensure the survival of life itself.

Summary

The quest to understand the origin and nature of life on Earth continues, but we can now say what chemicals living things are made from, and what properties of complex molecules like proteins, carbohydrates or enzymes enable living things to function. Science has established the links between living things: physical links such as similarities or differences of body form, and ecological links such as food webs and chains. The dynamic interaction of the creatures in a habitat with each other and their environment can lead to such changes as the increase of some types of creature at the expense of others, or the extinction of whole groups. We know that small differences between individuals can affect whether they survive or not, and that such differences are transmitted to offspring in the genetic code of parents. Those that survive are in effect copied to produce the next generation. They are the ones that best fit the environment.

By looking at similarities between living things, we can discern groups that are related as families. Classifying living things in this way helps us to understand and appreciate the diversity of life on Earth. In destroying habitats, we are at risk of losing the diversity of life that characterises Earth. Individual creatures, or even whole species, may seem insignificant, but a balance of plants, animals and fungi and bacteria is essential for human existence. Our aim as teachers must be to ensure that children value the diversity of life on Earth.

Further information and teaching resources can be found at the end of the 'Ideas for practice' section.

Part 2: Ideas for practice

Topic: Living and non-living

Age group: **Lower primary**

Scientific view

The world is full of living and non-living things, but what distinguishes one from the other? Some living things and non-living things look similar: for example, some toy animals can look very much like the real thing. But we know that living things have some profound similarities which set them apart from non-living things. Living things can move, respire, grow, take in nutrition and excrete waste products, reproduce and sense the world in ways that non-living things cannot.

Scientific enquiry skills

In these activities children will:

- raise and try to find answers to questions;
- use first-hand experience and simple information sources to answer questions;
- explore using their senses and record observations using ICT;
- communicate what happened using simple graphs, drawings and photographs;
- make simple comparisons and identify simple patterns and associations.

Exploratory stage

Children's talk involves trying out their own ideas

Setting the scene

I can hide like a snail

And I swim like a whale

I can bark like a dog

I can jump like a frog

Read children poems or picture stories about living things. Ask children to write their own poems about what they can do.

Scientific enquiry

Children can compare the things that they can do with other animals. Provide photographs of a range of animals familiar to the children. Include vertebrates and invertebrates from different groups. Ask the children to talk about what the animals can do.

Talking points: true, false or not sure?

- All animals are furry.
- All animals move in the same way.
- Humans can see better than other animals.
- A sense of smell is important for living things.
- There are many different ways that animals feed.
- We can say three things that all animals do.
- We can tell if something is a living thing.

Puzzle

Provide a range of toys which move and make noises. Ask children to explore how the toys work and what they can do; ask them to decide whether the toys are living or non-living things, and say how they know. Share ideas with the class.

Formative assessment

Listen to children's ideas to help decide what they need to learn in the next stage.

Re-describing stage

Children's talk involves making sense of scientific ideas

Children can be helped to recognise characteristics of living things. Start, for example, with a focus on the ability to grow. Compare *changes* over time that happen to a baby with changes that are likely to happen to toys. The baby will grow and change – toys will remain the same, or become damaged in ways that they cannot repair themselves. Using plant samples and pictures, discuss with children their ability to grow and develop. Decide whether plants are living or non-living. Help the children to develop a reliable list of things that living things have in common.

Ask children to consider the following scenario. In the corner of a field are a young oak tree and a car. No one goes near the field for fifty years. Draw a picture to show the corner of the field. What has happened to the oak tree? What has happened to the car? Label or annotate with key ideas to distinguish living from non-living things.

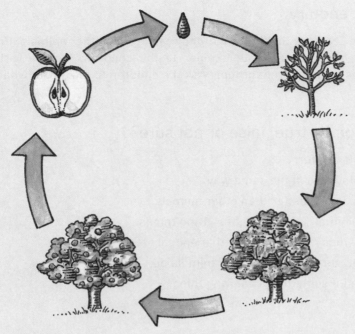

The life cycle of an apple tree: apple trees are large plants that
go through a similar life cycle to other smaller flowering plants
Source: Simone End / © Dorling Kindersley / DK Images

Assessment and further learning

Use children's drawings to assess their progress. What else would they like to find
out? Children can raise their own questions for further learning.

Application stage

Children's talk involves trying out scientific ideas

Scientific enquiry and links to mathematics

Take the children into the school grounds, or to a park or woodland to undertake
a photographic survey of the things which can be found there. *Talk together* about
which are living and which are not living. In class, create displays of the outdoor area
which focus on the range of living and non-living things found there. Categories
of 'not sure' and 'once-lived' could also be used if they are appropriate. Children can
construct simple graphs to represent and compare the numbers of different types of
living things found in the woodland.

Link to literacy

Children can write poems about what particular living things can do. Children could write poems about spiders, butterflies, plants or more abstract ideas such as 'growing up' or 'flowering'.

Assessment

Ask children to reflect on the topic and assess their own progress. They can list five key facts and five questions which they would like to ask about living and non-living things.

Topic: **Diversity amongst vertebrates**

Age group: **Upper primary**

Scientific view

Animals with an internal skeleton are called vertebrates. The five vertebrate groups of animals are mammals, birds, reptiles, amphibians and fish. Numerically, vertebrates represent only a very small percentage of the living things in the world. But their size, mobility and intellect often allow them to dominate their environment. There is a large diversity of different species of vertebrates. Each has adapted to its environment in ways which enable it to survive.

Scientific enquiry skills

In these activities children will:

● raise and try to find answers to questions;
● use a range of information sources to answer a question;
● use diagrams and ICT to present their findings;
● use scientific knowledge and understanding to explain their findings;
● review their work and work of others.

Exploration stage

Children's talk involves trying out their own ideas

Setting the scene

Ask children to bring in photographs of themselves at different ages. *Talk together* about how people change. Display photographs and ask children to put them in order from youngest to oldest. Discuss the children's reasoning.

Scientific enquiry

Explain that humans are vertebrates; with the class, decide on some functions of the skeleton. Find out if the children can suggest other animals that are vertebrates; if they can describe how vertebrates grow and change.

Divide the class into five groups and assign a different vertebrate to each group of children.

1. Frog (amphibian)
2. Snake (reptile)
3. Robin (bird)
4. Elephant (mammal)
5. Salmon (fish).

Ask the children to consider the changes that happen in 'their' animal as they grow into an adult. Their task is to use books and electronic resources to find information about growth and development, and present their ideas to the rest of the class. They should focus on thinking about the problems a creature might have at different stages of growth, and identifying the advantages of the life cycle of the animal. Ask children to present their ideas to the class as a brief dramatisation, or create a set of annotated illustrations or an electronic presentation. Children can draw a cartoon storyboard of the life cycle of their animal, annotating with facts about how they live and grow.

Puzzle

Compare animals that lay eggs with those that give birth to live young. What are the advantages of laying eggs? Why do some animals lay eggs and others give birth to live young?

Formative assessment

Use children's presentations, storyboards and responses to the puzzle to assess their progress. Decide what the children know and what they need to learn in the next stage.

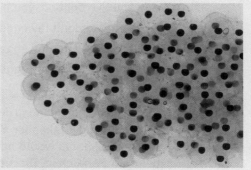

Eggs come in all shapes and sizes. Whose eggs are these? Which other animals lay eggs?
Source: Roger Philips (top left); Frank Greenaway (top right); DK Images (bottom left) / © Dorling Kindersley / DK Images

Re-describing stage

Children's talk involves making sense of scientific ideas

Discuss the reasons why some animals lay eggs and others give birth to live young. For some animals such as birds it is an advantage to lay eggs. For mammals such as elephants the disadvantage of egg-laying would affect their chances of survival.

Talking points: true, false or not sure?

- Elephants don't lay eggs because they can't make nests.
- Birds would be more successful if they had live young.
- Elephants don't lay eggs because baby elephants take too long to hatch.
- Eggs are the animal version of seeds.
- Many things can destroy a nest of eggs.
- Having live young makes life easier for mammals.
- Bird chicks and elephant calves need the same amount of help to survive.
- If you live in water, you have to lay eggs on land.

- If you live on land, you have to lay eggs on land.
- Elephants don't lay eggs because they are clumsy and would break them.
- Elephants don't lay eggs because baby elephants are too big.
- Elephants don't lay eggs because they couldn't keep them safe from predators.

Ask the class to share responses to the talking points. Discuss how long it takes for the chicks to form and grow inside the egg (in chickens this is 21 days). Compare this with how long it takes for a baby elephant to grow inside its mother (22 months). This means elephants would have to keep their eggs warm and safe for nearly two years before they hatched. Discuss the implications of this for life in their habitat. Elephants are constantly on the move in search of food. They need to eat enormous amounts of vegetation. How would they keep their eggs safe? Does it make more sense to carry their young inside their bodies until they can walk?

Ask children to *work collaboratively* to decide reasons why it is an advantage for some vertebrates, such as birds, to lay eggs. Provide information so that children can compare the eggs of amphibians, reptiles and birds. Ask children to relate the structure of different eggs to the environment in which the animal lives.

Assessment and further learning

Use children's responses to the tasks to assess their progress. What else would they like to find out? Children can raise and investigate their own questions.

Application stage

Children's talk involves trying out scientific ideas

Redesigning nature with links to art

Ask groups of children to imagine that they are scientists studying a remote environment. They can choose if this is very cold, hot, wet, dry, dark, sunny, seawater, freshwater, a cave, a desert, a jungle, snowy, and so on. The scientists come across an egg. They study it over a year to see how it grows and develops.

The task is to make the egg out of clay or modelling clay, then to make the imaginary creature that emerges and classify it in a vertebrate group. Finally the children can make what it changes into as an adult. The group must decide why the changes take place and what conditions are necessary to sustain the life of the creature. They must consider the creature's need for shelter and food, and its predator–prey relationships, and design it accordingly.

Ask groups to display their work and explain their ideas to the rest of the class. Explain that scientists must communicate with one another in this way. Prepare the class to ask other groups questions about the creature's growth, development and behaviour.

Assessment

To assess their understanding of the topic, ask the children to provide positive feedback on the work of other groups, or to examine and analyse the models and leave sticky notes with positive comments.

Information and teaching resources

Books

- Hollins, M. and Whitby, V. (2001) *Progression in Primary Science*, London: David Fulton Publishers, Chapter 2: Life processes and living things.
- Wenham, M. (2005) *Understanding Primary Science*, London: Paul Chapman Publishing Ltd, Chapter 2: Life and living processes.

Primary science review articles (Association of Science Education)

- PSR 101 (January/February 2008), 'Teaching life process' (Wobbly Corner) by Leigh Hoath.
- PSR 75 (November/December 2002), 'What's inside a seed?' by Natalie Jewell.

Useful information and interactive websites

- Nature Grid, Resources for Environmental Education: www.naturegrid.org
- ASE website: www.schoolscience.co.uk/ages_5-7/for_teachers.cfm
- Science stories about animals: www.highlightskids.com/Science/Stories/h13sciStoryArch_Animals.asp
- Useful information site: http://animals.howstuffworks.com/

CHAPTER 12
ADAPTATION AND EVOLUTION

This chapter discusses the key ideas about adaptation and evolution. Starting with Charles Darwin's work we look at how he arrived at his theory of natural selection, and then provide case studies to exemplify how his theory applies to both plants and animals. The chapter concludes by looking at the problems that rapid environmental change presents for many animals and plants.

Topics discussed in this chapter:

- Darwin's theory of natural selection
- Survival of the fittest and adaptation
- Adaptation in flowering plants
- Adaptation in animals
- The effects of changing habitats

Part 1: Subject knowledge

Darwin's theory of natural selection

Who was Charles Darwin?

Charles Darwin was born in 1809, at a time when the Industrial Revolution had just begun in England. The big northern cities were starting to develop but most of the country was still very rural. The Church was responsible for spiritual and pastoral care, education and spiritual guidance. A Christian view of the natural world was that God had created every species of animal and plant and these species were immutable. They could not change.

Darwin was born into a middle-class and privileged family who were interested in the natural world. His father Robert was a country doctor. His grandfather Erasmus was a surgeon, naturalist and poet who had published his own ideas about the nature of evolution in a book called *Zoonomia*. As a child Darwin was fascinated by nature and he collected animals and plants. He was unhappy at school where he was considered idle and ordinary. There was no indication of his creative mind and the contribution he was going to make to science in the future.

How Darwin developed a passion for biology

Robert Darwin was determined that his son should follow in the family footsteps and become a doctor. At the age of 16, Darwin was sent to Edinburgh University to study medicine. Unfortunately he did not share his family's enthusiasm for medicine. When he saw an operation being performed without anaesthetic on a child, he was deeply upset and refused to continue his studies. But through his childhood interest in collecting insects and shells, he met a Scottish zoologist – Robert Grant. They went out regularly collecting together. Darwin also met a freed Guyanan slave called John Edmonstone, who made his living by teaching taxidermy – the art of preparing, stuffing and mounting the skins of animals, including birds. Darwin became one of Edmonstone's pupils, and the skills he learnt were to become very useful on his future voyage to South America.

Since it was clear that Darwin was not going to become a doctor, his father decided he should become a clergyman and he was sent to Cambridge to study theology. Darwin once again had little enthusiasm for his studies. He was introduced to the Reverend John Henslow, a professor of botany, and started to accompany him on field trips. He attended Henslow's lectures and his interest in the natural world developed into a passion. Despite his lack of interest in theology, Darwin still managed to pass his degree.

Darwin sets sail for South America

In 1831, Henslow introduced Darwin to Robert Fitzroy, the Captain of HMS *Beagle*. The *Beagle* was due to set sail for South America to carry out a geographical survey of the coastline. Victorian conventions meant that Fitzroy could not socialise with the officers

Portrait of the young Charles Darwin
Source: © The Gallery Collection / Corbis

on his ship. He needed someone to act as the ship's naturalist but he also needed that person to be his intellectual equal, someone with whom he could share his dinner table. Darwin was chosen and the *Beagle* left England on 27 December that year.

Darwin was not a good sailor and he was often unwell. He was over six foot tall and his cabin was so low he could not stand up straight in it. The cabin also served as the map room, and part of one of the masts went through it. When he was not on his expeditions, it was in these very cramped conditions that Darwin had to examine, prepare and label the specimens he collected.

Darwin's experiences changed the way he imagined the world to be

As the *Beagle* progressed down the coast of South America, Darwin was dropped ashore for several days or weeks at a time while the ship carried out its survey of that part of the coastline. His collecting started in the jungle around Rio de Janeiro, where he was overwhelmed by the sights and sounds. He had never seen such a variety

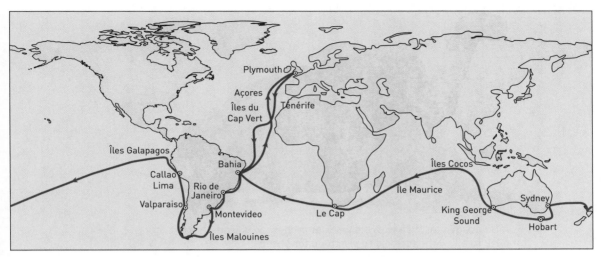

The voyage of the *Beagle from 1831–1836*

of plants and animals. As the journey continued, he found large fossilised bones that were bigger than any animal he knew. In the Andes he found fossilised sea shells 12,000 feet up in the mountains. To explain these observations, Darwin speculated that the whole landscape had been changed by a huge force. He experienced an earthquake for the first time and he saw how the landscape could be changed. Through these experiences and through studying the work of the geologist Charles Lyell, Darwin's knowledge and understanding of geology grew considerably. His study of fossils was crucial in helping him to develop his theory of evolution.

Darwin was puzzled by the variety of animals on the Galapagos Islands

In September 1835, nearly four years after leaving England, the *Beagle* arrived in the Galapagos Islands, a small group of islands off the coast of Ecuador. Some of the plants and animals on the islands were similar to those he had seen on the mainland, but they were not the same species. He found that each of the small islands in the group had their own unique animals. He saw animals that he had never seen before, such as giant tortoises, and on each island the tortoises had their own distinct characteristics. Where the islands were grassy the shells were close to the tortoises' necks, but on the islands where there was little grass and the tortoises had to eat shrubs, the shell was arched away from the neck to allow it to stretch up. He found a number of 'strange' animals, like marine iguanas, that were excellent swimmers and grazed on underwater plants but spent most of their life on the rocky shores.

Something to think about

Imagine how the tortoises developed different shaped shells. What further developments may have advantaged the shrub-eating tortoise?

A Galapagos tortoise with a shell that arches away from the neck to allow the tortoise to reach up for shrubs
Source: © Dorling Kindersley / DK Images

How did Darwin develop the theory of natural selection?

In December 1836, the *Beagle* arrived back in England. The voyage made Darwin famous and he was elected as a Fellow of the Royal Geographical Society. He returned to Cambridge and spent two years classifying and cataloguing his collection.

Among the specimens Darwin collected in the Galapagos was a collection of birds that he thought were finches, blackbirds and wrens. He sent these specimens to another scientist, John Gould, for examination. Gould recognised that they were in fact all finches and their distinguishing features were the size and shape of their beaks. Darwin hypothesised that all these birds had arisen from one species of finch that had arrived in the islands from the mainland of South America. He thought the size of the beaks was related to particular conditions on the islands, but his notes were incomplete and he had not labelled some of the birds properly. He did not know which birds came from which island and this meant he did not have good evidence to support his theory.

The variations in animals on the different islands made Darwin start to question the immutability of species. He set about collecting more systematic evidence. His studies over the next twenty years led him to develop three major theories:

1. Organisms produce more offspring than can survive. Large numbers die due to lack of food, disease and predation.

2. While all organisms in a species are similar, they are not identical; there are small variations in their characteristics. Those organisms whose characteristics were best suited to, or adapted to, a particular environment survived and passed on these characteristics to the next generation. Individuals less well adapted died out. Their characteristics were not passed on to the next generation. This is described as the 'survival of the fittest'.

3. Over very long periods of time, the impact in selecting characteristics gives rise to new species; the species evolves.

Darwin needed evidence to support his theory

Because Darwin did not think it was possible to see evolution happening in nature, he developed a scientific model to investigate the effect of selected characteristics being passed down from one generation to the next. He started to breed pigeons. Darwin gathered a great deal of scientific evidence and kept rigorous notes on his work. He found that eventually, through selective breeding, the offspring were so different from the original birds that they could be considered a new species. He extrapolated his results to suggest that this could happen of its own accord in nature. These findings challenged the biblical view that species were unchangeable and, knowing that this theory would cause controversy, he initially kept his ideas to himself.

Charles Darwin was not the first person to suggest that animals evolved, but, based on the evidence he collected during his pigeon breeding and combined with his experiences in the Galapagos, he was the first person to offer a scientifically plausible mechanism for evolution. He called this the theory of **natural selection**.

Something to think about

For many years people have bred different varieties of farm animals. Could an agricultural show be used to provide evidence for Darwin's theory?

Mr. Esquilant's Short-faced Baldheads.   Mr. W. Smith's White Pouters.   Mr. Wicking's Jacobin, Magpie, and Swallow.
Mr. Hayne's Carrier Cock.   Mr. Wicking's Magpie and Jacobin.
Mr. Harrison Weir's White Fantails.   Mr. Wicking's Brunswick and Nun.   Mr. Percival's Turbit.
PRIZE PIGEONS AT THE SHOW OF THE PHILO-PERISTERON SOCIETY, RECENTLY HELD IN FREEMASONS' HALL.

Breeding pigeons helped Darwin to develop his theory of evolution
Source: © Dorling Kindersley / DK Images

A letter persuaded Darwin it was time to publish his work

Alfred Russel Wallace was a naturalist and an admirer of Darwin. Wallace studied plants and animals in the Malay Archipelago and in February 1858 he sent Darwin a paper based on his studies. He presented ideas on evolution that were very similar to Darwin's. Although Darwin did not want to cause controversy, neither did he want to be upstaged by Wallace, so he decided to publish his ideas on natural selection. Their work was presented jointly to the Linnean Society of London in July 1858. In 1859 Darwin published his famous book *On the Origin of Species by means of Natural Selection*. Darwin's authority in the subject was based on rigorous analysis of evidence, which he used to support his theory.

The book caused the expected furore because it challenged the biblical view that God was the creator and designer of the world. Darwin developed his ideas further and his book *The Descent of Man* was published in 1871. He made comparisons between man and ape. He did not suggest that man had developed from apes but that they had a common ancestor. Even so, this challenged the view that man was created in God's image.

Scientists continue to develop and clarify Darwin's ideas

Our understanding of genetics, adaptation and evolution has developed considerably since Darwin's time. Mendel (1822–84) developed his Laws of **Inheritance** through the research he carried out on breeding peas. He suggested that inheritable characteristics were either *dominant* or *recessive* and this affected how they were passed on to future generations of peas. He published his work in 1865 but, even though they lived at the same time, Darwin was unaware of it. If he had been, he would have been able to explain more fully his theory of the 'survival of the fittest'. During the twentieth century there was an explosion of research into genetics. Genes are sections of **DNA (deoxyribonucleic acid)**, a large molecule that carries genetic information. Rosalind Franklin (1920–58) took X-ray images of DNA and this contributed significantly to Crick and Watson's discovery of its structure in 1953. They were awarded the Nobel Prize in recognition of the importance of this discovery. Subsequent work on genetics, including the Human Genome Project, which was completed in 2003, has given us a more detailed understanding of the laws of inheritance and provides us with a clear picture of how natural selection works.

Survival of the fittest and adaptation

What do scientists mean by survival of the fittest?

In any species there is variation. Some humans are tall and some are short. Some have brown eyes and some blue. We come from different ethnic backgrounds and this determines, among other things, our skin colour and facial features. There are clear differences but we are all easily recognisable as humans; we come from the same species. Similarly, other animals and plants exhibit variation.

Finches showing how beaks have changed through adaptation
Source: © Dorling Kindersley / DK Images

When considering Darwin's theory of 'survival of the fittest', it is a common misconception that fittest means healthiest. Fittest, in the context of **adaptation**, means best suited to or adapted to the particular environment in which the organism lives. An example is provided by Rosemary and Peter Grant who started a long-term project on Darwin's finches in the Galapagos Islands in 1973. They found that each island had its own particular species of finch, and there was a direct relationship between the size and shape of the birds' beaks and their diet.

The ground finches have crushing beaks to eat the seeds that are available. The bigger and stronger the beak, the bigger the seeds they can eat. The tree finches have grasping beaks to capture the insects. The warbler, woodpecker and cactus finches have probing beaks. In any species there is natural variation and those birds whose beaks enabled them to compete for the food supply available on their islands survived. On islands where there was a supply of large hard seeds the finches with naturally larger beaks survived and passed on this characteristic. Gradually the finches with smaller beaks died out. The species evolved. In times of food shortages, a difference of 1mm in the size of the beak can mean the difference between the birds being able to eat the available food and starving to death. All these different species of finches have evolved from a single species of finch that arrived in the islands from the mainland. Those birds which have been successful in competing for the available food on the island survived and passed their favourable characteristics to their offspring.

Which characteristics can be inherited?

Lamarck (1744–1829), a French scientist, proposed that through repeatedly stretching their necks to reach the taller trees, giraffes could make their necks longer and that they could pass on these longer necks to their offspring. This is not correct. Adaptation refers only to inheritable characteristics that are determined by our genes. Giraffes whose genes determined they had long necks survived when food was in short supply because they could reach the branches that shorter giraffes could not reach. They survived to pass on their 'long neck' gene. Characteristics acquired during our lifetime are not determined by our genes and cannot be inherited. For example, a weightlifter will train to develop his or her muscles in order to lift heavy weights, but these big muscles are not an inheritable characteristic and they will not be passed on to future generations. Adaptation is a slow process that takes place over many generations.

Adaptation in flowering plants

Just as there is variation within animal species there is variation within plant species. Flowering plants first appeared in the Cretaceous period when dinosaurs still existed. To survive, plants need to be attractive to pollinators and there is competition for these pollinators. The plants that have survived are those which have been successful in this competition.

Something to think about

Think about a bee flying over a field of wild flowers. How does it decide which flowers to land on?

There has to be a reason for a pollinator to visit a plant. Some plants contain nectar, a good food source for animals. The flowers advertise nectar by being brightly coloured or perfumed. The shape of the flowers on a plant will in some ways determine the type of pollinator that is attracted to it.

Flowers that do not contain nectar have to attract pollinators in a different way. Some orchids produce pheromones to attract insects. The bee orchid looks like a bee, and bees land on them thinking that they have found a mate. The corpse flower emits a smell of rotten flesh which can be detected up to 100 metres away, and it is pollinated by flesh-eating beetles which are attracted by the smell.

Plants cannot actively think about how best to attract pollinators, but the plants with flowers that are attractive to pollinators will be pollinated and produce offspring, which will inherit these attractive characteristics. Over generations, through the process of natural selection, the appearance of the flower changes. Plants and pollinators well adapted to one another and the local environmental conditions are best fitted to survive.

Bees prefer warm purple flowers

In order to warm up enough to be able to fly, bees 'shiver' the flight muscles at the base of their wings. It takes a great deal of energy for a bee to take off from a flower so they need to make sure that they collect pollen and nectar in the most efficient way possible.

The bee orchid attracts bees who think they have found a mate
Source: Derek Hall / © Dorling Kindersley / DK Images

Dyer et al. (2006) carried out a study of the colour preference of a population of young bumble bees and found that they preferred purple flowers. When these flowers were examined they were found to have a high nectar content, but the nectar content of a flower was not the only thing to attract bees. They found that bees preferred to visit warm flowers with a high nectar content. They have hypothesised that drinking this warmer nectar and being on or in a warmer flower enables the bees to warm their bodies. This is a great advantage to them because they save the energy they would otherwise have used to warm themselves. Flowers that track the sun, those which have heat-absorbing pigments and those with specialised cell structures that can warm the flower are all at an advantage when it comes to attracting bees. From an evolutionary point of view, successful plants are those which maximise their opportunities for reproduction.

Adaptation in animals

Why can camels survive in the desert?

The conditions that animals have to contend with in a desert are extremes of temperature, blowing sand, very infrequent water and food supplies, and sandy conditions underfoot.

We are familiar with pictures of caravans of camels walking across the desert and the camels are well adapted to the harsh conditions in a number of ways. The reserve

The camel has slit-like nostrils and thick eyelashes that keep out the blowing sand
Source: Jerry Young / © Dorling Kindersley / DK Images

of body fat stored in their hump means they can survive for a number of weeks without eating or drinking. Their fur keeps the Sun off their backs during the day and keeps them warm at night. Their feet are broad and this spreads their weight out and enables them to grip the moving sand. They are able to close their slit-like nostrils and they have very long thick eyelashes, both of which protect them against blowing sand. One of the ways in which camels adjust their body temperature is by diverting the blood supply to the nostrils where it is cooled before passing up to the brain, and this means they lose very little water through sweating.

Something to think about

Imagine you need to cross a desert and you only have a horse to carry you and your baggage. What problems would you have? Do you think you and the horse would survive?

What other animals have adapted to life in the desert?

A wide range of animals is adapted to life in the desert. Every group of animals is represented. There are species of mammals, birds, reptiles, amphibians, spiders, insects, and even fish where there are pools and streams. Reptiles such as lizards and snakes survive well in desert areas because they are 'cold blooded' and largely rely on the Sun to warm their bodies. Small mammals such as rats and bats also survive well. Most feed at night and shelter from the heat of the Sun during the day. Whatever the environmental conditions some living things will adapt and survive.

Effects of changing habitats

What is a habitat?

'Habitat' is a term used to describe the natural home of a group of plants and animals; the organisms within a habitat depend on each other. It can also be used to describe the specific set of conditions to which the animals and plants that live there have successfully adapted. It is a place where organisms live and reproduce. Factors that influence which animals and plants will thrive in a habitat include climate, light, seasonal changes, food supply, vegetation and predators.

Habitats are not unchangeable. For example, saplings are not big enough to support birds' nests and they cannot provide shelter for other common animals such as squirrels. Their canopies are very small and there is still light on the ground underneath them, which means a wide range of plants can grow there. As the trees mature, their trunk and branches offer food and shelter for a range of animals of different sizes. In a woodland, as the canopy starts to block out the sunlight, only plants that can tolerate shade will grow underneath them. The environment has changed and specific habitats within the environment change too.

Some changes are not so visible

There is currently international concern about the amount of carbon dioxide humans are emitting into the atmosphere and the impact this will have on life on Earth. One

Light penetrating the developing canopy of a woodland
Source: Barrie Watts / © Dorling Kindersley / DK Images

of the probable effects of increasing levels of carbon dioxide in the atmosphere is excessive global warming. This is causing an increase in the temperature of the seas. This is observable in the polar regions where the warmer waters are already causing glaciers and ice sheets to melt. Ice packs are becoming smaller and cannot support larger animals such as polar bears which need to move onto the ice to catch seals. As the seas become warmer, some marine animals that thrive in the icy waters will not be able to tolerate increases in temperature as small as 2 degrees Celsius. They will die out. As the habitat changes, different species will move in to replace those organisms that are not able to adapt to the changing conditions.

Some of the animals and plants in a tropical coral reef will be similarly intolerant of small rises in sea temperature, but coral reefs are also vulnerable to another change that is taking place. As the amount of carbon dioxide in the atmosphere increases, the amount of carbon dioxide being absorbed by the oceans is increasing. If this happens, there is a danger that the oceans will become slightly acidic and rapid changes could mean that corals will not have enough time to adapt to the changes in conditions. In more acidic waters they will not be able to form their skeletons. If the corals are threatened, all the plants and animals that depend on them will also be threatened.

Phytoplankton, which are microscopic green plants, are also susceptible to acidity levels. Phytoplankton cover large areas of the oceans and, because they are plants,

Coral and some of the fish that depend on it for food and shelter
Source: David Peart / © Dorling Kindersley / DK Images

they photosynthesise and produce oxygen: about 50% of the oxygen available on Earth. If they were to die out, the impact would be potentially catastrophic.

Summary

Charles Darwin's theory of evolution explains how organisms change over time. The term 'survival of the fittest' refers to how well adapted an organism is, not how healthy it is. Animals and plants that are well adapted to their environment survive and pass on their characteristics to the next generation. Characteristics acquired during an organism's lifetime are not inheritable. Through studying peas, Gregor Mendel was the first to explain how characteristics might be inherited. Studies into DNA have provided a clear picture of the mechanism by which this occurs.

When there are slow changes to the environment, organisms adapt slowly over many generations in order to survive in these new conditions. Owing to the behaviour of humans, environmental changes are happening rapidly and there are concerns that some organisms may not have the time they need to adapt. Large reductions in the numbers of plants on Earth will increase the rate of climate change as less carbon dioxide will be removed from the atmosphere and less oxygen will be released into the atmosphere through photosynthesis. The loss of habitat and the effects of rapid climate change are potentially devastating for the current balance of life on Earth.

Further information and teaching resources can be found at the end of the 'Ideas for practice' section.

Part 2: Ideas for practice

Topic: Teeth and beaks

Age group: Lower primary

Scientific point of view

In order for animals to survive, they need to be able to compete for the available resources including food. The mouth parts of an animal determine the type of food it eats. Different teeth have different shapes and sizes and their function relates to their shape. The functions are cutting, tearing, crushing and grinding. Beaks also have different shapes and sizes and this determines the food that birds can eat.

Scientific enquiry skills

In these activities children will:

- raise and try to find answers to questions;
- use first-hand experience and simple information sources to answer a question;
- explore using their senses and make and record observations;
- make simple comparisons and identify associations;
- compare what happened with what they expected and try to explain by drawing on their scientific knowledge.

Exploration stage

Children's talk involves trying out their own ideas

Setting the scene

Show the children video footage of animals such as lions, tigers, elephants in the wild. Talk about the children's favourite animals. Contrast similarities and differences. The children can play the role of their favourite animal. They can move and make noises like the animals they saw on the video.

Scientific enquiry

Talk together about what the animals eat. Provide resources which enable the children to compare the animals' teeth. There are lots of pictures on the Web. Can the children guess what the animals eat from the shape of their teeth? Which animals have the biggest teeth? Which animals have the sharpest teeth?

Focus on the skulls of lions and tigers. Compare the shape of the teeth with the children's own teeth. If appropriate, children can inspect each other's teeth and use mirrors to look at their own. Compare with a 3-D model. Children can make simple drawings of the shape of their own teeth. *Talk together* about similarities and differences between their teeth and those of the lions and tigers.

Talking points: true, false or not sure?

- Lions' teeth help them to catch and eat their food.
- Our teeth are no good for hunting.
- You can tell what a creature eats by studying its teeth.
- All teeth are basically the same.
- We can draw different teeth shapes and say what each type is for.
- If a wild lion loses its teeth, it dies.

Puzzle

Discuss children's responses to the talking points. Why are our teeth not the same as those of other animals like lions and tigers?

Formative assessment

Use children's responses to the talking points and puzzle to decide what they know and what they need to learn in the next stage.

Re-describing stage

Children's talk involves making sense of scientific ideas

Scientific enquiry

Ask children to record what they ate yesterday. What did they use to help them? Did they use a knife to cut up their food? Use information sources to find out what a lion is likely to eat. How does it cut up its food? Demonstrate how we need to use a very sharp knife to cut up raw meat. How sharp must a lion's teeth be?

Talk together about the purpose of different shaped teeth and how they are used by various animals. Find out why carnivores like lions and tigers need sharp incisors, and why they have fang-like canines. They also have molars, which have a flat surface for crushing and grinding. Carnivores sometimes use their claws to hold on to their prey and to help in tearing the flesh.

Talk about why we don't need teeth like a tiger's and help the children resolve the puzzle. Children can use information sources to explore other animals which do not have teeth for killing and cutting up their food. Children can collect pictures of the skulls of plant-eating animals and create a display which contrasts the teeth of carnivores and herbivores.

Assessment and further learning

Encourage the children to explain their displays and use their responses to assess their progress. What else would they like to find out? Children can raise their own questions for further learning.

Application stage

Children's talk involves trying out scientific ideas

Scientific enquiry

Show the children pictures of different shaped beaks and ask them to predict what each bird eats. Include pictures of distinctive beaks such as those of woodpeckers, pelicans, parrots, ducks and eagles. *Talk together* about how the shape of the beak is important because it helps the bird eat particular types of food.

Set up an investigation by giving the children different types of food and a range of implements to represent the beak. (If any children have a nut allergy you could use large sunflower seeds as an alternative to peanuts. The 'worms' are liquorice strings or something similar.) Challenge them to see how much they can 'eat' with their 'beak' in 30 seconds. 'Eating' in this activity means using one of the implements to get food from the tray into a cup.

Results could be recorded in a table such as the one shown.

	Rice	Peanuts	Nectar	Worms
Chopsticks				
Pegs				
Tweezers				
Pliers				
Straws				

Talk about which shape of beak is most suitable for eating a particular food and establish the link between the shape of its beak and what a bird eats.

Children investigating the best 'beak' for eating the available foods
Source: Peter Loxley

Link to design technology

Give the children a different type of food and challenge them to design and make a suitable beak for eating this food. The beak could be designed to fit on the thumb and index finger. This could lead to the children designing a puppet of their animal with a moving beak.

Assessment

Use feedback from the scientific enquiry and the children's justification for their beak design to assess their understanding of the topic.

Topic: Body colours and patterns

Age group: Upper primary

Scientific view

Successful animals are those whose characteristics enable them to survive and reproduce in their habitat. If the most brightly coloured animals survive, then this characteristic is passed on to subsequent generations. Over time the species develops brighter and brighter colours. The same applies to animals which survive best by camouflage. The ones with the best camouflage survive and these characteristics are passed on to successive generations.

Scientific enquiry skills

In these activities children will:

- raise and try to find answers to questions;
- think creatively to try and explain how living things work, and to establish a link between cause and effect;
- use a range of information sources to find an answer to a question;
- make systematic observations and record using ICT;
- use scientific knowledge and understanding to explain observations.

Exploration stage

Children's talk involves trying out their own ideas

Setting the scene

Read *How the Leopard Got its Spots by* Rudyard Kipling or a similar story involving an animal with spots. In Kipling's story some vocabulary would not now be considered acceptable. You might want to change some of the words before sharing the story with the children. Encourage them to discuss why the leopard was successful in the first part of the story and why it needed to change in the second part. *Talk together*

The spots on a peacock butterfly make it look like an owl in
order to scare off predators
Source: © Dorling Kindersley / DK Images

about whether stripes or spots provide better camouflage in a forest. Why are they
both better than being 'golden-yellow from head to heel'? Children can draw pictures
to illustrate their arguments.

The story illustrates the need for animals to be camouflaged, but it suggests that
animals can change their skin colourings instantly. Ask the children whether they
think this is possible.

Puzzle

It is not only leopards that have spots. Other animals such as fish, ladybirds, butterflies
and peacocks also have spots. But these spots are not for camouflage purposes: they
are bright colourful spots which are easily seen by predators. Lots of animals are
brightly coloured, including types of bees, wasps and frogs. Why? Is this a problem or
an advantage?

Talking points: true, false or not sure?

- Ladybirds have spots to look good and attract a mate.
- Some butterflies have spots to frighten predators.
- Some frogs are brightly coloured to encourage predators to eat them.
- The bright dark and yellow stripes on some wasps and bees warn predators that
  they may get stung.

Formative assessment

Explore children's responses to the talking points and the puzzle. Use the feedback
to decide what the children know and what they need to learn in the next stage.

Re-describing stage

Children's talk involves making sense of scientific ideas

The purpose of this stage is to make children aware that animals use body colours and patterns in different ways.

Talking and painting

Provide children with a range of coloured and patterned backgrounds, for example different fabrics, pictures from colour magazines, a range of wrapping papers. Alternatively, create a board with a range of coloured backgrounds. Ask children to design a butterfly, a lion and a fish, camouflaged for protection in its habitat. Also ask them to design a dangerous spider, a poisonous tree frog and a wasp, all of which must stand out to stop other creatures eating them.

Enquiry using information sources

Talk about the puzzle and whether the bright colours and patterns could be designed to scare away predators. Children can use information sources to find out how animals such as peacock butterflies, ladybirds, bees and types of frogs use their colourings to scare away predators. They can start by exploring which of their answers to the talking points were consistent with the scientific view. Their research can be widened to include other animals such as tigers and why they need to be camouflaged.

Talk together about how the animals' characteristics help them survive and reproduce in their habitat. Reflect on how they pass on these successful characteristics to their offspring. From this perspective, ask the children to create a more reliable, scientific story of *How the Leopard Got its Spots*.

Assessment and further learning

Use children's responses to your questions and the content of their stories to assess their progress. What else would they like to find out? Children can raise their own questions for further learning.

Application stage

Children's talk involves trying out scientific ideas

Scientific enquiry

Children can apply their developing understanding to design an experiment. The idea is to decorate an egg using colours and markings which will prevent it from being eaten by local animals. This can be done in the school grounds, children's gardens at

Warning signals painted on an egg
Source: Peter Loxley

home or nearby woodland. Children need to start by surveying the chosen area to find a place where they intend to leave the egg. They can then either camouflage the egg so it is difficult to see or paint warning signals on it to scare off local animals. Photographs can be taken to record each stage and the outcomes of the enquiry. Results are unpredictable but will provide discussion opportunities. Remember animals have ways of detecting food other than their sense of sight.

Links to geography, art and design technology

Give groups of children different habitats to research, for example woodland, tropical rainforest, desert, river and arctic regions. Can they find out about some of the animals that live there and suggest how they are adapted to their habitat? How do they keep safe?

Now ask them to design an imaginary animal which would be suited to a particular habitat. Give it a name and describe its characteristics. What would it eat? What would be its predators? How would it keep safe? Children can create a 3-D model of the habitat and the imaginary animal. The group can present their model and explain how the animal is well suited or adapted to living there. From an art point of view, there could be a focus on use of colour and pattern to create a desired effect.

Assessment

Use feedback from discussion of the enquiry and the presentation of their 3-D model to assess children's understanding of the topic.

Information and teaching resources

Books

- Farrow, S. (2006) *The Really Useful Science Book*, Abingdon: Falmer Press, Chapter 2.5: Adaptation to environment.
- Wenham, M. (2005) *Understanding Primary Science*, London: Paul Chapman Publishing Ltd, Chapter 5: Variety, adaptation and interdependence.

Primary science review articles (Association of Science Education)

- PSR 107 (March/April 2009)

  This issue focuses on the work of Darwin and related issues.

Useful information and interactive websites

Arkive is a collection of thousands of videos, images and fact files illustrating the world's species. Visit: www.arkive.org and www.arkiveeducation.org, which now includes the Planet Arkive site and offers a good range of resources for teachers and children.

CHAPTER 13
HEALTH AND WELL-BEING

This chapter examines factors which influence the health and well-being of humans and other animals. We look at how our understanding of animal body systems and the ways in which they interconnect have developed slowly through history. Animals cannot manufacture their food in the way that plants do, and so for most animals their way of life and continuing existence is limited by their ability to consume as widely as possible. Most humans, however, are able to make choices about what they eat and the ways in which they live, and the decisions they make will impact upon their health and development.

Topics discussed in this chapter:

- Historical context
- Animal growth
- Animal nutrition – the digestive system
- The cardiovascular system
- Keeping healthy

Part 1: Subject knowledge

Historical context

Balancing the humours

Until the sixteenth century our understanding of anatomical systems was dominated by the work of a Roman physician of Greek origin, Claudius Galen (*c.* 129–*c.* 216 CE). Because the dissection of human beings was considered unacceptable, Galen's work was based on clinical observation and the dissection of pigs and apes. Poor health was often diagnosed as the result of imbalance between the four humours – blood, phlegm, yellow bile and blood bile. Bloodletting was a common remedy for supposedly restoring the body's balance and remained so well into the eighteenth century.

Understanding of human disease was hampered by the persistence of Galen's four humours theory throughout Western medicine. The nature of infection and the transmission of contagious diseases were not fully understood and doctors were unable to cope with the epidemics that swept Western Europe in the Middle Ages.

In Arab cultures physiological investigation and medical trials were well known from the ninth century onwards. The philosopher and doctor Avicenna, also known as Ibn Sina (980–1037 CE), is thought, for example, to be responsible for the identification of a range of infectious diseases and a systematic approach to their treatment. Many of the hospitals established by religious orders in the medieval period owe their foundation to the medical practices witnessed by the soldiers and priests who returned from the crusades in the Middle East.

Human dissection led to major advances

In the early sixteenth century Galen's ideas were increasingly questioned. Wider acceptance of human dissection enabled physicians to revise and review his ideas. In 1542 Andreas Vesalius (1514–64) published a volume on human anatomy which raised the status of anatomy and surgery and led directly to Harvey's classic explanation of the dual circulation of the blood in 1578. However even Harvey (1578–1657) still believed in the mystical nature of the human body and the 'vital spark' that sustained life. It was René Descartes (1596–1650) in 1637 who initially described the heart as a mechanical pump and the body as a machine. Our knowledge of the process by which nutrition and breathing come together to provide the energy to sustain life was not developed until Antoine Lavoisier's (1743–94) descriptions of the role of oxygen in combustion. This led to an understanding of the way in which energy is released through respiration in each cell to yield the energy needed for growth and to repair and drive the body's systems. There was a gradual realisation that animals are made up of interrelated and complex systems which govern their well-being.

Animal growth

How do we and other animals grow?

Growth in animals takes place through **cell division**. In the moments after fertilisation, the fertilised egg begins to divide into 2, 4, 8, 16 cells and so on. Cell division begins with the replication of the genetic material, the chromosomes, in the nucleus. Following this the cell splits into two to produce two identical daughter cells, each containing the same genetic material as the parent cell.

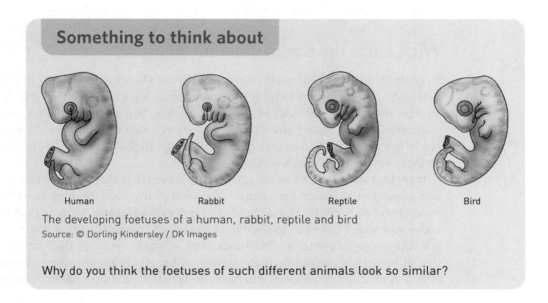

Something to think about

Human   Rabbit   Reptile   Bird

The developing foetuses of a human, rabbit, reptile and bird
Source: © Dorling Kindersley / DK Images

Why do you think the foetuses of such different animals look so similar?

How do we grow and why do we stop growing?

Different parts of an animal grow at different rates. A human baby's head grows quickly before birth to house and protect the developing brain whilst the limbs grow more quickly after birth. As the cells that make up muscle tissue and organ systems divide, the skeleton itself needs to grow to accommodate the growing organism. Eventually this process stops and the adult ceases growing. However, there will always be some cells that need to be replaced in the body. New blood cells for example are formed in the bone marrow throughout life. When the body is damaged, cells at the site begin dividing again, wounds heal and damaged tissue is replaced.

What are bones made from?

Human babies are born with over 300 bones but by the time a child becomes an adult these have reduced to 206. This reduction occurs because the infant bones are mostly cartilaginous and not made from the hard calcium-based bone material. **Cartilage** is a form of dense **connective tissue** and is flexible. Over time this is converted to bone by a process known as **ossification**. This flexibility allows for movement and growth and for fusing of bone material most notably in the skull, which is made up of separate plates in the uterus to enable slight compression and distortion of the head during birth. It is the cartilaginous nature of the infant bones that enable growth. The long bones of the body (such as the femur) grow from each end in areas called growth plates. This happens when the cartilage cells divide and increase in number. The new cartilage cells push the older cells towards the middle of the bone where they die and the space they occupied is replaced by bone. When a bone has reached its full size, its growth plates are also converted into bone and growth stops.

What limits the size of different animals?

To grow large an animal needs a strong internal skeleton to support it. The dinosaur skeletons found in many natural history museums are testament to this. The largest aquatic mammals, the whales, grow to such a size because their body weight is supported by the water. Even though they have strong skeletons, beached whales are in great danger and unless quickly returned to the sea their internal organs will collapse under their own weight.

Invertebrates such as earth worms that have no skeletons are restricted in size, and some live in water for support. On land many invertebrates tend to be slow-moving and vulnerable. Those that have hard **exoskeletons**, such as crabs, can move with more speed but need to shed their skeletons in order to grow and at these times are vulnerable to predators. **Molluscs** such as snails grow as their shells grow. The size of insects is limited by their inefficient breathing mechanisms. In **vertebrates** oxygen is efficiently transported to the cells by the circulatory system. However, insects rely on oxygen being delivered directly through a series of dead-end tracheal tubes, bottlenecks which limit the amount of oxygen that can be received at the insect's extremities. It is thought that the large insects that lived during the Palaeozoic era (543 to 248 million years ago) only did so because atmospheric oxygen levels were then at a record high.

Animal nutrition – the digestive system

Animals need food to live

In order to live all animals need energy. The ultimate source of this energy is the food produced by plants through photosynthesis (see Chapter 10). Animals need a mechanism to release energy from the food they eat. Energy is used for growth, repair and to keep vital internal systems working. Animals can consume a wide range of foods. Those that have the greatest range, normally the omnivores, are the most likely to survive successfully. Those that consume higher up the food chain (see Chapter 10), the carnivores, need only spend a fraction of their time finding food as the meat they eat is high in energy. For example, lions may well only hunt every few days and the boa constrictor can survive for months without eating. This is in contrast to the **ruminants**, the herbivorous mammals such as cattle that need to graze constantly in order to consume sufficient food to release enough energy to survive. Giant pandas (part of the bear family) consume a highly restricted diet mainly of bamboo. As a result, they need to spend most of their time feeding and cannot build up sufficient energy reserves to hibernate through the worst of the winter, as bears in temperate climates generally do. As a result, pandas struggle to survive in winter when the leaves that are available are often frozen and difficult to consume. From a survival point of view, an animal that has a highly specialised and restricted intake is vulnerable to alterations in the environment, either naturally or as a result of human actions.

Something to think about

Myth has it that we are never more than a few feet away from a rat. Why do rats survive so successfully? Is this anything to do with their diet?

What happens to the food that we eat?

Animals need to process their food so that it can be used effectively throughout the body to sustain life. The higher order vertebrates – that is, birds, reptiles, fish, amphibians and mammals – have the most complex digestive systems, particularly those that are capable of eating a wide range of foodstuffs including both vegetation and meat.

Human digestion – where does it begin?

Digestion begins mechanically through biting, gnawing, chewing and swallowing. Swallowing is aided by a process of muscle contraction, known as **peristalsis**, that forces food down the oesophagus or gullet towards the stomach. The process of digestion begins with saliva (a mixture of mucus to lubricate and amylase to break down starch) in the mouth and continues as the food passes to the stomach, which secretes **gastric juices** (hydrochloric acid and pepsin to break down the proteins) that attack the ingested food. The acid in a human stomach is highly corrosive with a pH of between 1 and 2. Depending on its nature, food will remain in the stomach for a variable amount of time. Water passes through quickly whilst more complex foods – that is, those that contain proteins, carbohydrates and fats – will remain for two to three hours.

Beyond the stomach

As the food passes out of the stomach into the duodenum, **bile** and other digestive juices stored in the gall bladder and pancreas help to break down the complex foods

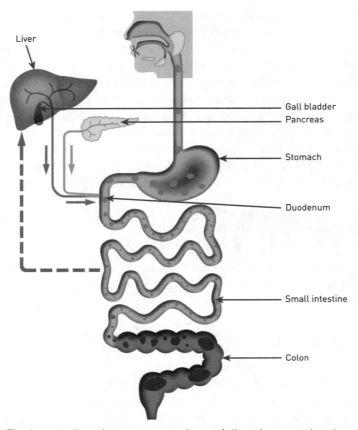

The human digestive system: products of digestion are taken by
the blood to the liver

Source: Kevin Jones / © Dorling Kindersley / DK Images

into soluble forms that can pass through the intestinal lining and directly into the
bloodstream. The small intestine or ileum is long and has a large absorbing surface
which is greatly increased by the thousands of tiny finger-like projections called 'villi'.
Any undigested food and water passes into the colon where the water is absorbed
into the bloodstream. The semi-solid waste remaining (the faeces) is passed into the
rectum by peristalsis and is expelled at intervals through the anus.

Why can't humans eat grass?

At the end of the caecum, connecting the ileum with the colon, humans have a vestigial
organ, the appendix. This structure is more prominent and important in herbivorous
mammals where it contains the bacteria essential for the digestion of cellulose.
Without these bacteria, the outer cellulose shell of sweetcorn, for example, passes
through the human digestive tract virtually untouched. It seems likely that the human
appendix is an evolutionary relic from the times when human ancestors existed on
mainly herbivorous diets.

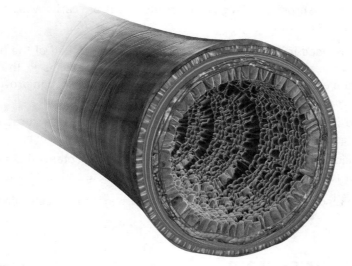

The human intestine and villi
Source: © Dorling Kindersley / DK Images

Snail watch

It can be fascinating to observe digestion first-hand in snails. Giant African land snails have a nearly transparent gut. Feeding them on strawberries for a time will enable you to watch the passage of food through the snail's gut and even observe the muscular contractions that move the food forward towards the stomach.

Digestion releases nutrients into the bloodstream

Whatever the actual process of digestion, the outcome is the presence in the blood-stream of various dissolved **compounds** that can be transported around the body. Some of these will be vitamins and minerals essential for continued health and well-being: for example, calcium from dairy products to support healthy bones and teeth, or vitamin C from citrus fruit to produce and repair connective tissues. The main purpose

Great African land snail
Source: Dave King / © Dorling Kindersley / DK Images

of digestion, however, is to ensure a constant supply of fuel to all cells for the process of respiration. The products of digestion are glucose (from carbohydrates), amino acids (from proteins) and fats:

- Glucose: is used in the process of respiration in every cell of the body. Here it is oxidised releasing energy to drive the chemical processes in the cells. Carbon dioxide and water are by-products of this reaction. Respiration provides energy for growth, living and renewal.
- Fats: are incorporated into cell membranes and other structures in the cells or used in respiration, releasing twice as much energy as glucose.
- Amino acids: absorbed by cells and used to build the proteins that form cell membranes or form enzymes which control and coordinate chemical activity in the cells.

Respiration also requires oxygen which is also brought to the cells via the circulation of the blood.

The cardiovascular system

How is oxygen transported around the body?

The heart (as a pump), the lungs (for the supply of oxygen) and the blood vessels (arteries, veins and capillaries) make up the cardiovascular system. Blood is able to transport dissolved oxygen, food and the waste products of respiration around the body. Deoxygenated blood flows from every tissue of the body to the right side of the heart where it is pumped to the lungs. Here the carbon dioxide produced as a by-product of respiration diffuses out of the blood plasma into the lungs, and oxygen **diffuses** from the lungs into the blood where it combines with **haemoglobin** in the red corpuscles. Oxygenated blood returns to the left side of the heart and is pumped around the body. The two circulations run simultaneously, giving the characteristic double heartbeat with which we are all familiar. Flow of the blood in the heart is controlled by non-return valves. Contractions of the left side of the heart (systolic) are stronger than those of the right (diastolic) because oxygenated blood has to be pumped around the whole body. This contraction can be felt as a 'pulse' in various locations (neck, wrist, behind the knee) where blood vessels carrying this blood run just below the surface of the skin. The normal adult human heart contracts about 70 times a minute, increasing to 100 times a minute during activity. In smaller animals such as mice the heartbeat can be as high as 600 times a minute whilst an elephant's heart beats only about 30 times a minute.

Something to think about

Mice live on average 3 years and elephants 60. Do you think there is a connection between the rate at which an animal's heart beats and its longevity? What implications does this have for humans?

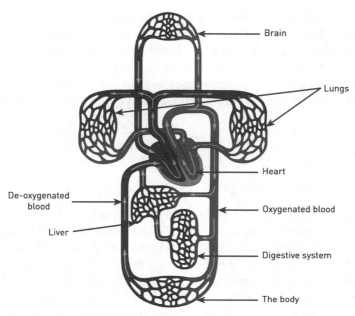

Brain

Lungs

Heart

De-oxygenated blood

Oxygenated blood

Liver

Digestive system

The body

Double circulation with the heart as a pump
Source: © Dorling Kindersley / DK Images

Respiration

Respiration takes place in every living cell of every organism – animals and plants. It is the process by which glucose is oxidised to form carbon dioxide and water and energy is released to maintain the organism's vital functions. This process happens most efficiently in the presence of oxygen (aerobic respiration). The oxygen is supplied via the lungs and the bloodstream through the process of breathing. The fuel, glucose, comes via the digestive system and the bloodstream.

Aerobic respiration can be described as:

glucose + oxygen → carbon dioxide + water + energy transfer

$$C_6H_{12}O_6 + \quad 6O_2 \quad \rightarrow \quad 6CO_2 \quad + 6H_2O$$

About 60% of the energy gained from aerobic respiration is in the form of heat. In 'warm blooded' animals this maintains the body temperature. Remaining energy is used for growth and repair or for muscular movement such as in locomotion, heartbeat or breathing. As activity increases, the need for oxygen to support respiration also increases. As a result, the heart beats faster to deliver oxygen more quickly to the cells and breathing rate increases to supply this. Certain **hormones** will also increase the heart rate: for example, adrenaline which is known as the 'fight, fright and flight' hormone. As well as increasing the blood sugar levels, adrenaline increases the heart rate, which allows an animal to react quickly to what are perceived as dangerous situations. Heart rate may also increase in colder conditions so that a greater amount of heat can be produced to compensate. If the demand for oxygen through vigorous exercise becomes greater than the rate at which the body is able to supply it, then anaerobic respiration will take place. The process is less efficient than aerobic respiration and as a result lactic acid is produced as a waste product. In humans this can happen during strenuous exercise. The lactic acid accumulates in muscle tissue and can cause stiffness and aching ('cramps'). In plants anaerobic respiration can result in the production of ethanol (alcohol) and carbon dioxide. This reaction is used in the brewing industry.

Keeping healthy

Limeys, sauerkraut and gum rot

On sea voyages prior to the mid-eighteenth century, many more sailors died due to poor health than any other reason. In the 1740s, for example, when Admiral Anson's expedition to the Pacific Ocean eventually returned, well over half the sailors aboard had perished. The majority of these deaths were due to the sailor's scourge, the dreaded illness, scurvy. In desperation the Admiralty in London invited scientists to suggest manageable ways of staving off the onset of this debilitating condition during the increasingly long voyages that were being undertaken.

It was considered at the time that scurvy was the result of poor sanitation, diet, living conditions aboard ship or even feebleness of mind in the sailors themselves. Although it was known that foods such as sauerkraut could combat the development of scurvy, there was no understanding that it was a deficiency condition resulting from lack of a vital vitamin. Sailors lacked vitamin C, which maintains the health of connective tissues in the body. Without it wounds do not heal, gums rot, lethargy and depression set in and eventually sailors die. Many weird and wonderful solutions were proposed, such as burying the sailor up to the neck in sand or drinking sulphuric acid, but it was James Lind, a naval surgeon, who in 1747 conducted a carefully structured investigation to prove conclusively that lack of a vital element in the diet caused scurvy. In doing so Lind provided the first recorded example of a clinical trial using control subjects. He introduced a much needed rigour into medical research. As a result of his work the provision of green vegetables and citrus fruits became commonplace on British naval vessels, earning the sailors the nickname 'limeys' and in the process saving untold numbers of lives.

Factors which influence health and well-being

The health and well-being of animals depends on a number of factors. For most animals these are the ability to find and consume appropriate amounts of food, freedom from disease or debilitating injury, shelter from adverse weather conditions and safety from predators. Today we have a clear understanding of the nature of infection and communicable bacteriological diseases and the role **micro-organisms** play in human health. In the eighteenth and nineteenth century the Industrial Revolution saw rural populations move to the cities to live in crowded and insanitary conditions. Public health became a matter of real concern when in 1848 an epidemic of cholera led to the death of 14,000 people in London. The writings of Charles Dickens and others exposed the problems associated with poor diet and sanitation and helped to bring about the development of great engineering works such as the building of the London sewerage system by Joseph Bazalgette. This effectively lifted the scourge of water-borne diseases from the city. In the early twentieth century the mass mobilisation of men to fight in two world wars exposed the impact of poor nutrition on the population and brought a clearer understanding of the importance of diet in promoting health and general well-being.

Humans are able to make choices about the food they consume and the ways in which they live and these can have a direct impact on health and well-being. Some choices are personal ones for which we can take direct responsibility – whether we eat a balanced diet or give up smoking. Some choices we may feel are beyond our direct control – industrial pollution, exposure to epidemics or the predicted outcomes of increased global warming.

There is an increased emphasis within education on the ways in which individuals can take responsibility for the impact of lifestyle on health and well-being. With growing levels of childhood obesity and falling levels of exercise, children need to be aware of the ways in which they can determine their future well-being. However, these are sensitive issues and need careful and measured treatment in the primary context.

What is a balanced diet?

We know that a variety of different foods is essential to support our body systems and maintain our health. The human body uses carbohydrates as a source of energy for growth, movement and repair. We eat carbohydrates in the form of sugars or starch (found in grains such as rice and wheat). These are broken down through the process of digestion and changed into glucose, which is the main energy source for respiration. Our bodies cannot store excess carbohydrate so if more sugar and starch is eaten than the body can use, it is stored as fat. Similarly the fats that we eat are broken down and used by the body to fuel respiration. Proteins either from meat or pulses yield a range of chemicals that are used to replace and repair damaged tissue. They also provide some of the enzymes that control our metabolic rate. Within a balanced diet we also need to consume foods rich in vitamins to help control reactions within the body, and minerals, such as calcium, to support the building of bones and maintain nerve function. Living tissue is made up mostly of water so we need to replace water lost through urination, sweating and exhalation. Finally although we can no longer digest cellulose (fibre found in vegetables, fruits, whole grains), it still forms an essential part of our daily diet as our bodies need it to speed up the passage of food through the gut. This fibre is also known as roughage.

Poor diet is a global issue. In areas of poverty and deprivation people are often malnourished and underweight, whereas in developed countries the abundance and relative cheapness of foodstuffs has led to a growing concern about rising levels of obesity. Many foods are highly processed and contain high levels of sugars, fats and salt. Maintaining a healthy lifestyle requires good nutrition and exercise and children need to be encouraged to recognise the link between the two.

Bread, other cereals and potatoes

Milk and dairy foods

Foods containing fat and sugar

Meat, fish and alternatives

Fruits and vegetables

A balanced diet: the balance of good health is based on five food groups
Source: Maximilian Stock Ltd / Science Photo Library Ltd

Summary

Developments in understanding of the way in which our bodies function, combined with understanding of the nature of disease, have led to improvements in health and well-being. Food contains stored energy which was originally captured by plants from the Sun, and the digestive system enables animals to break down these foods into soluble forms. The blood carries dissolved food, along with oxygen, through the circulatory system to all animal cells. Respiration is the process by which this energy is released and made available for animals to carry out all of the life processes. Respiration takes place in all cells.

Animals produce offspring that are similar to themselves. Growth occurs through the process of cell division and each new cell contains the same genetic material as the parent cell. The skeleton supports and protects an animal's body and determines its size. Continuing health and well-being depends on the choices we make about what we consume and how we live our lives.

Further information and teaching resources can be found at the end of the 'Ideas for practice' section.

Part 2: Ideas for practice

Topic: Healthy eating

Age group: Lower primary

Scientific view

We obtain everything that we need to grow and develop healthily from the foods we eat. Food is not only enjoyable but also serves a vital function in providing our bodies with the means of staying healthy and of getting energy to grow and function. To keep healthy we must choose a balanced diet from the different food groups.

Scientific enquiry skills

In these activities children will:

- raise and try to find answers to questions;
- make simple comparisons;
- communicate their choices using pictograms;
- review their work and explain them to others.

Exploratory stage

Children's talk involves trying out their own ideas

Setting the scene

Read the story of *The Very Hungry Caterpillar* by Eric Carle. *Talk together* about what it ate each day. Were the children surprised that the caterpillar had stomach-ache on Saturday? Which of the foods are best for a growing caterpillar? Which foods will keep it healthy? Is it best to eat lots of fruit or lots of things like chocolate cake, ice cream and sausages? If the children could choose, which foods would they eat? Explain why.

PSHE activity

Ask the children what they would eat if they could choose their own meals for a week. How would they make their decisions? Would it be based only on what they like best or would they choose 'healthy foods'? Children can *work collaboratively* in groups to plan their meals for a week. They must come to an agreement for the whole group because they will have to eat the same things. Younger children can plan for a shorter time and use drawings to record their choices. The groups should compare and justify their choice of meals.

Puzzle

How do we know which are the best foods to choose? Which foods keep us healthy?

Formative assessment

Listen to children's justifications for their meals and their responses to the puzzle to decide what the children know and what they need to learn in the next stage.

Re-describing stage

Children's talk involves making sense of scientific ideas

The purpose of this part is to introduce the children to the different food groups so that they can make informed choices about what they should eat.

Scientific enquiry

Provide the children with pictures of foods from all the major food groups.

Food from the major food groups
Source: Martin Brigdale / © Dorling Kindersley / DK Images

a) Fruit and vegetables

b) Meat, fish and alternatives

c) Foods containing fat and sugars

d) Milk and dairy foods

e) Bread, other cereals and potatoes

Which of these were included in the children's choice of meals? How many children chose to eat lots of fruit and vegetables? How many chose lots of foods containing fats and sugars such as crisps, chips and cakes. Which was the most popular choice? Help the children match their foods to each of the groups. Use pictograms to record how frequently they choose a particular type of food.

Make children aware that their bodies perform best when they eat a balance of these foods. Use a food pyramid diagram to talk about the balance. They can use this information to decide whether their choices of food provided a healthy diet or whether they would likely end up with stomach-ache like the caterpillar! What changes do they need to make to their original choices?

Assessment and further learning

Review the changes children made to their choices of meals and assess their progress. What else would they like to find out? Children can raise their own questions for further learning.

Application stage

Children's talk involves trying out scientific ideas

Links to design technology and mathematics

An enjoyable way of further developing children's understanding would be to involve them in planning, shopping for and preparing a balanced meal for a picnic or other occasion. *Working collaboratively* in groups, children can decide what they would like to eat on the picnic and then justify their choices with regard to a healthy balance.

Once a decision has been made children can be taken to the local supermarket to choose and buy their food. Back in the classroom they can then prepare their picnic. Issues of hygiene and special diets can be brought into the discussion. Calculation of costs of the meals could be included. While on their picnic they could go on a caterpillar hunt and photograph what the caterpillars are eating.

Assessment

Listen to conversations and children's justifications for their choices to assess their understanding of the topic.

Topic: Benefits of exercise

Age group: Upper primary

Scientific view

The circulatory system is the means by which blood is pumped by the heart around our bodies. The blood carries food to every cell where it is used as a fuel in the process of respiration, which releases energy to support the body's natural functions. The blood also carries oxygen from the lungs to our cells to support respiration and takes away waste products – water and carbon dioxide. As we make greater demands on our bodies through exercise then the heart pumps more quickly to supply additional energy.

Scientific enquiry skills

In these activities children will:

- raise and try to find answers to questions;
- decide what kind of evidence to collect and equipment to use;
- make systematic observations and measurements;
- use observations, measurements and other data to draw conclusions;
- use their scientific knowledge and understanding to explain observations and measurements.

Exploration stage

Children's talk involves trying out their own ideas

Setting the scene

Start with video footage of athletes competing in a recent event, a world championship, a marathon or the Olympics, for example. Ask the children to watch them closely and discuss how they might be feeling when they finish their race. Do they notice if the athlete is sweating or breathing heavily or even falls on the ground as they finish?

Scientific enquiry

Talk together about how the children feel when they have been exercising – during PE in school, for example. Do they experience similar effects to the Olympic athletes?

In a PE session ask the children to undertake a series of simple exercises. This may well need to be adapted to meet the needs of particular children in the class. This could be a simple circuit-training exercise, for example, with set numbers of star jumps, running on the spot, step-ups, etc. for 2 minutes altogether. When the children have finished ask them to sit immediately and discuss in pairs how they feel. Encourage the children to be more precise about how they describe this.

Children can discuss:

- whether they feel hot;
- whether they are sweating;
- whether their heart is beating faster;
- whether they ache;
- what has happened to their breathing.

Discuss children's responses and focus on how their heartbeat changes during exercise. Time spent practising finding and recording a pulse before the investigation will be well spent. The children can work in pairs to alternately exercise and measure pulses for each other. They need to be reminded that the idea is not to tire themselves completely; moderate exercise is enough.

The children will need to record in some detail the changes that occur during exercise. To do this they will need to measure and record their at-rest results for heart rate and breathing. They could also describe their appearance and use a fore-head thermometer to take their temperature. Once they have the base data, the pairs

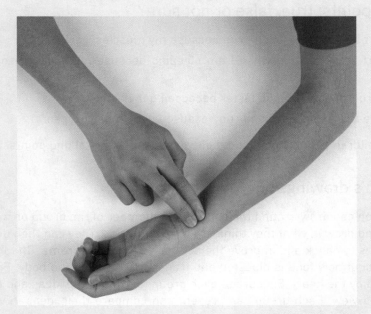

Taking a pulse at the wrist
Source: Tim Ridley / © Dorling Kindersley / DK Images

can take it in turns to exercise and record physiological readings. At this point it would also be useful to ask the children to take the same readings five minutes after exercising has finished to see if anything has changed.

Puzzle

Prompt the children to suggest reasons for why the changes occur, relating this back to existing knowledge about the body's need for energy. Why does our pulse rate rise and why do we breathe more heavily when exercising? Why do we get hot?

Formative assessment

Explore children's responses to the puzzle and decide what the children know and what they need to learn in the next stage.

Re-describing stage

Children's talk involves making sense of scientific ideas

The purpose of this stage is to help children understand that we get energy from our food, which is used to make our limbs move and also to warm our bodies. The faster or longer we run the more energy our bodies require.

Talking points: true, false or not sure?

- My heart beats faster when I run because my muscles work harder.
- My heart stops beating when I am sleeping because my body doesn't need any energy.
- When I run my heart beats faster because I get excited.
- I breathe more deeply when I run because I need more oxygen.

Discuss children's thinking behind their responses to the talking points.

Children's drawings

The children can draw around the body of one member of the group on a large piece of paper and draw in what they think are the key organs. They can then use information sources to check and improve the accuracy of their diagrams. Children can *talk together* about how food is digested and transported around the body. Focus on the role played by the heart. Encourage each group to explore the ideas and try to arrive at a shared view. Each group can present and compare their ideas in whole-class discussion.

Modelling

Based on the children's ideas, introduce the process of respiration and its requirements. How do the children's ideas fit in with this scientific explanation? Respiration is a difficult concept to teach as we cannot observe it directly. Use a simple model of the circulation system and explain how food combines with oxygen in the muscles (cells) to release energy for movement and heat. Children can modify their drawings in light of what they have learnt from the research.

Assessment and further learning

Use the children's responses to the talking points and discussion of their modified drawings to assess their progress. What else would they like to find out? Children can raise their own questions for further learning.

Application stage

Children's talk involves trying out scientific ideas

Links to physical education and design technology

The children can investigate through information sources the diets and training routines of athletes. What effects are the routines designed to have on their bodies and performances? Does exercise increase breathing rate or an athlete's ability to take in more oxygen at each breath: in other words, does lung capacity increase? Does the diet help to build muscle or provide the energy to perform better? As part of the project children can design and make high-energy meals which are designed for sprinting or endurance running. They can compare these with the diets of top athletes.

Links to music

Review with the children the different stages as food passes through our bodies. Children use musical instruments to compose a piece of music based on the journey of the food as it passes stage by stage through the body. The children can choose a musical theme, maybe based on heartbeat or breathing, which continues throughout their piece and on which other sounds which represent the different stages are imposed (idea based on *Explore Music through Science* by David Wheway and Shelagh Thomson, 1993).

Assessment

Listen to conversations and use feedback from the activities to assess children's understanding of the topic.

Information and teaching resources

Books

- Roden, J., Ward, H. and Ritchie, H. (2007) *Extending Knowledge in Practice: Primary Science*, Exeter: Learning Matters, Chapter 4: Humans and other animals.
- Wenham, M. (2005) *Understanding Primary Science*, London: Paul Chapman Publishing Ltd, Chapter 3: Humans and other animals.

Primary science review articles (Association of Science Education)

- PSR 102 (March/April 2008), 'The benefits of being physically active' by Sue Chedzoy and Craig Williams.
- PSR 97 (March/April 2007), 'What big teeth you have' by David Aston.
- PSR 86 (January/February 2005), 'Exploring the meaning of healthy' by Jonathan Whitewell.
- PSR 86 (January/February 2005), 'What drugs have you taken this week?' by Barbara Wyvill.
- PSR 85 (November/December 2004), 'Where does the drink go?' by Sue Dale Tunnicliffe.

Useful information and interactive websites

- Food a fact of life website – lots of activities: www.foodafactoflife.org.uk/
- BBC clips for schools: www.bbc.co.uk/schools/scienceclips/ages/6_7/health_growth.shtml
- Wide range of activities: www.bbc.co.uk/science/humanbody/ (interactive)
- Well designed website for children: http://kidshealth.org/kid/index.jsp
- Interactive website designed for primary education: www.childrensuniversity.manchester.ac.uk/interactives/science/bodyandmedicine/

CHAPTER 14
THE PARTICLE NATURE
OF MATERIALS

In everyday contexts we heat water to make tea or melt chocolate to cover a cake. Puddles on the pavement dry up in the sunshine and water turns into ice cubes in the freezer. The words that we use to describe what we observe, such as solidifying, melting, boiling and condensing, label these events in scientific terms but give no explanation of the processes taking place. In order to help to explain why materials such as water change their properties when they change from a solid to a liquid and to a gas, we need to offer a story or a model which will help in visualising the processes involved. This chapter explores the particle nature of matter and how this can be used to make sense of phenomena such as ice cubes melting and sugar dissolving in water.

Topics discussed in this chapter:

- Historical context
- Properties of materials
- The particle model of matter
- Reversible and physical changes

Part 1: Subject knowledge

Historical context

What the ancient Greeks believed

The idea that matter is not continuous but can be understood as being made up of tiny particles originally came to us from Greek thinking. The philosopher Democritus (460–370 BCE) proposed a thought experiment to ask what would happen if we try to divide matter (a piece of gold, say) into smaller and smaller pieces by continually cutting it in half. He suggested there would be a limit to the number of times this could be done and that eventually the smallest possible piece would result and that this would be indivisible. This he named an atom, meaning 'cannot be cut'. He proposed that these atoms were very small, hard particles that were different in size and shape for each different material but were capable of moving about and joining together.

However, Democritus' ideas were ignored in favour of the 'four elements' theory supported by more eminent Greek philosophers such as Aristotle and Plato. This idea, that matter is made up of differing proportions of the elements earth, fire, air and water, and that matter could be transmuted from one form to another, formed the basis of alchemy. The pursuit of alchemy and the search for the magical 'philosopher's stone' that would transform base metals into gold was ultimately a dead end in our developing understanding of the nature of matter, although many eminent scientists, including Newton, became fascinated with its study.

New ideas emerge in the nineteenth century

In the early nineteenth century the atomic ideas of Democritus were resurrected by the work of John Dalton, who calculated the relative sizes and characteristics of atoms and laid the foundations for modern chemistry. Our understanding of the form that these atoms actually take was later refined by the research of J. J. Thomson and Ernest Rutherford, and culminated in Niels Bohr presenting his 'solar system' model of the atom in 1913 (see Chapter 15). Nowadays we see the atom as no longer indivisible but comprised of **protons**, **neutrons** and **electrons** and other particles which determine the nature of matter itself.

Properties of materials

Common experiences

The common materials with which we come into contact in everyday life exist in one of three familiar forms: as a solid e.g. wood, a liquid e.g. water or as a gas such as oxygen. There are obvious physical features that distinguish a solid from a liquid. Solids tend to have a shape of their own which they maintain without support. Even a malleable solid such as play dough will retain its new shape once manipulated. A liquid, however, flows and takes on the shape of its container or, if let to run freely, will spread out into a thin film on a level surface. The extent to which a liquid spreads is dependent on its viscosity: water and syrup offer two contrasting examples of this. Defining the properties of gases in a similar way is more problematic. Experience of blowing up balloons tells us that a gas, like liquid, has no shape of its own but unlike liquid will fill a container completely rather than collecting at the bottom.

Something to think about

Consider the gas that fills the rooms we live in. Wherever we are in the room we can breathe easily, whether we're up a ladder changing a light bulb or lying on the floor watching TV. How does air get everywhere?

Solid or liquid or gas?

Some solids like sand and flour can mimic the behaviour of liquids. We can pour flour and see the flow of sand. Does this mean that sand and flour should be classified as liquids?

If we investigate the structure of sand and flour more closely by looking through a magnifying glass or digital microscope, we can see the individual bits of solid material or grains from which they are made. An analogy is to compare a sack of sand or a bag of flour with a bag of marbles. Each is a mixture made up of solid pieces of material and air. Each grain of sand or flour is classified as a solid. A bag of sand or flour is a **mixture** of a solid and a gas, and the ability to flow is a property of the mixture. An observable property that distinguishes a gas from a liquid or a solid is that it can be squashed or compressed. Generally, solids and liquids are difficult to compress, whilst gases are springy and compress easily.

Something to think about

A sponge holds its own shape but is obviously squashy. Does this mean that some solids are easily squashed or is there another way of looking at it?

The need for a model

The previous discussion draws on features of solids, liquids and gases which we can observe but offers no explanation about why these differences occur. How can we offer an explanation when we cannot see what is causing materials to behave as they do? To do this we need to think creatively and imagine what the structure of the materials may look like. To help us do this we need a model which behaves in the same way as the materials. The particle model of matter offers a fairly simple and understandable way of explaining the behaviour of materials.

Something to think about

Imagine you have been given a block of chocolate and asked to divide it into as many pieces as possible. Imagine using finer and finer instruments until you are working at a microscopic level, rather like a surgeon performing intricate keyhole surgery using a microscope to focus on the operation site. As you continue cutting what do you imagine the chocolate would look like? When you look through the microscope what would you see? Could you imagine going on like this forever?

The particle model of matter

What you would end up with would be individual 'particles' of chocolate that are the smallest pieces possible and can no longer be divided – but are still chocolate. Every substance has unique particles that are different from the particles of any other substance. These particles are not static; they have energy, are in constant motion and are attracted to each other by very strong electrical forces. Energy in the form of heat will affect the speed of the particles. The higher the temperature the more energy the particles have and so the quicker they move. In a small square of chocolate there will be many millions of particles. When the chocolate is in a solid block we can imagine particles arranged in a tightly packed uniform structure, rather like a lattice, with the particles held firmly in place by the mutual attraction between them. They can vibrate but cannot move freely. This structure is rigid and not easily pressed out of shape. A solid is **dense** because the particles are packed tightly together. It has a fixed volume and its shape is fixed unless subjected to a force (think of plasticene being moulded). Solids are difficult to compress as there is no empty space between the particles.

Something to think about

Imagine what happens if you now decide to make a chocolate cake and so heat a block of chocolate in a microwave oven. What will happen to it as it gains more energy?

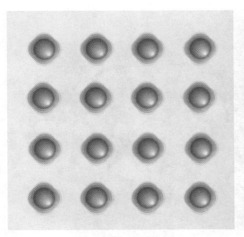 

Model of a solid

Source: © Dorling Kindersley / DK Images (left); © Leslie Morris / Photographers Direct (right)

More to think about

In the model above imagine the supermarket shelf is shaken from side to side (given more energy). The regular arrangement of the stacked apples will break down and the apples will roll across the floor. Compare the behaviour of the apples to the behaviour of chocolate when it is heated. Do you think this is a useful model?

How do solids change into liquids?

As we heat materials we give more energy to the particles. They are able to move apart from each other and are less constrained by the forces that attract them. They are freer to move randomly over and around each other. The chocolate can be poured out of the basin and will spread across a plate. A liquid will flow as the particles, although still close together, clump randomly and show no particular order. A liquid has a surface and fixed volume, although its shape is defined by its container. A liquid is not easily compressed as there is no empty space between the particles. An analogy is a children's ball pool. The balls take up the shape of the pool but there is little space between them and so they cannot be compressed. As the children play in the pool the balls roll over each other and become thoroughly mixed.

Why are gases easily compressed?

In a gas such as air the particles move with more energy and greater speed than in a liquid and are able to break the bonds that hold them together. A gas has no surface and no fixed shape or volume and will spread out to fill any container. Gases

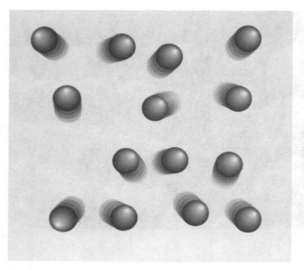 

Model of a liquid
Source: © Dorling Kindersley (left); Dave King / © Dorling Kindersley (right) / DK Images

are much less dense than solids or liquids. The particles move rapidly, bouncing off one another and off the sides of their container. There are wide gaps between the particles and the volume of gas becomes smaller as the size of the container decreases. A model for this might be the National Lottery balls in the drum of the machine.

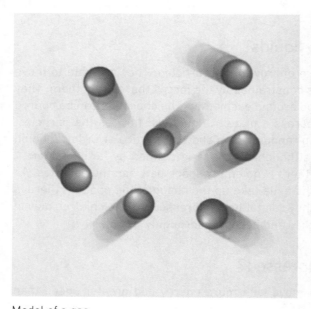 

Model of a gas
Source: © Dorling Kindersley / DK Images (left); Andy Marlin / Getty Images (right)

Something to think about

Imagine your chocolate cake is baking in the oven. How does the smell of the cake baking spread throughout the house?

How can the particle model explain melting and evaporation?

As a solid warms the particles begin to vibrate more vigorously until they are able to overcome the forces of attraction between them and move more freely. The solid has melted or liquefied to become a liquid: we call this a change of state. As warming continues the particles continue to gain energy until they move so vigorously that they break away from each other and escape as free-moving gas particles. The liquid evaporates and changes state. The amount of heat (and so energy) needed to achieve this change will be different for different substances. Evaporation does not always require high temperatures. For example, a saucer of water left on a windowsill will eventually 'dry up'. The water takes in heat from the surrounding air and so the water particles begin to move more quickly. Faster moving particles close to the surface have enough energy to resist the pull of the surrounding water particles and so escape the liquid. Evaporation happens more quickly if the surrounding air temperature is warmer and also if there is a greater surface area of water exposed to the air.

When materials are cooled the reverse happens. Cooling removes energy from the particles and so they slow down and are unable to overcome the attraction between them. Gases become liquids again by condensing and liquids return to solids by solidifying.

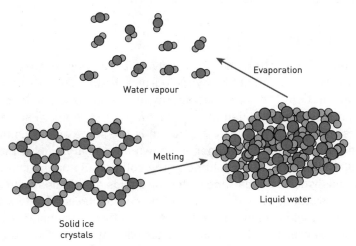

Water vapour

Evaporation

Melting

Liquid water

Solid ice
crystals

The changing structure of water

Reversible and physical changes

The change of state of a material from solid to liquid to gas is a *reversible change* and an example of a *physical change* to that material. Physical changes may alter the appearance and physical properties of a material but the nature of the particles involved stays essentially the same.

What other changes are reversible?

Sand and gravel, oil and vinegar, dust in the air and salt dissolved in water are all examples of mixtures of materials. The two (or more) substances are physically combined but remain chemically distinct and, in theory, can be separated by physical means. A mixture of sand and gravel is separated by sieving, oil and vinegar by settling and then pouring; dust can be removed from the air by a filter and salt and water separated by evaporation. Most methods of separation are one-step, mechanical processes such as sieving (sand and gravel), filtering (coffee grinds and water) or pouring off (fat from gravy). However, other mixtures may require an intermediate step such as the addition of water. For example, to separate a mixture of sand and salt it is first mixed with water. The mixture can then be filtered to remove the insoluble solid (sand) and evaporated to separate out the soluble solid (salt).

Solutions and suspensions

When materials such as sugar or salt dissolve a solution is formed. A solution is a clear liquid which is often but not always colourless. Instant coffee, for example, gives a clear, brown solution. The liquid which forms a solution is called a **solvent** and the substance that dissolves is called the solute. Water is a common solvent. Weighing reveals that although the **weight** of a solution is the same as the combined weight of the solvent and solute (a phenomenon known as conservation of mass), there is no appreciable difference in the volume of the solution. Solutions can be formed of solids and liquids, such as sugar and water, or liquids and liquids such as water and alcohol, or liquids and gases such as water and carbon dioxide (soda water).

Not all materials will dissolve in each other. Initially a suspension is formed when they are mixed but over time the solid particles will settle out. Examples of suspensions are muddy water, dust particles in air, and fog, which is water suspended in air.

Some liquids will not mix: for example, oil and vinegar separate out in salad dressings. The more similar two liquids are in density and size and composition of particles the more likely they are to mix.

Something to think about

We can mix flour, sand, gravel, paperclips and salt. How can we retrieve all the constituents? How many different separation techniques would be needed to achieve this?

An example of dissolving – where did the sugar go?

Water and sugar are made up of tiny particles. The particles in the solid sugar are held in tight arrays whilst those of the liquid water are freer to move around each other. The water particles have more energy than the sugar particles as they have been able to break the strong bonds of attraction between them. The individual sugar particles are grouped together into granules, their size depending on the type of sugar: granulated, caster, icing, etc. When the sugar is added to the water, we can imagine the more energetic water particles knocking and bumping against the particles on the surface of the solid sugar. Gradually these particles will be dislodged from the sugar granule and then slip into the spaces between the water particles. Gradually more particles are dislodged, slip into the spaces and eventually a solution is created. This explains why the mass of the resultant solution increases, but its volume does not.

What difference does heat make?

When we make instant coffee we use hot water and stir. How can we explain this in terms of the particle nature of materials? If the water is hotter then the water particles will have more energy and so move faster and bump into the coffee granules with more energy, breaking them down more quickly. Similarly, stirring will impart more

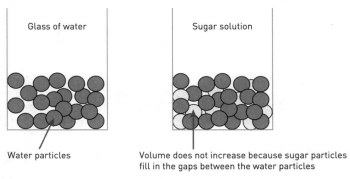

Simplified model of a sugar solution

energy to the water and speed up the mechanical breaking down of the coffee granules. The smaller the granules the quicker they will dissolve, as smaller granules have proportionally greater surface area for their volume. The particle model also helps to explain why there is a limit to the amount of sugar we can dissolve in our tea. When there is no more space between the water particles the solution is described as 'saturated' and the sugar particles drop to the bottom of the cup.

Summary

All matter exists either as a solid, a liquid or a gas: these are known as states of matter. Many substances are capable of changing from one form to another when they are either heated or cooled. The amount of heating or cooling needed to produce a change of state differs for each material. Changes of state are reversible or physical changes.

These processes can be explained by imagining materials made up ultimately of tiny indivisible particles that are held together by mutual attraction. This is the particle model. When a solid is heated the particles gain energy and start to move away from each other and in doing so the solid becomes a liquid. As a liquid gains energy the particles are able to break away from each other and become a gas. The reverse happens when the material is cooled. As they gain or lose energy (through heating or cooling) the physical properties of the material itself change.

When solutions are formed the particles of the solute slip into the spaces between the particles of solvent. The volume of a solution is the same as the initial volume of the solvent. The mass of a solution is the same as the combined masses of the solvent and solute. This phenomenon is known as the conservation of mass.

Further information and teaching resources can be found at the end of the 'Ideas for practice' section.

Part 2: Ideas for practice

Topic: Ice and water

Age group: Lower primary

Scientific view

Water can exist as a solid or a liquid. Liquids and solids behave differently and have different properties. The temperature of water determines whether it becomes a solid or a liquid. Liquid water turns into solid ice when it is cooled below 0°C. Ice becomes a liquid when it is heated above 0°C.

Scientific enquiry skills

In these activities children will:

- raise and try to find answers to questions;
- use first-hand experience to find answers to a question;
- think about what might happen before deciding what to do;
- record and communicate what happened using drawings;
- compare what happened with what they expected would happen and try to explain it.

Exploration stage

Children's talk involves trying out their own ideas

Setting the scene

Ice balloons have their own built-in 'wow' factor and never fail to prompt an excited response from children, especially if they are presented as 'ice animals'. Make ice balloons in various shapes and sizes, one for each group.

Scientific enquiry

Children can spend time initially observing, drawing, photographing or describing their ice balloon. What does it look like? What does it feel like? Does it make any sounds? Children can listen to the balloons as they crinkle and crack in the warm classroom

Ice balloons
Source: Peter Loxley

atmosphere. Make a list of all the key words which children use to describe the properties, such as hard, heavy, cold, freezing, etc.

Talking points: true, false or not sure?

- The ice balloon is made from water.
- If left for a long time the ice will melt.
- The ice is too cold to melt.
- We can stop it melting by wrapping it up in a woolly coat.

Use the talking points to encourage the children to share their understanding of the properties of ice. Discuss children's reasons for their answers.

Children's drawings

Ask the children to predict what may happen to their ice balloon if they left it in the classroom overnight. Groups can *work collaboratively* to hypothesise about what will happen overnight and produce annotated drawings to illustrate their ideas. Next day children describe the changes. Were their predictions right? Make a list of key words used by children and compare them with the words they used to describe the ice balloon.

Puzzle

How would we now describe the ice balloon? What has happened to it?

Formative assessment

Explore children's responses to the puzzle and, together with the feedback from the talking points, decide what the children know and what they need to learn in the next stage.

Re-describing stage

Children's talk involves making sense of scientific ideas

The purpose of this stage is to help the children think about the puzzle from a scientific point of view and to realise that the temperature of water determines whether it is solid or liquid.

Scientific enquiry

Start by encouraging the children to compare the properties of ice and water. Ask them to use as many words as they can to describe the properties. Use simple thermometers to measure the temperature of ice and the temperature of tap water. Establish that ice is much colder than tap water. *Talk together* about how the tap water could be turned into ice.

Where would the children put water-filled balloons to turn them into ice balloons? They can use thermometers to compare temperatures inside a freezer, inside the cooler section of the fridge and in different parts of the classroom. Discuss reasons for their responses, together with the scientific view. Children's reasoning provides insights into their developing understanding. They should test out their ideas and describe the effect the different temperatures have on the ice balloons.

Further explorations

Provide children with ice balloons with the balloon removed. *Talk together* about which part of the balloon they think will melt first. Discuss the reasons for the children's answers. The children can predict which part of the ice balloon would be coldest – the inside or the outside. Test children's predictions by measuring relevant temperatures. Encourage children to suggest ways that they could stop their ice balloons melting.

Children can experiment to see whether their ice balloons would be able to float in water. Compare different temperatures of water and how they affect the ice balloons. *Talk together* to explain the effects warmer water may have on them. Encourage the children to use their developing understanding to explain their observations.

Assessment and further learning

Listen to children's conversations while they are doing the further explorations and assess their progress. What else would they like to find out? Children can raise their own questions for further learning.

Application stage

Children's talk involves trying out scientific ideas

Snowflakes
Source: © Dorling Kindersley / DK Images

Read the story of *The Snowman* by Raymond Briggs or a similar story. *Talk together* about the climatic conditions which turn rain into snow (liquid into a solid). Find some interesting pictures or video clips showing heavy snowfalls and snowy landscapes. Encourage the children to share their experiences of playing in the snow. Encourage the children to explain why snow melts. Where does it go after it melts?

Role-play and link to dance

Explore pictures of snowflakes in all their beautiful diversity. Ask the children to imagine they are individual snowflakes and to model how they combine to make snow. They can demonstrate how snowflakes might be combined to make a snowball or a snowman.

Groups of children could then look at developing a snowflake dance, thinking about appropriate music to convey the different stages of the snowflake's life. They can model through dance how the snowflakes form when the weather is cold and how they 'melt' as the temperature rises.

Links to art and creative writing

The children can make models of snowflakes or create their own paintings. Use information sources to explore the different patterns. They can also write their own stories or poems inspired by their experiences of snow and the ephemeral beauty of snowflakes.

Assessment

Listen to conversations and ask the children to describe the effects different temperatures will have on the snowflakes to assess children's understanding of the topic.

Topic: Melting icebergs

Age group: Upper primary

Scientific view

The particle model of the structure of materials is one of science's biggest ideas. The model can be used to explain the different behaviours of solids, liquids and gases. When ice melts into water its volume decreases because its particles move closer together. This explains why melting icebergs do not raise sea levels.

Scientific enquiry skills

In these activities children will:

- ask questions to be investigated and decide how to find answers;
- plan a fair test;
- make systematic observations and measurements and record them using tables and graphs;
- use observations and measurements to draw conclusions;
- use scientific knowledge and understanding to explain observations.

Exploration stage

Children's talk involves trying out their own ideas

Setting the scene

Show children a video of icebergs in the Arctic or Antarctic regions. What do the children know about icebergs? What are they made from? How are they formed? Why are they found only in very cold regions? Are any of them melting? At what temperature will they melt?

Scientific enquiry

Focus on how global warming may be causing ice in the Arctic and Antarctic regions to melt. Use pictures, videos and information sources to explore what scientists have found out. *Talk together* about whether the melting of icebergs will cause the sea levels to rise. Children can make their own predictions and design an experiment to find out if they are right.

Have ready frozen water-filled balloons to make big icebergs. Strip off the rubber skin. They can be floated in tanks of warm water. Children can mark the level of the water before the icebergs start to melt. At intervals in time they record any changes in the water level. The same experiment could be done on a smaller scale with ice cubes and plastic beakers.

Puzzle

The children will discover that the water level does not change. This is a puzzle which needs some explanation. Explore the children's ideas.

Formative assessment

Explore children's responses to the scientific enquiry and the puzzle. Decide what the children know and what they need to learn in the next stage.

Ice balloons floating in water
Source: Peter Loxley

Re-describing stage

Children's talk involves making sense of scientific ideas

Before the puzzle can be solved the children need to know something about the structure of ice and water. The purpose of this stage is use the particle model to illustrate how the volume of solid water (ice) can be greater than the liquid. This provides a solution to the puzzle.

Exploring through talking and drawing

Talk together about how the behaviour of an object is influenced by its structure. For example, flour flows freely because the grains are loose and not bonded together. However, when it is mixed with water and baked in an oven it becomes solid because the heat causes the grains to stick together. Children can compare the properties of flour and bread. Use hand magnifiers or electronic microscopes to explore and draw pictures of their structure. Ask the children to imagine and describe how the grains of flour could be arranged to form bread. Children could represent grains of flour and very simply role-model how the grains could be arranged to form a solid piece of bread. Explain this is a simplified model, but useful for explaining the different properties. In reality the structure of bread is similar but more complex.

Modelling

Explain that scientists use models when it is impossible to see the real thing. Illustrate how particles are arranged to form a solid with simple analogies such as stacking apples. Talk about what would happen if the stack of apples was pushed over. The apples would roll along the table in a similar way to a liquid. Use this analogy to talk about the different particle structure for ice (solid) and water (liquid).

Children can take on the role of the particles. Groups can model the structure and behaviour of ice and water. They can model how heating solids make the particles vibrate vigorously, resulting in a collapse of the solid structure into that of a liquid. Children can explore through modelling how it is possible for the water to have a smaller volume than ice. Discuss how this provides a solution to the puzzle.

Return to the puzzle and establish that when ice melts into water its volume reduces so that it only has the volume previously taken up by that part of the iceberg beneath the water. This is why the volume of the water does not rise when ice melts. *Talk together* about why melting icebergs cannot be responsible for increases in sea levels. Children can use information sources to find out why scientists believe global warming will cause sea levels to rise.

Further scientific enquiry

Children can design and carry out their own enquiries into how increases in temperature affect the rate of melting of icebergs.

Assessment and further learning

Use children's explanations and responses to their modelling to assess their progress. What else would they like to find out? Children can raise their own questions for further learning.

Application stage

Children's talk involves trying out scientific ideas

Scientific enquiry and links to mathematics

Children can use their understanding of the particle model to explain what happens to sugar or salt after it is dissolved in water. Why can't we see the salt or sugar after it is dissolved?

Children can carry out a fair-test enquiry into the factors that affect the rate at which the sugar or salt dissolves. The enquiry requires accurate measurements and the graphical representation of the data. Children can explain their results using appropriate particle modelling techniques.

Assessment

Listen to conversations and use children's explanations of their results to assess their understanding of the particle model.

Information and teaching resources

Books

- Devereux, J. (2000) *Primary Science: Developing Subject Knowledge*, London: Paul Chapman, Chapter 2: Materials and their properties.
- Oliver, A. (2006) *Creative Teaching Science*, London: David Fulton, Chapter 8: Creative teaching and learning in 'Materials and their Properties'.
- Ward, H., Roden, J., Hewlett, C. and Foreman, J. (2005) *Teaching Science in the Primary Classroom*, London: Paul Chapman Publishing, Chapter 8: Using role-play to stimulate and develop children's understanding of scientific concepts.
- Royal Society of Chemistry (2000) *That's Chemistry*. A resource for primary school teachers about materials and their properties.

Primary science review articles (Association of Science Education)

- PSR 89 (September/October 2005), 'Teaching about stuff' by Keith Scamp.
- PSR 82 (March/April 2004), 'Atoms and molecules do they have a place in primary science?' by Kam-Wah Lucille Lee and Swee-Ngin Tan.
- PSR 63 (May/June 2000) Issue focuses on everyday materials.

Useful information and interactive websites

- abpi resources for schools: www.abpischools.org.uk/page/modules/solids-liquids-gases/
- ASE resource website: www.schoolscience.co.uk/

CHAPTER 15
CHANGING MATERIALS

It has always been the alchemist's desire to turn base metals, such as lead, into gold and silver. The legendary tool supposedly capable of achieving this was the philosopher's stone. Although the alchemists never succeeded, their work led to the development of what we now call chemistry. This chapter looks at how substances can be chemically combined to form new materials and uses the particle model to explain the nature of the changes involved.

Topics discussed in this chapter:

- Historical context
- Elements, compounds and mixtures
- The periodic table
- The formation of materials
- Spectacular chemical reactions

Part 1: Subject knowledge

Historical context

The plum pudding model

John Dalton (1766–1844) suggested that all known substances could be formed from different combinations of tiny particles (see Chapter 14). He was convinced by the evidence available that the atom was truly indivisible. However, this was later found not to be true and we now know that atoms can be split up into even smaller particles.

The mystery of the atom and its true nature began to unravel in the late nineteenth century when the physicist J. J. Thompson (1856–1940) discovered within matter a negatively charged particle, which was named the electron. This led to a new way of visualising an atom. Instead of imagining it to be a solid sphere, Thompson visualised it as a mass of positive matter with negative electrons scattered throughout like plums in a suet pudding.

From plum pudding to solar system model

In 1909 the New Zealand physicist Ernest Rutherford (1871–1937) and his colleagues tested Thompson's 'plum pudding' model. Their investigation showed the plum pudding

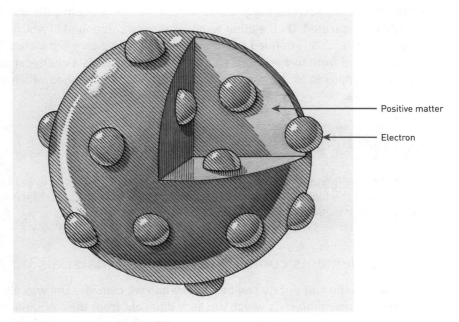

The plum pudding model of the atom
Source: John Woodcock / © Dorling Kindersley / DK Images

model was inadequate in explaining their results. As a result, Rutherford suggested a 'solar system' model with a cloud of negatively charged electrons orbiting a tiny, densely packed, positively charged nucleus. Rutherford's subsequent work led in 1918 to the discovery of the proton, the positively charged particles within the nucleus that neutralise the negatively charged electrons surrounding it. However, measurement of the mass of atoms indicated that a further, neutral particle must exist within the nucleus. This constituent of the atom, the neutron, proved harder to find and it wasn't until 1932 that James Chadwick identified what was seen as the last piece in the atomic puzzle.

However, it is now known that both the neutron and the proton are in fact made of even smaller particles known as quarks. Today scientists continue to seek the most fundamental particles from which materials are constructed. The Large Hadron Collider at CERN (The European Organisation for Nuclear Research) in Geneva has been designed to answer questions about the nature of quarks and to explore in greater depth their composition and formation.

Elements, compounds and mixtures

What is our world made of?

The materials which make up the Earth are **elements**, mixtures or compounds.

An element is a pure substance consisting of one type of atom. There are 118 known elements such as hydrogen, oxygen, gold and lead. These elements are combined in different ways to form all the materials which make up the Earth. In a mixture like air the elements such as oxygen and nitrogen are not chemically bonded together and can be separated. On the other hand, water is a compound in which hydrogen and oxygen are chemically bonded together and cannot be easily separated. The creation of a compound from two or more elements is described as a chemical or permanent change, as opposed to the non-chemical or reversible changes which we associate with mixtures.

Something to think about

Common salt, which we have used for centuries to add flavour to food, is a combination of the highly volatile metal sodium and the noxious gas chlorine. Why isn't salt more of a danger to our health?

How do elements combine to make new materials?

An answer to the salt puzzle can be found when we consider the way elements combine to form new materials which are very different from their original constituents. Rutherford's model of the atom allows us to tell convincing stories of the ways in which elements combine to form new substances.

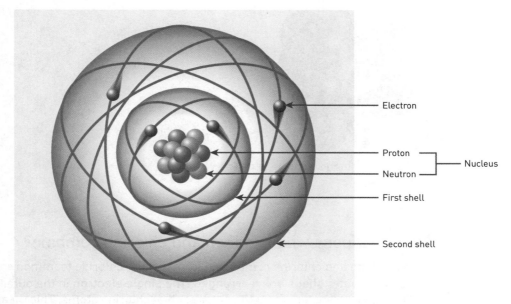

The solar system model of the atom – a single atom of carbon
Source: Robin Hunter / © Dorling Kindersley / DK Images

Imagine the atom as a central nucleus surrounded by a cloud of negatively charged electrons. The resultant charge is always neutral, so the number of protons in the nucleus must equal the number of electrons. Each of the known elements has a unique number of protons and corresponding electrons. Hydrogen, the simplest atom of all, has a nucleus containing just one proton and so has one orbiting electron. The much heavier silver atom has 47 neutrons and 61 protons in its nucleus and so 61 orbiting electrons.

Why are some elements, like sodium, very reactive?

It is the arrangement of the orbiting electrons that determines the reactivity of an element. Electrons are confined to orbit in particular arrangements. The first orbital shell (see diagram above) cannot contain more than 2 electrons; the second cannot contain more than 8; the maximum number is also 8 for the third shell. If the outer shell of an atom is not complete, it will combine easily with other elements until it is 'filled up'. The ease with which this takes place is largely due to the number of spaces on the outer shells. For example, sodium has an outer shell with 1 single electron where 8 are possible and therefore is highly reactive. Chlorine is reactive because it has only 7 electrons in its outer shell and needs an additional 1 to make it stable. Atoms that have full shells do not tend to react easily with other chemicals. For example the noble gases, helium (2 electrons), neon (10 electrons) and argon (18 electrons) all have full outer shells and are all odourless, colourless and unreactive.

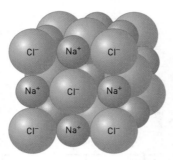

Sodium and chlorine combine to make common salt

What happens when sodium and chlorine combine?

When sodium and chlorine combine to form sodium chloride (common salt) the electrons in the outer shells are rearranged. The single electron in the outer shell of the sodium atoms transfers to fill the outer shell of chlorine atoms. This means that both atoms now have full outer shells and are therefore much less reactive. The atoms of chlorine and sodium are then bonded together by electrical forces to form sodium chloride molecules, which have their own unique properties.

What does an atom really look like?

Scientists do not know what an atom actually looks like. The solar system model provides us with a useful way of visualising it, but scientists do not actually think that it looks this way in reality. There are, however, some things that scientists are certain about. Firstly, they believe that the majority of the mass of an atom is contained in its nucleus – the electrons can be considered to have negligible mass. Although the nucleus is so massive, its volume is believed to be small compared to the size of the atom. The majority of the volume occupied by the atom is empty space, as the orbits of the electrons extend far beyond the nucleus. The atom overall is believed to be about 100,000 times bigger than the nucleus.

Something to think about

Imagine you needed to make a scale model of an atom. If you used a ping-pong ball to represent the nucleus, how far away would you place the orbiting electrons?

The periodic table

In 1869 the Russian chemist Dmitri Mendeleev succeeded in representing the known elements in a graphical format, the periodic table. The elements were grouped in the

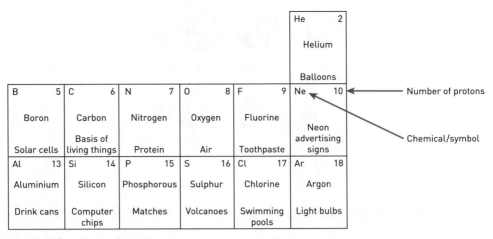

Part of the periodic table (simplified)

table according to their atomic structure and other properties. The first table had gaps which Mendeleev believed belonged to elements which had not yet been discovered. Some of the first missing elements to be discovered were gallium (1875) and scandium (1879). These discoveries demonstrated to scientists the immense value of the periodic table in helping to develop their understanding of the structure of matter.

The periodic table has become one of the icons of science. Using atomic mass to order the elements means that reactive elements are grouped on the left-hand side of the table and the stable elements on the right. Within the table all the metals are grouped together. Metals are distinguished by their ability to conduct electrical charge. This charge is carried on electrons, and in metals the electrons in the outer shell are only loosely attracted to the nucleus. This allows the electrons to exist in what is often termed a 'sea of electrons', free to move in response to an externally applied voltage. For example, when a length of copper wire is attached to the opposite ends of a battery, negatively charged electrons are free to move round the circuit.

The formation of materials

Atoms rarely exist on their own

Individual atoms of elements tend not to exist singly: they clump together into arrangements that are called molecules. Oxygen, for example, is always written as O_2 because it occurs naturally as two oxygen atoms joined together into a stable molecule. When hydrogen joins with oxygen to form water the resulting molecule is made up of two hydrogen atoms and one oxygen atom. Oxygen has 8 electrons in total – so there are two empty spaces in its outer electron shells. The two hydrogen atoms slot neatly into place, their single electrons filling the gaps. The resulting water molecule is written as H_2O.

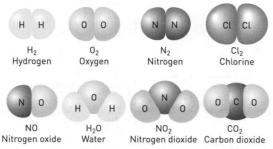

Some common molecules

Can the same atoms be used to produce different materials?

When atoms combine together they form continuous structures that give us the materials with which we are familiar. The ways in which these structures form will often define the properties of the material itself. For example, diamond, which is made from densely packed carbon atoms, has a very rigid internal structure which gives it hardness and durability. In contrast, graphite, which is softer and much less durable than diamond, is made from carbon atoms joined together in layers. The bonds between the layers are relatively weak, which means that the layers can slide across each other. Graphite is a useful material for drawing with because it is soft, slippery and the layers of carbon are easily rubbed off onto the paper.

> ### Something to think about
>
> Clay used for making pottery is a layered compound of silicon, oxygen, aluminium and hydrogen. When wet, water molecules can get between the layers and the clay is slippery and malleable. When the clay is dried the water evaporates, but the structure of the clay remains the same so it is crumbly. If it is wetted it will once again be workable. However, if the clay is fired in a kiln a chemical reaction takes place and a new, stronger material is produced. Can you imagine what the firing does to the atomic structure of the clay to change its properties so radically?

Does energy always play a part in the formation of new materials?

Whether a change in materials is physical or chemical, energy will always play its part. For example, rolling and shaping play dough takes energy, as does squeezing water out of a sponge. When dissolving sugar in water, the movement energy of the water molecules helps to break down the solid lumps of sugar. These changes are relatively easily reversed. However, the changes that occur when two or more substances join together chemically are not easily reversed and usually take place as a result of an exchange of energy. Everyday examples of chemical change include baking a cake, frying an egg and firing clay.

Energy is released when new materials are formed by burning

Heating involves raising the temperature of a material: for example, to melt gold so that it can be cast into different solid shapes. This can be reversed. Burning involves a chemical change that results in the formation of new substances: for example, when a common fuel such as wood burns. Carbon and hydrogen from the wood combine with oxygen in the air to produce carbon dioxide and water. A residue, ash, results. Burning is an irreversible chemical reaction that requires fuel, oxygen and a high enough temperature. This is described as the 'fire triangle' and all three have to be present for burning to occur. The reaction is capable of emitting huge amounts of energy and has proved useful to humans over a long time.

What happens to the original materials when things burn?

Things appear to diminish as they burn. A candle decreases in size and wood disintegrates to ash. We see burning as a destructive process. However, in chemical terms it is in fact a constructive process since it results in the formation of new materials. It is difficult to demonstrate that mass is conserved when things burn, but this is so.

Something to think about

Candle wax is a hydrocarbon – a carbon-based material. If mass is conserved when materials burn, can you think what happens to the wax when the candle is lit?

A candle burning
Source: Steve Gorton / © Dorling Kindersley / DK Images

Other chemical changes involving oxygen

Chemical changes involving the combination of oxygen with other materials are described as oxidising reactions. Respiration is an important example of **oxidation**. This is the process by which energy is released to the body when carbohydrate molecules combine with oxygen in our cells (see Chapter 13). This is an example of oxidation which does not involve burning. Another example is rusting. Most metals will react with oxygen: for example, the oxidisation of copper creates a green discolouration, which is easily removed. 'Rusting' happens when iron and steel oxidise. Rusting iron can weaken built structures and cause irreversible damage. For oxidation of iron to occur water needs to be present. Water is always present in the atmosphere, but rusting is more rapid in damp climates or when salt is present to speed up the reaction. There are a number of ways to prevent rusting: for example, painting the iron or mixing it with a metal that is resistant to oxidation such as chrome to form stainless steel.

Spectacular chemical reactions

Mixing bicarbonate of soda and vinegar is a popular way of creating a spectacular volcano effect.

A vivid description of the fate of Pompeii during a topic on the Romans encouraged a class of 8-year-olds to try to recreate the eruption of Vesuvius. They built a model from papier mâché and then wondered how to model the eruption itself. A mixture of bicarbonate of soda and vinegar, with red powder paint for authenticity, gave a satisfying result, with the lava bubbling out of the crater and pouring down the mountainside.

The volcano effect
Source: Peter Loxley

What causes the volcano effect?

Bicarbonate of soda is an alkaline substance; its constituents are hydrogen, carbon and oxygen and the reactive metal sodium. Vinegar is an acid. Highly alkaline and highly acidic substances are dangerous but we use milder forms of them in many household contexts. Toothpaste is alkaline to combat the acidity of saliva. Acidic lemon imparts a tart flavour to foods whilst vinegar kills bacteria and so is useful in preserving food. Generally an acid will react with an alkaline to produce a new substance and, typically, a gas – carbon dioxide – will be produced. It is the release of the gas which causes the mixture of vinegar and bicarbonate of soda to bubble up and create the volcano effect. Another example of this can be seen when an effervescent vitamin C tablet is placed in water. The tablet contains a dry mixture of vitamin C, an alkaline material such as sodium bicarbonate and citric acid. When placed in water the tablet dissolves and the citric acid and sodium bicarbonate combine chemically. New substances are produced, including carbon dioxide which provides the fizz.

Could we use the volcano effect to prove that mass is conserved?

Mix sodium bicarbonate and citric acid in a small plastic bag and weigh it. Weigh some water, add this to the bag and seal it. The mixture will bubble and the bag will expand. Weighing again should demonstrate that, although the constituents have combined and changed and new substances have been produced (carbon dioxide, for example), the overall mass has remained the same. The conservation of mass is one of science's big ideas because it applies to all types of chemical and physical changes, regardless of the materials involved.

Mass is conserved in a chemical reaction
Source: Peter Loxley

Something to think about

If you held the plastic bag while the reaction was taking place you would have noticed a change in temperature of the mixture. What may have caused it?

Summary

As research into the nature of materials continues, our understanding of the complexity of the structure of atoms continues to develop. Materials can exist as elements, compounds and mixtures. The periodic table is a classification of elements based on their atomic mass, and the position of an element in the table will indicate its properties. The fundamental structure of atoms of different elements determines their properties and how they combine together to form more complex materials. The resulting compounds often have very different properties from their constituent elements. Energy is a part of the process of forming new compounds as electrons are either exchanged or shared by the atoms. When new compounds are formed the mass of the resulting materials is the same as the combined mass of the reacting materials – mass is conserved. Mixtures consist of elements or compounds which do not react chemically together and they can be relatively easily separated.

Further information and teaching resources can be found at the end of the 'Ideas for practice' section.

Part 2: Ideas for practice

Topic: Making new materials

Age group: Lower primary

Scientific view

Heating a material can change its properties permanently. For example, baking dough in a hot oven or making porridge in a microwave changes the substance and produces new materials. Heating can cause irreversible change.

Scientific enquiry skills

In these activities children will:

- decide how to find answers to the enquiry questions;
- use first-hand experience to answer questions;
- make simple comparisons;
- use simple equipment to collect data;
- explain their data, drawing on their knowledge and understanding.

Exploration stage

Children's talk involves trying out their own ideas

Setting the scene

Retell the tale of Goldilocks and *talk together* about whether the children like to eat porridge. What does it taste like? What does it look like? What is porridge made from? Show children some pictures of oats growing in a field and talk about how it is a special type of grass that we can eat. We eat its seeds (grains) which we call cereals. Porridge is a breakfast cereal made from oats.

Scientific enquiry

Bring some oats into school for children to explore. Let the children explore what rolled-oat cereal looks like using a hand lens. Encourage the children to describe the properties of the rolled oats. Compare these with pictures of unprocessed oat grains. Children can talk about what they think might have happened to the rolled oats to make them so flat.

How can the oats be made into porridge? Is there a special 'just right' temperature for making porridge? Use a quick-make variety of porridge. Heat the mixture in a microwave for the recommended length of time. Use simple thermometers to measure the temperature before and after heating. Children can describe the properties of the porridge and compare with rolled oats. What is the best temperature for making porridge? *Talk together* to interpret the children's observations and discuss the effects heat has on the porridge.

Puzzle

When cooled can we separate the porridge and milk? Can we get our porridge oats back again?

Scientific enquiry

Review what happened to the porridge after it was heated. Children can hypothesise about how they could separate the rolled oats and milk from the sticky porridge once it had cooled. They can test out their ideas to see if it is possible. This could be messy, but fun.

Formative assessment

Use the children's responses to the puzzle and the outcomes of the enquiry to assess what they know about permanent changes. Decide what they need to learn in the next stage.

Re-describing stage

Children's talk involves making sense of scientific ideas

The purpose of this stage is to present the scientific view in ways that young children can make sense of it. We want to make them aware of how new things (materials) can be made from mixing and heating different ingredients. Once new materials have been made it is not easy to get the old ingredients back again.

Children's drawings

Establish that it is not possible to separate the oats and milk from the porridge after it has been heated. *Talk together* about what the children think has happened to the milk and oats. Where has the milk gone? *Working collaboratively*, children can draw pictures to explain what has happened to milk and oats to turn them into porridge.

Role-modelling

Children can role-play what they think has happened. Some children can represent the oats and others the milk. When mixed together, before heating, their arms are firmly folded across their chests and they can wander about within the mixture. Heating caused their arms to come loose and they are able to grab hold of each other. The oats lock arms with the milk and vice versa until most of the children are stuck together. Based on the modelling, children can review and modify their pictures. *Talk together* about the meanings of the term 'permanent change' in this context. Talk about how the porridge is a new material because it behaves differently and we will never be able to get the original ingredients back again. Children can modify their pictures in light of the modelling.

Assessment and further learning

Use the children's pictures to assess their progress. What else would they like to find out? Children can raise their own questions for further learning.

Application stage

Children's talk involves trying out scientific ideas

Links to geography and design technology

Scientific enquiry

Children can explore different types of bread to find out in which parts of the world they are made. Provide a range of different breads from the local supermarket which are representative of different cultures. Children can test the properties of the breads including texture, colour and weight and taste. Produce a table of the similarities and differences between them.

Examine different types of flour and compare the properties of the flour with those of the bread. Children can then be shown how to make small bread rolls. Explore the effects of adding yeast. Discuss how the properties of the materials change in each stage.

1. Properties of individual ingredients.
2. Properties of the mixture (dough).
3. Properties of the bread rolls after baking.

Children can compare the properties of their baked rolls with the flour from which they were made. Some dough can be left uncooked to compare with the cooked bread. Discuss the role heat plays in transforming a dough mixture into bread. Children can use their scientific knowledge to explain their observations. Do you they think bread is a new material? Can it be easily changed back into its ingredients?

Design and make

Children can design their own bread – or perhaps make pizzas.

Assessment

Listen to children's conversations and question what they think is happening in each stage of the baking process.

Topic: Burning and pollution

Age group: Upper primary

Scientific view

Burning is a process in which an existing material chemically combines with oxygen to produce a new material. Heat energy is released as part of the process. Carbon-based materials such as oil, wood, coal and paper readily burn in oxygen to produce gases which can be harmful and pollute the atmosphere.

Scientific enquiry skills

In these activities children will:

- raise and try to find answers to questions;
- consider what sources of information they will use to answer questions;
- use simple equipment and materials appropriately and take action to control risks;
- make comparisons and identify simple patterns in their observations;
- use their scientific knowledge and understanding to explain observations.

Exploration stage

Children's talk involves trying out their own ideas

Setting the scene

One of the earliest scientific attempts to explain burning (combustion) was made by Johannes Baptista van Helmont (1580–1644), a Flemish physician and alchemist. Van Helmont carefully observed how different materials burnt and concluded it involved the escape of a 'wild spirit' (*spiritus silvestre*).

Van Helmont played an important role in the development of modern science by challenging the Ancient Greek and medieval ideas (see Chapter 7). He was the first person to understand that air is not a single substance but is a mixture of substances which he called gases. He discovered the gas carbon dioxide and showed that it is produced both in the burning of coal and in the fermentation process of winemaking.

Introduce the children to the work of Johannes Baptista van Helmont. Focus on his work on gases and burning, especially his belief that burning involved the escape of a 'wild spirit'.

Puzzle

Talk together about what van Helmont may have meant by a 'wild spirit'. What *does* escape during burning?

Scientific enquiry

Children can talk about how they can find an answer to the puzzle. They can plan an experiment to find out what is released into air when things are burnt. In a well-ventilated room children can burn various things such as small pieces of paper, wood and nuts. If they weigh the objects before and after burning they can collect data to answer part of the puzzle. (Use sand trays, safety candles and fire-proof tongs. Refer to the ASE publication *Be safe* when planning this investigation.)

Establish that burning the materials creates a substance which is released into the air. Discuss children's ideas about what the substance is and what they think it is made from.

Re-describing stage

Children's talk involves making sense of scientific ideas

The purpose of this stage is to help children to visualise the role played by gases in the air in the burning process.

Modelling

Start with children's ideas and ask them to model what they think is happening when a candle burns. Remind them that all materials are made of particles. They can represent a solid (candle wax) by bunching together and holding on to each other. Now what happens? How does the wax burn? Is there something else involved which we cannot see? *Talk together* about the possibility of some invisible substance being involved. What happens when a scented candle is burnt? How is the scent transferred around the room? What substances do the children know exist but cannot be easily seen? Pick up on children's references to the air and gases. How could we find out whether the air is involved?

The water rises because something is used up in burning
Source: Susanna Price (left); Mike Dunning (right) / © Dorling Kindersley / DK Images

Scientific enquiry

Use a sand tray, candles and different sized glass jars to demonstrate that some-thing in the air is used for burning. Invert a jar full of air over a burning candle. The candle goes out: evidence that a constituent of the air has been used up. With bigger jars, which contain more air, we would expect the candle to burn for longer. It is important not to allow any more air to get into the jar after it is placed over the candle. If a burning candle stands in a tray full of water and a jar is put over it, what do the children notice happens to the water as the candle burns and goes out? Ask the children to draw an illustration to show the demonstration, annotating it with their ideas about the process.

Children can use information sources to find out more about burning and how it can release carbon dioxide and other substances into the air.

Assessment and further learning

Ask the children to draw pictures to show how coal burns. *Talk together* about their pictures to assess their progress. What else would they like to find out? Children can raise their own questions for further learning.

Application stage

Children's talk involves trying out scientific ideas

Links to maths and design technology

This activity will help the children to apply their understanding of burning and make them aware of the problems associated with burning fossil fuels.

Bring in a 2-litre water bottle. Tell the children that if it was filled with petrol it would weigh approximately the same. Ask the children to guess its mass in kilograms. Children can try to lift the bottle and review their estimate. The children can research how many litre bottles it would take to fill a typical family car. Establish there must be a lot of 'stuff' in a tank full of petrol. How long would it take to use a tank full of petrol? How far could the car go? Discuss what will happen to all the petrol after it has been burnt in the engine of the car. Talk about the car journeys we take each week and work out an estimate of how many kilograms of petrol are used by the average family in one week. Estimates for the whole school could be calculated.

Modelling and explaining

Help children to apply their understanding of burning to explain how cars pollute the air. Talk about how the process of burning in the engine involves the combination of petrol and oxygen particles from the air to create carbon dioxide and other particles which can be dangerous. Focus their attention on exhaust fumes and how a large part of this poisonous material ends up in the air. Encourage children to imagine burning as a way of littering the air with potentially dangerous gases. How much 'litter' does the average car produce in a week? It is not only cars which are polluting the atmosphere. Children can research and present a scientific report on other sources of air pollution.

Design project

Children can research recent developments into the possibility of designing 'pollution-free' cars. They could use their finding and imaginations to design the pollution-free car of tomorrow. They can design posters to advertise the design features and the benefits their cars will have for society.

Assessment

Listen to conversations and use the children's reports to assess their progress.

Information and teaching resources

Books

- Devereux, J. (2000) *Primary Science: Developing Subject Knowledge*, London: Paul Chapman, Chapter 2: Materials and their properties.
- Royal Society of Chemistry (2000) *That's Chemistry.* A resource for primary school teachers about materials and their properties.

Primary science review articles (Association of Science Education)

- PSR 88 (May/June 2005), 'Crunchier on the outside – investigating bread' by Sarah Marks and Emma Ranger.
- PSR 90 (November/December 2005), 'Snow in the nursery' by Collyer and Ross.

CHAPTER 16
ELECTRICITY AND MAGNETISM

Analogies are used to help visualise concepts such as electrical current, voltage and resistance. Analogies are an important meaning-making tool in science because they enable learners to use familiar images and experiences to make sense of unfamiliar scientific concepts. However, it is important to remember that the analogies presented do not provide exact representations of electricity and therefore have limited explanatory power. When teaching electricity we need to be aware of the limitations of the analogies and discuss them with the children.

Topics discussed in this chapter:

- Historical context
- Static electricity
- Electrical circuits
- The mysteries of voltage explained
- Electrical resistance
- Links between magnetism and electricity

Part 1: Subject knowledge

Historical context

Around 2,600 years ago the ancient Greeks discovered that rubbing amber on lamb's wool produced **static electricity**. Once rubbed the wool attracted materials such as feathers and straw. If rubbed hard enough, small sparks could be generated.

Although static electricity was demonstrated in the times of the ancient Greeks, little progress was made until the eighteenth century when Benjamin Franklin (1706–90) demonstrated that electricity could travel between objects. He demonstrated that electricity acted like a fluid (current) travelling from what he called a positive object to a negative one.

In 1800 Alessandro Volta (1745–1827) discovered how to produce electricity using zinc and copper discs. This discovery was the forerunner of the dry-cell battery and was a dependable and safe source of **electrical current**. Hans Christian Oersted (1777–1851) demonstrated the relationship between electricity and magnetism. He realised that when electricity flows in a wire it creates a magnetic field around the wire which can be detected by a simple magnetic compass. André Marie Ampère (1775–1836) used this discovery as a way of measuring electric current, which led to the development of instruments such as the ammeter and voltmeter.

Static electricity

Why does rubbing create static electricity?

Rubbing a balloon against your sweatshirt will make you and a balloon stick together. How does this work?

The force of attraction between a sweatshirt and the balloon is caused by static electricity. Rubbing the surface of the balloon with fabric creates a build-up of negative charge on the balloon and a build-up of positive charge on the fabric. Since negative and positive charges attract each other, the balloon sticks to the sweatshirt.

Where do the positive and negative charges come from?

All atoms are made up of positive and negative charges. The nucleus of an atom has a positive charge and the electrons which surround it are negatively charged. Atoms are usually neutral because the combined negative charge of the electrons balances the positive charge of the nucleus. When a balloon is rubbed with a cloth a great number of the electrons from the atoms in the cloth are transferred to the balloon. This increases the amount of negative charge on the surface of the balloon. At the same time the amount of negative charge on the surface of the cloth is reduced and

Static electricity in action
Source: Peter Loxley

the cloth becomes positively charged. In this way both the balloon and cloth have become electrified. Static electricity is so called because it is only the *surface* of the cloth and balloon which are electrified. The charge does not flow in the materials.

Something to think about

You may have experienced the effects of static electricity when you brushed your hair on a dry day. Imagine what happens to your hair to create static electricity. Where does the static charge go eventually?

The build-up of static electricity can create lightning

Throughout history different cultures have developed mythological stories to explain lightning. For example, the ancient Greeks thought it was a weapon used by Zeus, the king of all gods. We associate lightning with thunderstorms, but it has also been

Static electricity causes lightning
Source: © Dorling Kindersley / DK Images

seen during volcanic eruptions, the testing of nuclear weapons, heavy snowstorms, extremely intense forest fires, and large hurricanes.

Lightning is a gigantic discharge of static electricity. It is similar to the electric shock you sometimes get when you touch a doorknob, but on a massively larger scale. Lightning is caused by a build-up of negative charge in the atmosphere which discharges down to the ground through the air. In doing so, it creates a large amount of heat and light.

Electrical circuits

Electrical current refers to the movement or flow of electricity. Batteries enable **circuits** to be created in which a steady flow of electrical current can be maintained. The electrical current in a circuit is created by the flow of negative charge (electrons) in the connecting wires. Connecting wires are usually made from copper which contains electrons which are free to move inside the metal. These mobile electrons are drawn to the positive terminal of the battery, creating a flow of negative charge. At the same time the negative terminal of the battery feeds new electrons into the circuit so maintaining the flow.

How do children visualise electric current?

Children imagine electric current in different ways. Some see it as little bright sparks that run through wires. Others imagine it to be like flashes of lightning, while some children imagine it to be like a fluid flowing from the battery to the bulb.

Clashing Currents   Current is used up   Some of the current is used up

Children's ideas about electrical circuits (Osborne and Freyberg, 1985)

Generally, children's ideas derive from the belief that electricity is stored in the battery and flows down the wires to the bulb. The 'clashing current' idea is based on the belief that electricity flows out from both ends of the battery and collides in the bulb causing it to light up. Another common misconception is that electricity flows along one wire only and is then used up in the bulb. The 'some current used' model is a sort of compromise, when children realise that an electric circuit will not work without a return path from the bulb to the battery. They imagine that any spare electricity would be returned to the battery via the second wire.

How do children's views differ from the scientific model?

Although the children's explanatory models are not scientifically correct, they are nevertheless quite powerful and can provide quite convincing explanations. The problem with these models is that they are not consistent with more detailed observations and do not stand up to rigorous testing. If instruments that measure the flow of electricity are used, we find that the flow (electrical current) is the same in all parts of the circuit. In other words the same amount of electricity that flows out of the battery flows back into its other end. That is, the flow of electricity is conserved in all parts of the circuit.

What causes the bulb to light?

To understand how an electrical circuit lights up the bulb we can use the analogy of an energy transport system. We can compare the battery to an energy storage depot and the electrical current to the flow of transporters or trucks which carry the energy from the depot (battery) to the bulb. Each of the transporters picks up energy at the depot and transfers it to the bulb. It then returns to the depot to collect more energy. The bulb shines brightly as long as the transporters provide it with enough energy.

Something to think about

Imagine if there was a problem which slowed down the flow of transporters. What would happen to the brightness of the bulb? Can you think of other events that would influence how brightly the bulb would shine?

Electrical current is the same in all parts of the circuit

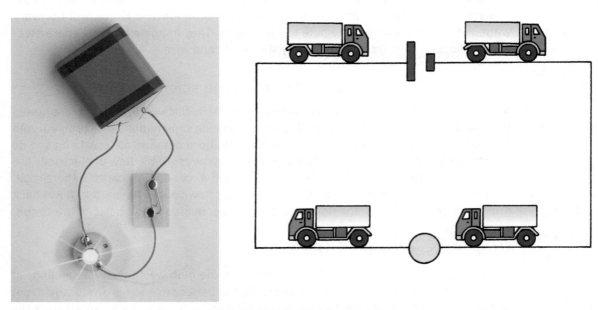

Energy transport model – the circuit (left); energy transport model (right)
Source: Dave King / © Dorling Kindersley / DK Images (left)

What happens inside the wires?

Inside a wire the mobile electrons which are part of the metal act as transporters. Large numbers of mobile electrons exist inside the conducting wires. Imagine tiny energy transporters travelling in the wires that connect the bulb to the battery.

When connected in a circuit the mobile electrons move energy from where it is stored in the battery to the bulb. The flow of electrons around the circuit is called an electrical current, measured in amps (A). Because the numbers of electrons are

Random movement of
electrons when the wire is
not connected in a circuit

Flow of electrons when the wire
is connected in a circuit

Mobile electrons are part of the structure of wires

so large, we measure electric current by the number of coulombs of charge which flow in the circuit. One coulomb (C) of charge consists of approximately six million, million, million electrons. A current of 1 amp indicates that 1 coulomb of electrons flow through the bulb every second. If the current increases to 2 amps, the rate of flow of electrons is twice as much, and so on. The coulomb is named after the scientist Charles-Augustin de Coulomb (1736–1806) and the amp is named after André Marie Ampère (1775–1836). Both made major contributions to our understanding of the behaviour of electricity.

With regard to the transport analogy, each transporter represents one coulomb of charge. When the current is increased, each coulomb of charge flows more quickly around the circuit delivering more energy to the bulb each second.

Connecting bulbs in series and parallel circuits

Bulbs can be connected together to form either a series or parallel circuit. In a series circuit, current flows through each bulb in turn (see diagram below). Adding bulbs in series reduces their brightness. The more bulbs we connect in series the less brightly they shine. This is because the transporters have to share their energy between the bulbs. Two bulbs in series shine less brightly than a single bulb.

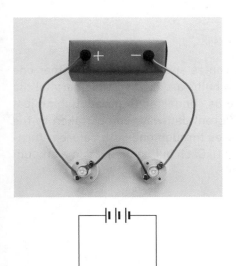

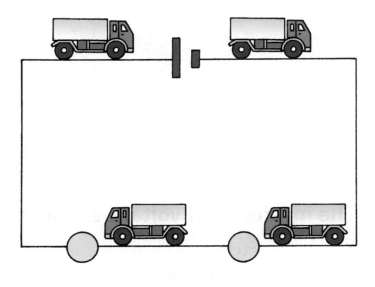

Series circuit
Source: Clive Streeter / © Dorling Kindersley / Courtesy of The Science Museum, London (left)

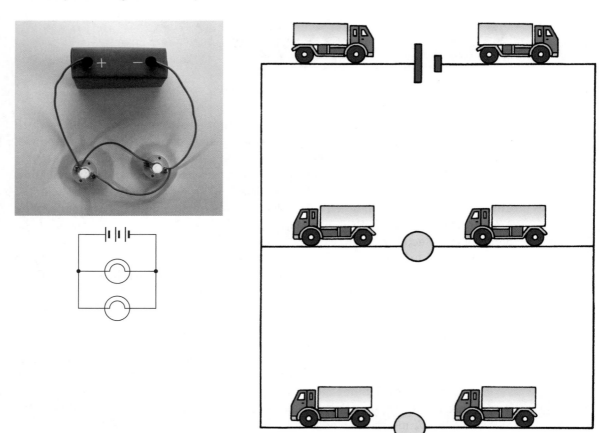

Parallel circuit
Source: Clive Streeter / © Dorling Kindersley / Courtesy of The Science Museum, London (left)

In a parallel circuit, current has a choice of routes and flows through either one or other of the bulbs (see diagram above). When bulbs are connected in parallel the brightness of the bulbs is not affected. Two bulbs connected in parallel shine just as brightly as a single bulb. This is because different pathways can be taken by the transporters. Each of the transporters only passes through one bulb before returning to collect more energy from the battery (depot). Each bulb gets the same amount of energy as if it were the only bulb in the circuit.

The mysteries of voltage explained

Matching bulbs to batteries

Batteries are made up of cells. In common dry-cell batteries each cell has an **electrical voltage** of 1.5. Two cells combine to make 3 volts, four cells to make 6 volts and six cells to make 9 volts. As we increase the voltage in a circuit by adding more cells, the brightness of the bulb increases. However, if we increase the voltage too much, there is a danger that the filament of the bulb will overheat and 'blow'. Bulbs are labelled to indicate their recommended voltage. When connected to its recommended voltage a bulb will shine brightly and is less likely to be damaged.

Something to think about

Imagine that you have a 9-volt battery and three 3-volt bulbs. How would you connect them together so that the bulbs would shine as brightly as possible without blowing?

What is voltage?

To help us imagine the nature of voltage, we can again use the energy transport analogy. Think of the voltage of the battery as an indication of how much energy each of the transporters will carry from the battery to the bulb. For example, a 1.5-volt battery provides each transporter with 1.5 units of energy to carry to the bulb. When the transporters return to the battery, they are each given another 1.5 units of energy, and so on. A unit of energy is called a joule. A 3-volt battery therefore provides each transporter with 3 joules of energy, a 6-volt battery supplies 6 joules, and so on. The larger the voltage the more energy is carried by each of the transporters to the bulb.

Something to think about

All analogies have their limitations. What can't the transport analogy explain about the behaviour of an electrical circuit? Can you think of another analogy which could be used?

Electrical resistance

What happens inside a light bulb?

Chaos is caused by roadworks on a crowded motorway, as the motorists are forced to squeeze into one narrow lane. So we can imagine the energy transporters in a circuit trying to squeeze through the bulb's very thin filament wire. They will find little problem travelling through the spacious connecting wires, but hold-ups are inevitable owing to the crowded conditions they will experience inside the filament. The speed at which they travel through the filament will dictate the rate of flow of the transporters (electrical current) all around the circuit.

As the transporters enter the filament wire they are packed together and inevitably crash into its atomic structure. It is through these collisions that they pass on their energy to the filament, which becomes very hot and gives out heat and light. Collisions

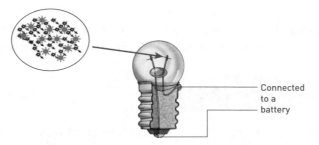

Collisions inside the filament wire

Source: Janos Marffy / © Dorling Kindersley / DK Images

with the atomic structure create **resistance** to the flow of electrical current. Thinner wires create more resistance because there are more collisions between the transporters and the atomic structure of the wire.

The difference between conductors and insulators

Conductors allow the passage of electrical current. Good conductors have a structure which provides a supply of mobile electrons (energy transporters). Metals are good conductors because they contain an abundance of mobile electrons. Generally, non-metals such as plastic, wood, wool, rubber and glass are insulators. These materials have structures which prevent the flow of electrons and therefore cannot provide an adequate supply of energy transporters. The exception is graphite, a non-metal, which has a structure through which electricity can flow.

Solutions which contain sugar, salt or lemon juice are fairly good conductors. This is because, when these materials dissolve, they produce a large supply of positive and negative energy transporters which can travel relatively easily through the liquid.

Links between magnetism and electricity

Which materials are magnetic?

Magnets are surrounded by an invisible force field. The magnetic field is strongest at the poles of the magnet. Not all materials are attracted to magnets; only objects made of iron, cobalt or nickel are magnetic.

Something to think about

What are the differences between magnetic and gravitational force fields? Do you think it curious that magnets can attract and repel each other, while gravity can only act in one way? Is it possible that there could be a gravitational force which repels objects?

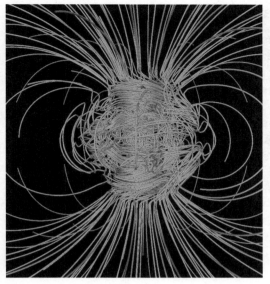 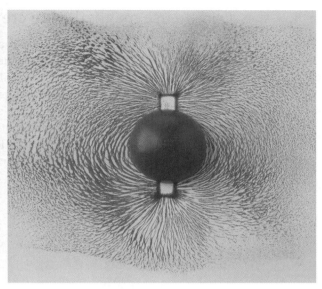

Earth's magnetic field – computer image (left); magnetic field of bar magnet (right)
Sources: Courtesy of Gary A. Glatzmaier (left); Mike Dunning / © Dorling Kindersley / DK Images (right)

The Earth is a giant magnet

The Earth behaves like a giant magnet. Its magnetic field is similar to that of a bar magnet which is tilted 11 degrees from Earth's axis.

Scientists think that the rotation of the Earth plays a part in creating its magnetic field. The rotation of the Earth generates electrical currents in its iron core which are thought to be the cause of the magnetic field. How the currents and magnetic field are created is not clear, but it is known that Venus does not have such a strong magnetic field although it has an iron core similar to the Earth's. It seems that Venus, which takes 243 Earth days to rotate, does not spin fast enough to create a strong magnetic field.

Is there a connection between electricity and magnetism?

Hans Christian Oersted (1820) accidently discovered that when an electrical current flows it creates a magnetic field. He was demonstrating to friends the heating effect of electrical currents when he noticed that a nearby compass needle moved every time he turned on the circuit. This has become known as the electromagnetic effect. When a current flows through a wire it creates a magnetic field in the space around the wire. This discovery led to the development of electromagnets, which are made from coils of wire around an iron core. Increasing the number of coils increases the strength of the magnetic field.

Can we use magnetism to create electricity?

If electricity can be used to make magnetism, can magnetism be used to make electricity? In 1831, Michael Faraday demonstrated that by moving a magnet in and out of a coil of wire an electric current could be produced. Faraday's discovery led to the development of the electrical generator, which has had profound effects on the way that we live and work. Today's power stations use giant turbines to move magnets inside huge coils of wire (generators) to produce the electricity we need. Many of these power stations use fossils fuels such as coal, gas and oil to power the turbines. Alternative technologies include the use of wave power, wind power, tidal power, nuclear power and biofuels.

Summary

Electricity is a phenomenon made possible by the structure of materials. All materials are made up of atoms, which contain positive charges called protons and negative charges called electrons. Usually the two types of charge cancel each out and no electric effect can be detected. However, with various materials it is possible to remove some of the negative charges by rubbing the surface. Removing the negative charges leaves the surface of the material positively charged and creates static electricity.

In many metals the negative charges (electrons) are not firmly fixed to atoms and are free to move around inside the material. When a battery is connected to the metal filament in a bulb, the mobile negative charges travel away from the negative end of the battery towards the positive terminal. This creates an electric current. Electric currents carry energy from the battery to appliances such as light bulbs, motors and buzzers.

Materials that contain iron have magnetic properties. The Earth behaves like a giant magnet because of its iron core. There is a close connection between electricity and magnetism. When an electric current flows in a wire it creates a magnetic field. The reverse is also true. Moving a magnet inside a coil of wire can generate a voltage and cause an electric current to flow. The movement of a magnet inside a coil is the method by which electric power is produced in power stations.

Further information and teaching resources can be found at the end of the 'Ideas for practice' section.

Part 2: Ideas for practice

Topic: Electric circuits

Age group: Lower primary

Scientific view

A simple circuit is a one-way track around which electricity flows. The flow of electricity through the bulb causes it to light up. If the circuit is not a complete loop, the electricity is prevented from flowing and the bulb will not light up.

Scientific enquiry skills

In these activities children will:

● raise and try to find answers to questions;
● think creatively to explain how the circuit works and to establish links between cause and effects;
● compare what happened in the circuit with what they expected would happen;
● explain observations by drawing on their knowledge and understanding.

Exploration stage

Children's talk involves trying out their own ideas

Setting the scene

Read the children a story about a lighthouse such as *The Lighthouse Keeper's Lunch* (Armitage and Armitage, 2008). Show the children some pictures of real lighthouses and talk about their structure and purpose. Ask the children to *talk together* about how the lighthouse works. How does the lighthouse keeper turn on the bulb? Compare this to turning lights on at home. Establish that electricity is used to light the bulb in a lighthouse.

Show the children a model lighthouse which you can make from a cardboard tube. Use a simple electric circuit consisting of a bulb, battery and wires. Make sure the battery and wires are hidden inside the tube and the children can only see the bulb fixed to the top. Children can guess what must be inside the model lighthouse to light

Model lighthouse
Source: Peter Loxley

the bulb. *Working collaboratively*, children can talk about and draw a picture of what they think is inside the model which causes the bulb to light. Discuss children's pictures and compare to a torch. Establish that there must be a battery inside the model.

Scientific enquiry

Talk with the children about the purpose of the battery and how it can be connected to the bulb. Provide the children with a simple 1.5-volt battery and point out that it has a positive and negative end. Challenge the children to use the battery to light their 1.5-volt bulb. Encourage them to place the bulb in turn against each end of the battery. Ask them to suggest why the bulb does not light. What else do they need? Children can try to use one wire to light the bulb. When successful they can draw the circuit. Use magnifiers so the children can see the filament clearly and draw the part of the bulb which lights up. Children can consider why the bulb has to be connected in a loop to the battery to make it work. Once the children are familiar with the concept of an electrical circuit they can use bulb holders and battery holders to make a circuit. Explain that the holders make the job easier.

Making a simple circuit
Source: Peter Loxley

Puzzle

Talk together about why the bulbs would not light until they were connected in a circuit to both ends of the battery. Why do we need a complete circuit?

Formative assessment

Discuss children's responses to the puzzle and note misconceptions which need to be addressed. Decide what the children know and what they need to learn in the next stage.

Re-describing stage

Children's talk involves making sense of scientific ideas

The purpose of this stage is to provide an analogy which children can use to make sense of why a battery and bulb need to be connected in a complete circuit.

Modelling

A useful analogy for a circuit is a toy train carrying goods from the depot (battery) along the track (wires) to a station (bulb) and then returning to collect more goods. If the track is not a complete loop the train will get stuck and will not be able to complete its journey. A toy track can be set up in the classroom and compared with the circuit. Children can also role-model this analogy if a track is marked out in the playground.

Assessment and further learning

Listen to the children's conversations when they are modelling and ask them to explain the answer to the puzzle. Use their responses to assess their progress. What else would they like to find out? Children can raise their own enquiry questions.

Application stage

Children's talk involves trying out scientific ideas

Scientific enquiry

Children can make switches and use them to control a simple circuit. Use materials such as paper clips, paper fasteners, foil, card and wire to make simple switches to try their own designs. Encourage the children to draw their circuits and talk about how the switch turns the bulb on and off, using the train analogy.

Links to design technology

Children could design and make their model lighthouse, which is turned on and off by a simple switch.

Assessment

Listen to conversations and use the children's drawings and explanations to assess their understanding of the topic.

Topic: Series and parallel circuits

Age group: Upper primary

Scientific view

An electrical circuit can be visualised as a transport system which uses electrical current to transfer energy from the battery to the bulbs. A series circuit is a one-way track along which electricity flows to deliver energy to each of the bulbs. When bulbs are connected in a parallel the electrical current splits up in order to flow through each branch of the circuit. Bulbs shine brighter when connected in parallel because the arrangement allows more electrical current to flow and hence more energy per second is delivered to each bulb.

Scientific enquiry skills

In these activities children will:

- raise and try to find answers to questions;
- think creatively to explain how the circuits work and to establish links between cause and effects;
- make comparisons based on their observations;
- use scientific knowledge and understanding to explain observations.

Exploration stage

Children's talk involves trying out their own ideas

Setting the scene

Introduce the lesson by exploring pictures and models of different types of cars. Talk about the children's favourites. What do they like best about them? Discuss the main parts of a car and their purposes. Focus the discussion on the design criteria for the headlights. What should they be able to do? Talk about the source of energy which powers the lights. Establish there is a battery in the car which provides energy to light up the bulbs in the headlights.

Tell the children that they are going to design and make a model car with working headlights. Tell them that you will talk more about the design of the car later on, but first they need to work out how to connect the headlights together in an electrical circuit. Which is the best way?

Scientific enquiry

In small groups children can systematically test different circuits to discover the best circuit arrangement for headlights. They can start off with a circuit containing a 1.5-volt lamp and a 1.5-volt battery. Children can observe the brightness of the bulb. They can then test two 1.5-volt lamps and a 1.5-volt dry-cell battery connected in series. Why are the bulbs so dim? Children can *work collaboratively* to construct an explanation on which they can agree. Use a circuit diagram to record how they connected the bulbs.

Now challenge the children to find ways of connecting the two lamps together so that they shine brightly. Ask each group to draw a diagram of their successful circuit and compare to the diagram of the series circuit. Talk about the similarities and differences in the circuits and introduce the term 'parallel circuit'. Ask each group to list the differences between a parallel and a series circuit. What advantages do parallel circuits have over series circuits? Are there any disadvantages? What would happen if they used 6-volt bulbs and a 6-volt battery? Children can ask their own questions and test out their predictions.

Based on their investigations, ask the children to decide which circuit arrangement they will choose for their model car.

Puzzle

Why do bulbs become dimmer when connected in series and why do they shine so brightly when connected in parallel?

Formative assessment

Discuss children's responses to the puzzle and, together with the feedback from the enquiry, decide what the children know and what they need to learn in the next stage.

Children testing different circuits
Source: Peter Loxley

Re-describing stage

Children's talk involves making sense of scientific ideas

Role-modelling

Choose an analogy which you think will be most meaningful for your children. The transport analogy in which energy is stored in the battery and carried to the bulb by the flow of electricity is a useful one. Children can role-model this analogy using sweets as the energy which is stored in the battery (Asoko and de Boo, 2001). Discuss the concept of energy with the children. Energy is needed to make things happen. They can talk about what they are able to do when they have lots of energy. They can run about and do lots of work. Similarly a bulb needs energy, which it gets from the battery, to light up. Children can model the flow of electricity carrying the energy from the battery to the bulb before returning to load up with more energy.

When modelling a single-lamp circuit, each child transports two sweets from the battery to the single bulb. When modelling a two-lamp series circuit, each child carries two sweets from the battery which are shared between the two bulbs. Discuss the effect of sharing the energy on the brightness of the bulbs. It means each bulb only gets half the energy supplied by the battery. Children can use this analogy to predict what will happen if three bulbs are connected in series. Use the term 'electric current' to describe the flow of the children (electricity) around the circuit.

In a parallel arrangement each transporter only passes through one bulb before returning the battery. This means each bulb is supplied with a full load (two sweets) of energy, the same amount it would receive if it was the only bulb in the circuit. Children can hypothesise about the brightness of the bulbs if a third bulb was connected in parallel. Compare the energy drain on a battery when it is connected in parallel and series circuits.

Using drawings children can explain a solution to the puzzle. Can they think of any other analogies which could be used to help solve the puzzle?

Assessment and further learning

Use the children's drawings and explanations to assess their progress. What else would they like to find out? Children can raise their own enquiry questions.

Application stage

Children's talk involves trying out scientific ideas

Children can use the transport model to explain why we would expect bulbs to shine more brightly in the 6-volt circuit. They can also explain why 12-volt batteries are used to power headlights in real cars. Other combinations of batteries and bulbs can be used to enable children to practise using the transport model as an explanatory tool.

Links to design technology

Children can design and make a model car with working headlights. For a further challenge they could design one which is also powered by an electrical motor. This could link with a project into sustainable development, with a focus on recent developments of electric vehicle design.

Assessment

Listen to conversations and use the children's modelling and justifications for their headlights circuit to assess their understanding of the topic.

Information and teaching resources

Books

- Asoko, H. and de Boo, M. (2001) *Analogies and Illustrations: Presenting Ideas in Primary Science*, Hatfield: ASE Publications.
- Devereux, J. (2000) *Primary Science: Developing Subject Knowledge*, London: Paul Chapman, Chapter 8: Electricity and magnetism.
- Parker, S. and Buller, L. (2005) *Electricity*, London: Dorling Kindersley.

Primary science review articles (Association of Science Education)

- PSR 98 (May/June 2007), 'Understanding simple circuits' by Jenny Many and Helen Wilson.
- PSR 35 (December 1994), 'Using analogies of electricity flow in circuits to improve understanding' by Zuhra Jabin and Robin Smith.

Useful information and interactive websites

- BBC Science Clips (animations): www.bbc.co.uk/schools/scienceclips/
- The Nuffield Foundation Primary Design and Technology website: www.primarydandt.org/
- This website has a range of interesting interactive simulations including static electricity: http://phet.colorado.edu/simulations

CHAPTER 17
FORCES AND MOTION

Although we rarely think about forces they are part of everything that we do. On Earth it is not possible to imagine a situation in which forces are not involved. Gravity causes objects to fall to the ground; friction causes our shoes to wear out and, when cycling or driving in our cars, air resistance slows us down. This chapter looks at a range of situations in which forces are involved.

Topics discussed in this chapter:

- Historical context
- Relationship between force and motion
- Gravity and weight
- Air resistance
- Floating and sinking
- Friction

Part 1: Subject knowledge

Historical context

Our understanding of how **forces** control motion can be traced back to the time of the ancient Greeks and in particular to the work of Aristotle (384–322 BCE). Aristotle's ideas about why things moved were intuitive and based on common sense. For example, he thought objects could not move without a force to push them. This understanding was based on his everyday experience. If he rolled a rock along the ground it would stop after travelling a certain distance. The distance depended on how hard he pushed it. He concluded from this that the rock stopped because it ran out of force. Bigger forces lasted longer and hence the rock travelled further.

A more reliable view of force and motion

Aristotle's explanation of how forces control motion is a powerful view because it is built on observation and experience. However, it is not reliable because it does not predict the motion of objects accurately in a wide range of contexts. It was Sir Isaac Newton (1643–1727) who eventually provided us with more dependable understanding of forces and motion. Newton recognised that objects continue to move naturally without the help of forces. He realised that forces change motion. In other words, forces make objects go faster, or slower or change direction. If there are no forces acting on an object it will continue to move at a constant speed or remain at rest.

Relationship between force and motion

Imagine you are travelling on a spaceship towards Mars. The journey will take you nearly a year even though you are travelling very fast. The rockets which fired you into space have detached from the main capsule. What is keeping the spaceship moving so fast? Would we expect for the spaceship to slow down as it gradually 'runs out' of force?

From a scientific perspective, we should ask ourselves not what is keeping the spaceship going but if there is anything out there that could slow it down. On Earth objects that move are slowed down by air resistance and friction. If you travel fast on a bicycle you can feel the force of the air pushing against you. When you stop pedalling the force of the air will slow you down. In space there are no air particles to smash into and hence no force of air resistance to slow the spaceship down. Once travelling at a particular speed a spaceship will continue travelling at that speed. Some spaceships have small engines which can be used to create forces to alter their direction or speed. The same law of motion applies to the Earth; an object will continue moving at a constant speed until a force acts on it.

Space walk

Space walk

Now imagine that a fault develops on a radio aerial on the outside of the spaceship. You open the door and take a step outside while the ship is still travelling very fast. What would happen next?

1. Would you fall away from the spacecraft?

2. Would the spacecraft speed on past you, leaving you behind?

3. Would you continue moving alongside the spacecraft?

Remember that you were travelling at the same speed as the spaceship when you were inside it. As you step outside would that situation change? In space there is no air and hence nothing to bump into which will slow you down. If there are no forces to speed you up, slow you down or change the direction of your motion, then you will continue moving at the same speed as the spacecraft. Indeed, if you could only see the spacecraft you would not sense that you were moving.

Gravity holds the universe together

Have you ever thought why the Moon doesn't fly off into space? Why does it keep moving around the Earth? Isaac Newton worked out the answer to this question when he realised that the force of gravity pulls the Moon around the Earth. To explain how it works Newton imagined a cannon ball being fired from the top of a very high mountain.

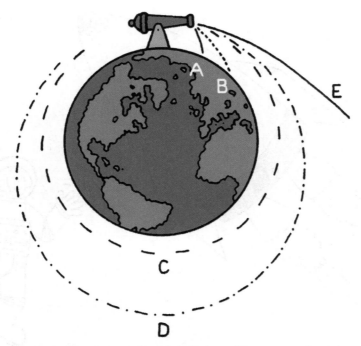

Newton's thought experiment: A–E show different speeds of the cannon ball

When fired, gravity would pull the ball down towards the ground. Where it lands would depend on how fast it was fired. If the speed of the cannon ball is too slow it will crash into the Earth. If the speed is too fast the cannon ball will fly off into space. But, if the speed is just right then the cannon ball will continually fall towards the Earth but never reach it – it will orbit the Earth. Because the Earth is curved, the cannon ball would fall all the way around. His thought experiment ignores the effects of air resistance which would influence the motion of the cannon ball. However, it explains the movement of the Moon because there is no air in space to affect its movement.

The force of gravity can act over very large distances and keeps all the planets orbiting around the Sun. Without the force of gravity the solar system would never have been formed (Chapter 8).

Gravity and weight

What is the weight of a 2 kg bag of sugar?

The concepts of weight and mass are often confused in everyday life. From a scientific point of view the mass of the sugar is 2 kg, but its weight is different because it is a measure of the force of gravity acting on it. For every kilogram of mass gravity exerts a force of 10 newtons (N). If an object has a mass of 2 kg then its weight will be 20 N. This means that you need to pull with a force of 20 N to lift the bag of sugar off the supermarket shelf.

 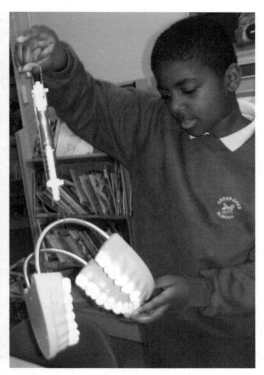

Using force meters
Source: Peter Loxley

Something to think about

Use force meters to compare the weights of different objects. What does a mobile phone weigh in newtons? Estimate before measuring with the force meter. Do this for a range of objects until you become skilled at estimating weights.

Gravity is a natural force

Scientists are not sure about what causes gravity. Gravity is a natural force that pulls objects together. All solid objects exert a gravitational force. The strength of the pull of gravity depends on the mass of the objects and the distance between them. All objects have gravitational attraction, but we may only notice the force of its pull when massive objects like the Earth are involved. If we take a bag of sugar into space we would not be able to detect its weight. It would become weightless because the force of gravity from Earth would be so weak. The sugar would be weightless but we would still have a mass of 2 kg to sweeten our tea. Mass is a measure of how much sugar there is in the bag measured in kilograms, while weight is a measure of the force of gravity pulling it down towards the Earth measured in newtons. In our everyday lives we commonly confuse mass and weight because they are so closely connected.

Something to think about

Imagine what it would be like living on a planet with an atmosphere similar to that on Earth but with one-tenth of the gravity. How would this affect the evolution of the animals and plants? What would a tree look like?

Air resistance

Why is it difficult to run with an open umbrella?

On Earth the motion of objects is controlled by a number of interacting forces. One of the most common forces is air resistance. When running with an open umbrella we feel the resistance that air creates to anything that moves through it. In effect, we live at the bottom of a sea of air, and in order to move we need to push the air in front of us out of the way. An open umbrella makes this task even more difficult because more air has to be pushed out of the way. The bigger the umbrella the harder it is to push the air out of the way and hence the greater the air resistance.

Something to think about

Imagine that you are an animal that lives on the seabed. Would you notice all the water around you? How would it affect your movement? Is living on the seabed comparable to living at the bottom of a sea of air?

Choosing the best words

Air resistance is a force created by collisions between the air and objects which push their way through it. Bigger objects create more air resistance because they have to push more air out of the way. Faster objects create more air resistance because they smash through the air more violently. Imagine what words you could use to explain the effect air has on the motion of objects. Explain the motion of a falling feather without using the words 'air resistance'. Which words do you think are appropriate?

Balanced and unbalanced forces

We can use arrows to depict the direction and magnitude of the forces which control the motion of an object. Consider a hippopotamus called Hypo who has just jumped out of a plane with a parachute on its back. Two forces control its motion. There is a

Air resistance

Weight of Hypo (force of gravity pulling her down)

Forces in action

downward force caused by the pull of gravity (Hypo's weight) which tends to speed it up, and an upward force caused by air resistance which tends to slow it down. In this case the opposing forces are unbalanced. That is, the pull of gravity is larger than the air resistance and consequently Hypo's speed will increase. If the air resistance which opposes its motion was greater than the force of gravity, Hypo would slow down (decelerate).

If Hypo's weight and the air resistance were of equal magnitude then she would fall at a constant speed because the effect of one force would be balanced by the other. Balanced forces do not change motion – they have the same effect as if there were no forces involved.

Something to think about

Imagine if gravity was turned off halfway through Hypo's fall. Describe what would happen.

Unbalanced forces change the motion of objects. Objects speed up when the forces are unbalanced in the same direction as their movement and slow down when the unbalanced forces act in the opposite direction. When the forces are balanced the motion of an object is unaffected: it will either continue moving at a constant speed or remain at rest. These are big ideas because they apply to all situations. The concept of balanced and unbalanced forces can be used to explain and predict the motion of all objects in every situation, including our next topic – floating and sinking.

Floating and sinking

Why is it hard to sink a beach ball?

Pushing a beach ball under the water in a pool or at the seaside is not easy. The bigger the ball the harder it is to push under the water. This is because water exerts an upward force on the beach ball. The bigger the ball the greater is the upward force or **upthrust** created by the water.

The forces that control the motion of an object in water are its weight and the upthrust exerted by the water. If the weight of the object exceeds the upthrust then the object will sink. If the forces are balanced the object will float.

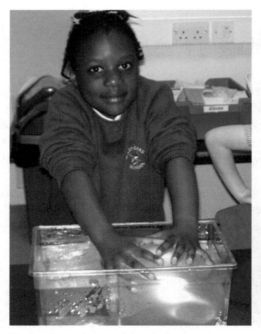 

Having fun trying to sink a balloon
Source: Peter Loxley

Factors which influence upthrust

The upthrust exerted on an object is dependent on the amount of water that the object pushes out of the way (displaces). The upthrust is dependent on the amount of space the object takes up in the water. Big objects create more upthrust because they take up more water space. Try submerging a big balloon and a small balloon. The upthrust created by the big balloon will be greater than the smaller one because it displaces more water.

The shapes of boats are designed to optimise the amount of space they take up in the water. Cargo boats are designed to float more deeply in the water when they are fully laden. This means they take up more space and hence create more upthrust to support the weight of the boat and its cargo.

Something to think about

Imagine how a submarine is made to sink and then rise to the surface again by taking in and letting out water. How can the concept of balanced and unbalanced forces explain the way the motion of a submarine is controlled?

Friction

Something to think about

Why do things wear out? A simple explanation is that things, such as shoes, wear out because of friction. However, this explanation is only meaningful if you understand how friction works. Can you explain why shoes wear out, without using the term 'friction'? Are words such as rubbing, rasping, grating, scratching, ripping, sliding, colliding and bumping appropriate?

Friction is caused by tiny 'potholes'

If you have driven a car on a very bumpy road with lots of potholes, you will know what it feels like when your wheels smash into the bumps and potholes.

Pothole analogy

Exploring the effects of friction
Source: Peter Loxley

Equivalent collisions happen when an object, such as a brick, is dragged over a rough surface. The roughness of both the base of the brick and the surface over which it is dragged are the cause of friction between the surfaces. No surfaces are perfectly smooth; if you look at most surfaces under a powerful microscope you will see they have bumps and 'potholes' in them.

To drag an object over a surface you need to apply a force to overcome friction. The amount of friction created will depend on the smoothness of the object and the surface. Very smooth surfaces such as that on an ice rink create little friction.

To help us move objects over rough surfaces we use wheels. Wheels make use of friction. It is the force of friction between the surface of the wheel and the surface of the road, that is, the 'grip' of tyres, that enables a vehicle to move forwards.

Something to think about

Imagine what life would be like without friction. Start by thinking about how friction helps you to run or walk up a hill.

Summary

The relationship between force and motion can be surprising. Our everyday experiences lead us to think that objects require a force to keep them moving. After all, when we stop pushing something on a flat surface we normally expect it to slow and stop. Science shows us that this is not the case. Things change their motion not because a force is used up or removed but because of the action of forces. For example, shopping trolleys slow down when we stop pushing them because frictional forces act on their wheels to stop them turning freely. If there were no forces acting on the trolley after we stop pushing, it would keep moving at a constant speed until it collided with something.

Forces owing to friction and air resistance can rarely be avoided on Earth, and so objects appear to slow down naturally when they are not being pushed or pulled along. Out in space the conditions are different. Objects can travel great distances at constant speeds without being pushed or pulled along. In the solar system the motion of objects, both natural and man-made, is mainly controlled by gravity. Planets, moons and manufactured satellites are kept in their orbits by the pull of gravity.

Further information and teaching resources can be found at the end of the 'Ideas for practice' section.

Part 2: Ideas for practice

Topic: Friction

Age group: Lower primary

Scientific view

Most things we do involve forces. For example, pushing forces help us jump and run. Rubbing or sliding forces help us slow down and stop. Forces even help warm our hands when we rub them together. Rubbing forces are also responsible for wearing out our clothes. When we walk and run our shoes rub against the ground and bits are torn off. Friction is another name for rubbing forces. Frictional forces can slow objects down and can scratch and damage surfaces. Friction can also help us to move by providing 'grip' between surfaces.

Scientific enquiry skills

In these activities children will:

- raise and try to find answers to questions;
- put forward their own ideas and make simple predictions;
- make simple comparisons and identify simple patterns;
- compare what happened with what they expected would happen;
- plan a fair test with help from their teacher;
- provide explanations for their observations.

Exploration stage

Children's talk involves trying out their own ideas

Setting the scene

Arrange for the children to bring their favourite shoes to school. *Talk together* about what the children like about their shoes. Why are they their favourites? When do they wear them? Why do they need to wear shoes? Why do we wear different types of shoes?

Puzzle

Show the children a shoe with a hole in it. *Talk together* about what could have caused the hole. Encourage the children to hypothesise why the soles of their shoes wear out. Explore types of activities such as running, sliding, jumping and dancing which are likely to wear shoes out more quickly. What causes our shoes to wear out?

Formative assessment

Use children's responses to the puzzle to decide what they know and what they need to learn about friction in the next stage.

Re-describing stage

Children's talk involves making sense of scientific ideas

The purpose of this stage is help children to imagine how rubbing forces (friction) cause their shoes to wear out.

Modelling

Children can make simple models of shoes. They can explore how the soles of shoes wear out by rubbing their model shoes against different textured surfaces. Children

How friction wears things out
Source: Peter Loxley

can *work collaboratively* to discover which surfaces are more likely to wear shoes out. Discuss their reasons. Encourage the children to use a range of words to describe the actions which wear out their shoes. Words such as rubbing, scratching, ripping, gripping, grating, scraping, cutting, scuffing are all appropriate. Children can draw pictures to show how rubbing or scraping causes things to wear out. They can explain their pictures to each other. Compare children's pictures with drawings which illustrate the scientific view.

Introduce the concepts of force and friction. Help the children re-describe the events using terms such as shoes are worn out by rubbing forces, scraping forces, scuffing forces, etc. Talk about how these forces are created by pulling or pushing the shoes across rough surfaces. Explain that another word for a rubbing force or scraping force is friction. *Talk together* about how friction can wear other things out.

Assessment and further learning

Talk together about how other things wear out – such as clothes, and tyres on their bicycles. Use the children's responses to assess their progress. What else would they like to find out? Children can raise their own questions for further learning.

Application stage

Children's talk involves trying out scientific ideas

Link to design technology

Children could apply their emerging understanding of friction to choose the best material from which to make a pair of sandals.

Talk together about the types of materials from which the soles of the sandals could be made. Discuss the properties of suitable materials. For example, suitable materials would need to be strong, hard-wearing, not too hard, etc. How can we make the soles of shoes both hard-wearing and comfortable?

Scientific enquiry

Children can sort and test a range of materials to choose the most suitable. They can test how quickly they are likely to wear out by rubbing them with a sandpaper block. Help children to ensure their tests are fair. Encourage children to explain their results in terms of their understanding of friction.

Designing and making

Children can use their understanding of the materials which they tested to design and make simple sandals. When designing focus on how the soles of the sandals can be made hard-wearing but also comfortable. Explore through information sources and products how commercial soles can be made from layers of different materials.

Assessment

Listen to conversations and ask children to explain why their sandals will not wear out too quickly. Probe their understanding of the types of forces involved.

Topic: Air resistance

Age group: Upper primary

Scientific view

Air is all around us. We live in a sea of air, like fish live in a sea of water. To move through air we need to push it out of the way, just like wading through water. Falling objects push air aside as they move towards the ground. The force with which objects push their way through air is called 'air resistance'. Air resistance is a force which impedes movement and is a type of friction.

Scientific enquiry skills

In these activities children will:

- raise and try to find answers to questions;
- think creatively to explain how air resistance works and to establish causes and effects;
- use first-hand experience to answer questions;
- use scientific knowledge and understanding to explain their observations;
- review their modelling to describe its significance and limitations.

Exploration stage

Children's talk involves trying out their own ideas

Setting the scene

Leonardo da Vinci was much more than just a painter: he was also a scientist, engineer, inventor, town-planner and sculptor. Children can use information sources to explore some of his inventions which included designs for flying machines and a parachute.

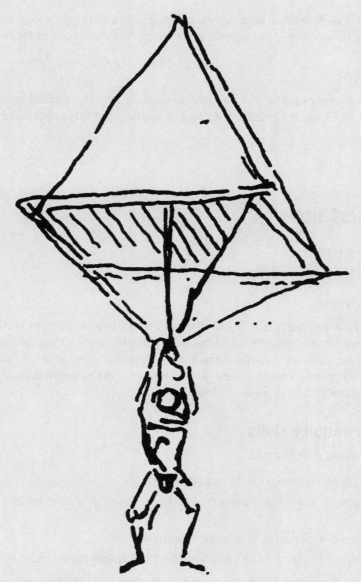

Leonardo da Vinci's parachute

Scientific enquiry

Children can *work collaboratively* to make and test a model of Leonardo's parachute design. *Talk together* about how it works and how the design could be improved. Children can make their own parachutes and compare their performance with Leonardo's design.

Talking points: true, false or not sure?

- Light parachutes fall faster.
- Small parachutes fall slower.
- Parachutes work because they catch the air.
- Round parachutes work better than square ones.

Discuss children's reasons for their responses to the talking points.

Puzzle

When discussing children's responses to the talking points, pick up on the use of the term 'air resistance'. Ask the children to explain what they mean without using the term. This is quite a challenge: often the term 'air resistance' is used as an explanation without the children really understanding how it works. Ask the children to explain what air resistance is. What does it look like?

Formative assessment

Use children's responses to the talking points and the puzzle to decide what they know and what they need to learn in the next stage.

Re-describing stage

Children's talk involves making sense of scientific ideas

The purpose of this part is to introduce the children to models which will help them visualise the nature of air resistance.

Scientific enquiry

To understand air resistance children need to experience its force. Explore the effect an open umbrella has on how fast children can run. Start by measuring how fast children can run without an umbrella and then compare when running with various sizes. Record and graph the results. Ask the children to describe how the running speed and size of umbrella influence the force exerted by the air. Share results of the enquiry and explore reasons why running through air with an open umbrella creates such a powerful force. *Talk together* about why air resistance increases with the speed and size of the umbrella.

It helps if the children have something tangible with which to compare air resistance. Encourage the children to compare moving through air to moving through water. Talk about living at the bottom of a sea of air and compare with moving through water. Can the children imagine what it would be like to live on the seabed like a crab? What

Experiencing the effects of air resistance
Source: Peter Loxley

would it feel like? After they got used to it, would they necessarily notice the water? To move around we have to push the air out of the way, just like moving through water. Encourage the children to use their own words to describe the forces involved, as well as scientific words such as 'air resistance' and 'water resistance'.

Modelling through role-play

Air resistance can be modelled using the children to represent air molecules. Children who represent the air stand relatively close together with little room for anyone to squeeze through. A child can then be chosen to gently push his/her way through the crowd. Encourage the children to visualise air resistance as a series of collisions between the moving object and the air. The collisions with the air create forces which oppose or resist the movement of the object. The faster the object moves the greater number of collisions and hence the greater is the air resistance. Can the model be used to explain why bigger objects create more air resistance? *Talk together* about whether the children think this is a good model. Could they think of another one?

Children's drawings

Give each group a feather to observe falling through the air. Ask them to describe its motion and to explain it with regard to the collisions it makes with the air particles. Children should draw pictures to illustrate their explanations. When talking about the pictures encourage the children to use their own words to describe the forces involved.

Assessment and further learning

Use children's explanations of their drawings to assess their progress. What else would they like to find out? Children can raise their own questions for further learning.

Application stage

Children's talk involves trying out scientific ideas

Links to design technology and mathematics

Children can apply their understanding of forces to parachute design. Make parachutes using polythene bags and string. Encourage children to draw diagrams which clearly

Testing out a parachute
Source: Peter Loxley

show the forces which control the motion of the parachute. Ask the children to predict how the shape and size of the parachute influences these forces. Children should justify their predictions based on their understanding of air resistance.

Scientific enquiry

Once the children have identified all the variables they can design a fair test. Comparing different sizes of parachute is quite easy. It is more difficult to fairly compare different shapes because the sizes need to be kept the same. This activity provides opportunities for children to apply their mathematical knowledge of shape and their understanding of how forces control the motion of the parachute.

Design, make and communicate findings

Children can explore the design of commercial parachutes from a range of information sources and perhaps compare them to Leonardo's original design. They can finally use the outcomes of their enquiry to help design and test their own toy parachute. Children can report their findings in the form of an advertising poster which promotes the efficiency of their design based on performance statistics, similar to the way new car designs are promoted.

Assessment

Listen to conversations and ask the children to describe the forces which control the motion of their parachutes.

Information and teaching resources

Books

- Devereux, J. (2000) *Primary Science: Developing Subject Knowledge*, London: Paul Chapman, Chapter 3: Forces.
- Wenham, M. (2005) *Understanding Primary Science*, London: Paul Chapman Publishing Ltd, Chapter 14: Forces and their effects.

Primary science review articles (Association of Science Education)

- PSR 103 (June 2008), 'Leonardo flies again – integrating science and art' by Ivor Hickey, Deirdre Robson, Mary Flanagan and Paula Campbell.
- PSR 70 (November/December 2001) The curriculum focus for this issue is *Forces*.

CHAPTER 18
LIGHT

Light is a fascinating physical phenomenon. Light travels at astonishing speed; it bounces off some objects and is absorbed by others. Because we can sense light, we see images, shadows and colour. Most living things rely on light for their survival. Plants need light to grow, and animals rely on plants for their food. Without light there would be no hope of survival for the majority of the living things that inhabit the Earth. In this chapter our main focus is on the behaviour of light as a form of radiant energy and how it helps living things to survive. We also look briefly at the language of light and how it has been used by writers to powerful effect.

Topics discussed in this chapter:

- Historical context
- The nature of light
- How living things sense light
- The language of light

Part 1: Subject knowledge

Historical context

What the ancient Greeks believed

The ancient Greeks knew that light travelled, but thought that vision worked by *intromission*, that is, that eyes send out beams which we see when they return to us. This idea is disproved by the way that we can see distant objects. Aristotle (384–322 BCE) puzzled over the nature of light and decided that light can be thought of as waves of energy similar to ocean waves. Other Greek scientists thought that light moved as particles. This dichotomy of ideas still exists: sometimes light appears to behave as a wave and sometimes as a particle. What these theories have in common are the key ideas that light travels; it needs no medium to travel through and it is a form of energy.

Newton and Huygens hold conflicting views

New ideas started to emerge during the seventeenth century. Dutch mathematician Christiaan Huygens (1629–95) thought that light travelled in waves. He believed light crossed space through the mysterious medium of ether – a weightless, invisible substance existing in space and the Earth's atmosphere. Huygens' contemporary Sir Isaac Newton (1642–1727) conducted a series of investigations into the nature of light and colour, which indicated that light travelled as particles. Newton was not wholly convinced that this was the complete picture but he was so influential that his 'corpuscular' theory took precedence. In his 1704 book *Opticks* Newton says: 'Light is never known to follow crooked passages nor to bend into the shadow'. Light as particles must always travel in straight lines.

Thomas Young provides a different picture

Newton's particle theory dominated optics until the nineteenth century when it was augmented by the wave theory of light. British physicist Thomas Young (1773–1829) showed that different wavelengths of light corresponded to different colours. This paved the way for new ways of explaining the nature of light, which eventually led to the development of the electromagnetic theory based on the work of James Clark Maxwell (1831–79). We now use both the wave and particle models of light to explain how it behaves in a range of contexts.

The nature of light

What do we know about light?

Light is radiant energy which we can sense with our eyes. Because we can see light, we literally have a vision of our surroundings. We interpret this vision, focusing on different aspects of what we see, and learn to make meaning of constantly changing images.

Something to think about

Imagine what the physical world would be like without light or without colour.

Light can be pictured as a type of **wave**. It has two key properties – intensity and wavelength. The light that we see is a part of a spectrum of **electromagnetic energy**; other wavelengths include radio and television waves, microwaves and infrared waves.

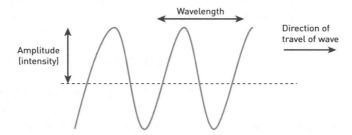

Light as a wave

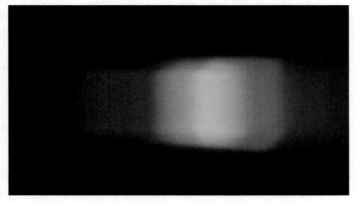

The visible part of the electromagnetic spectrum
Source: Dave King / © Dorling Kindersley / DK Images

311

Light travels through a vacuum at 300 million metres per second (700 million miles per hour) or seven times round the Earth in one second.

What is a light year?

A **light year** is a measure of distance, not time. A light year is the distance that light would travel in one Earth year, roughly 10 million, million kilometres or about 6 million, million miles. The extremely high speed at which light travels means that here on Earth we see light from nearby sources at practically the instant it is produced. This is not true of very distant, interplanetary objects; light takes eight minutes to reach us from the Sun. We see the Sun as it was eight minutes ago. Light from distant stars can take many thousands of years to arrive on Earth. When we look at distant stars we see them as they were many, many years ago.

Amazingly, light can travel through a vacuum

Light needs no material (solid, liquid or gas) to travel through. Space is empty; there is no air or anything else between us and the Sun, or the planets, but we see them because light waves move through a vacuum. In contrast, if the Sun or planets are making any sound, we cannot hear it because sound cannot travel across space like light. Sound needs something to move through.

Light can also travel through some materials

Light travels through clear air largely unaffected by the particles of its gases. Similarly light is transmitted through clean water. Particles and pollutants may scatter or absorb light, making air or water appear murky. Solid materials are interestingly varied in the way they do, or do not, let light through. Transparent solids such as glass, some plastics, some crystals and cellophane transmit light. Coloured glass or cellophane can be just as transparent as clear glass. Transparency is not to do with lack of colour, but with the ease of transmission of light. Some materials allow us to see light through them, but we cannot see clear images. These materials are translucent. Some plastics, tracing paper, obscure glass, ceramics and unpolished crystals are translucent. Other materials halt light entirely by absorbing or reflecting all of it. These materials are opaque. Metals, wood, cork, cardboard, clay and some fabrics are opaque.

What causes a shadow?

The importance of opaque materials is that they create distinct shadows by blocking out the light. A shadow is created when light from a source falls on an opaque object. Because light travels in straight lines, the area 'behind' the object is deprived of light.

How shadows are formed
Source: Peter Gardner / © Dorling Kindersley / DK Images

Something to think about

Where does your shadow go when you turn off the light? Can you make a red shadow? Can you make darker or lighter shadows?

Reflection enables us to see objects

Light falling on an object is transmitted through it, absorbed by it or **reflected** from it. When light is absorbed by materials its energy is used to heat the object. Some materials appear black because they absorb all the visible wavelengths, reflecting little into our eyes. White materials reflect the entire spectrum. Other materials reflect some colours and absorb others; a red book reflects red and absorbs the other colours or wavelengths.

Things which are not luminous are visible because they reflect light. Some surfaces such as that of a mirror or still water are almost perfect reflectors, bouncing back much of the light that lands on them. The mirrors we use in our homes reflect light extremely well, giving us a clear image of what is before them. They are usually 'plane' (flat) so that the images we see look like things as they are. Curved mirrors can invert, magnify or distort images and can be used for a range of purposes such as viewing mirrors on cars or as part of a telescope.

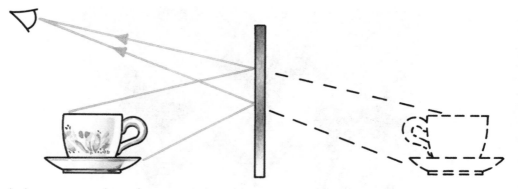

An image as seen in a mirror
Source: © Dorling Kindersley / DK Images

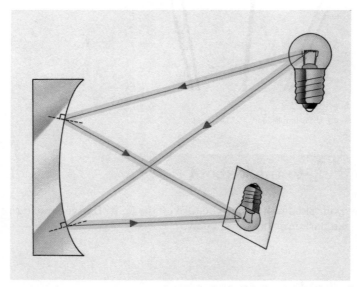

Light reflected from a concave surface such as a spoon
Source: © Dorling Kindersley / DK Images

Absorption can transform light energy into different forms

Solar cells (often used to power classroom calculators) absorb **radiant** light **energy**, which is then transferred into electrical energy. They need good levels of sunlight to work effectively. Solar water heaters work by absorbing heat energy from sunlight to directly heat water and will work even on dull days. Solar absorption panels of different types increasingly provide a form of sustainable energy.

Green plants absorb light (blue and red light, reflecting green) and fortunately for life on Earth have found a way of storing its energy. Inside the leaf a light-fuelled set of reactions goes on. This is photosynthesis – literally, *light used for making* (see

Chapter 10). The resources required are the simple particles of water and carbon dioxide; using these, in the presence of light and chlorophyll, plants produce simple sugars. These are used to make the more complex organic (carbon-based) proteins, carbohydrates, fats, oils and other materials that plants need to live and grow. Plants offer animals two life-sustaining things: a source of energy contained in compounds like sugars, and a source of oxygen.

How living things sense light

Worm's eye view

Some living things have the ability to sense light even though they don't have eyes. For example, scientists have discovered that worms have light-sensitive cells on the front and end of their bodies. It is thought that worms that live in soil use their light-sensitive cells to detect when they are close to the surface. Worms can detect not only the radiation wavelengths of visible light but also ultraviolet light.

Bees and birds can detect ultraviolet light

Humans have very complex eyes and we can be forgiven for thinking that our vision is among the best of all the animals. We classify the wavelengths of light that we can see as 'visible' light, which suggests that all other light is 'invisible'. This is not the case. Some animals, including birds and certain insects, can detect ultraviolet light and are able to sense more colours than we can. Birds and some invertebrates, such as bees and spiders, can sense different parts of the electromagnetic spectrum. What they 'see' is very different from what we see.

A primrose as seen by the human eye and a bee
Source: Bjorn Rorslett / Science Photo Library Ltd

Something to think about

What would our world look like to an alien whose eyes were only sensitive to ultraviolet light? Imagine trying to explain why you had to stop at traffic lights. What would be the advantages to an alien of eyes which were highly sensitive to infrared light? Think about how we use infrared cameras.

Can any animals see in the dark?

Cats are said to be able to 'see in the dark'. Does this mean cats do not need light to see? Confusion can stem from how we use the term 'dark'. Often we use 'dark' to mean dim light, not its total absence. Cats can vary the size of their pupils much more than humans; they can let in more light, or contract the pupil to a very small size to protect the eyes in bright sunlight. Cats also have special cells behind the retina which act as mirrors, reflecting light back through the retina; this gives their sensitive cells a second chance to absorb the light and gather information. Light reflecting from the back of cats' eyes seems to make them glow in the dark.

Cats can see about six times better than humans in dim light. Most sharks which live in dim and murky water can see even better. Sharks have extremely light-sensitive retinas and also reflect light back into their eyes. Since sharks can see about ten times better than us in murky water, it means that a shark will inevitably see you before you see it.

Cat's eye glowing in the dark
Source: © Dorling Kindersley / DK Images

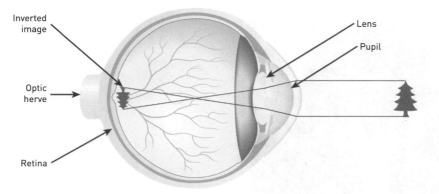

Diagram of the human eye
Source: Robin Hunter / © Dorling Kindersley / DK Images

How our eyes work

We can only see things because light travels; it has to move to get to us. Light entering the eye through the pupil is focused by a lens and its energy is captured by sensitive cells at the back of the eye. These cells, the rods and cones of the retina, respond to different wavelengths of light and different light intensities. The brain interprets the patterns made by light on the retina and so we see images, colours, shades and movement.

Because we have two eyes, we see the world in three dimensions; we are able to judge distances and understand textures, deciding whether things are solid or liquid. We have colour vision which allows us to note the warning colours of dangerous creatures that give other creatures the chance to camouflage themselves and hide. Ingenious uses of technology such as television and cinema enable us to see other lives and other scenes from around the world. Microscopes and telescopes magnify things so that we can see the very small or the very far away. Technology can enhance what we are able to see so that our view of the world, and our place in it, is enriched.

Our eyes control the amount of light which enters them

Some light sources have lots of energy and are intensely bright. Others have little energy and appear dim. Brightness and dimness are simple visual descriptions. The intensity of light is measured in units called **lux**. At 5 lux, things appear dim; at 500 lux, they are bright. Humans can see in an extremely wide range of light intensities, from starlight to spotlights, but our eyes are damaged by bright lights, which leave an after-image on the retina. The iris controls the amount of light which enters our eyes. In dim conditions the iris expands (dilates) to let in as much light as possible; when the light is very bright the iris contracts to prevent too much light entering.

Mixing light
Source: DK Images

What are colours?

White light, such as sunlight, is a mix of different wavelengths. Newton separated and recombined white light and went on to describe seven colours of the visible light spectrum as red, orange, yellow, green, blue, indigo and violet. Newton liked the number 7; but actually the colours merge into one another and can be described in other ways. The primary colours of light are red, blue and green. They are different from the primary colours of pigment which are red, blue and yellow.

If you look at a rainbow spectrum created by sunlight shining through rain, you can see that its colours could be described as red, yellow, green, cyan, blue and magenta. Rainbows are an optical illusion dependent on where an observer is standing; so everyone sees their own separate rainbow. We see colour because of cone cells in the retina which are sensitive to different wavelengths, which our brains interpret as different colours. The light we see is usually a mixture of wavelengths. If we look at a blue book cover, we are seeing reflected blue light and the cover is absorbing all other wavelengths which fall on it. Plant leaves absorb and use blue and red light, reflecting back to us mixtures of light from the middle of the spectrum, that is, different shades of green.

Something to think about

Look at the shiny side of a CD-ROM disc in bright light. Moving the disc creates different shapes of rainbow or spectra; it is possible to capture this with a digital camera. Think about the CD rainbows. What colours are there; in what order? Why do these colours appear? What other objects can be used to create a spectrum? How would you describe the order of the colours? Compare with Newton's observations.

A rainbow
Source: © Rowan Greenwood / DK Images

Coloured objects reflect some colours and absorb others
Source: Kuo Kang Chen / © Dorling Kindersley / DK Images

The language of light

Light influences how we think and talk about the world

Although light is a physical phenomenon, a radiant wave, our emotional response to light is dependent on what it tells us about our surroundings. We enjoy our sense of sight. We like colours, patterns, pictures, scenery, sunsets, certain arrangements of human features – that is, what we interpret as physical beauty. The idea of light is used as a metaphor for some things which are profoundly important to people; the Roman poet Catullus uses the phrase *brevis lux* – brief light – to describe life itself. The world's great religions relate light and life. 'Then spake Jesus again unto them, saying, "I am the light of the world: he that followeth me shall not walk in darkness, but shall have the light of life"' (John 8:12). The Hindu festival of Holi (colour) and the Indian and Nepalese festival of light or Diwali are examples of how people interpret and celebrate the ways that light changes as the world moves around the Sun. Children may have encountered the idea that light is a metaphor for life and have heard stories in which the concept of light is used when considering notions of spirituality.

Darkness represents a step into the unknown

Conversely we use the idea of darkness as a metaphor for things that are fearful or even evil. Children may think of darkness as having a substance of its own. People are rightly afraid of the dark. Darkness – absence of light – robs us of our ability to see where we are and what is happening, and this loss of perception means we have much less control or chance to make informed choices. It is not dark we fear but what happens 'under cover of darkness'. Put scientifically we would not imply that darkness is a cover or cloak, or that dark has agency and collaborates to offer concealment to villains: we would say that we fear what happens in the absence of light.

Colours also form important functions in figurative vocabulary. We see 'red', we feel 'blue' and we go through 'purple patches'. Light and dark, day and night, colour and reflection, all figure largely in stories and poems and offer ways into thinking about the physics of light. Helping children to understand the physical nature of light is an opportunity to help them distinguish real from imaginary fears, and to learn to cherish their sense of sight.

How the concepts of light and dark are used in stories

'Darkness fell . . .' 'Her face lit up . . .' Such phrases in stories may influence children's perception of light and dark. We commonly use the concepts of light and dark metaphorically: 'light streamed in', 'colour drained from her face', 'his eyes shone', 'the wizard was in a dark mood', 'the gold coins glowed'. A further source of confusion might be that *light* is also the opposite of *heavy*. Traditional stories make great use of light and dark, mirrors, crystals, rainbows and colour, and the changes that happen throughout a day or because of the seasons. The Sun, Moon and stars figure largely in traditional tales, as do magic potions that make things invisible and spells that cast darkness. Rainbows have a long tradition in stories, from the sign of hope seen by Noah to the pots of gold buried by leprechauns. Phases of the Moon, eclipses and the way the positions of the planets change all contribute excitement to stories. This is to our advantage as science teachers. Children's everyday ideas are valuable starting points for discussion and can lead on to activities which help to establish a more scientific point of view. We can tap into the power of stories and poems. We can also ensure that we encourage children to create hypothetical and testable concepts of how the world works, without dimming their capacity to enjoy fantasy. Imagination is a resource for science.

Summary

Light is a form of energy which travels as an electromagnetic wave, or as high-energy photon particles. It needs no medium to travel through. Our sense of vision is profoundly important. What we perceive as dark is absence of light. Green plants use trapped light energy to synthesise sugars, providing themselves and animals with a source of chemicals for respiration, growth and repair. The oxygen we breathe is a by-product of photosynthesis. Materials may be transparent, translucent or opaque, and opaque objects block light, creating shadows. White light comprises a spectrum of colours, with each colour of light having a slightly different wavelength. Blue light has more energy than red light. Different colours of light are absorbed by some surfaces and reflected by others. This creates the colourful world in which we live.

The concepts of light and dark lend texture to our use of language. A mix of stories and children's own ideas about light and dark can provide an interesting basis for considering a more scientific perspective.

Further information and teaching resources can be found at the end of the 'Ideas for practice' section.

Part 2: Ideas for practice

Topic: Shadows

Age group: Lower primary

Scientific view

Light enables us to see and recognise different objects and to make sense of the world in which we live. Without light the world would be dark. Shadows are formed when objects block out light to create areas of darkness.

Scientific enquiry skills

In these activities children will:

- raise and try to find answers to questions;
- use first-hand experience and information sources to find answers to questions;
- make simple comparisons and identify simple patterns;
- compare what happened with what they expected would happen and try to explain it, drawing on their knowledge and understanding.

Exploration stage

Children's talk involves trying out their own ideas

Setting the scene

Read the extract from *Peter Pan*. Mrs Darling has just spotted Peter. Nana is a big dog who looks after the children Wendy, John and Michael.

Peter Pan

Mrs. Darling screamed, and, as if in answer to a bell, the door opened, and Nana entered, returned from her evening out. She growled and sprang at the boy, who leapt lightly through the window. Again Mrs. Darling screamed, this time in distress for him, for she thought he was killed, and she ran down into the street to look for his little body, but it was not there; and she looked up, and in the black night she could see nothing but what she thought was a shooting star.

She returned to the nursery, and found Nana with something in her mouth, which proved to be the boy's shadow. As he leapt at the window Nana had closed it quickly, too late to catch him, but his shadow had not had time to get out; slam went the window and snapped it off.

You may be sure Mrs. Darling examined the shadow carefully, but it was quite the ordinary kind. Nana had no doubt of what was the best thing to do with this shadow. She hung it out at the window, meaning 'He is sure to come back for it; let us put it where he can get it easily without disturbing the children.'

But unfortunately Mrs. Darling could not leave it hanging out at the window. It looked so like the washing and lowered the whole tone of the house. She thought of showing it to Mr. Darling, but he was totting up winter great-coats for John and Michael, with a wet towel around his head to keep his brain clear, and it seemed a shame to trouble him; besides, she knew exactly what he would say: 'It all comes of having a dog for a nurse.'

She decided to roll the shadow up and put it away carefully in a drawer, until a fitting opportunity came for telling her husband.
Barrie (2007)

Puzzle

Ask the children whether they have ever lost their shadows like Peter Pan. If so, do they think a drawer would be a good place to keep it? Is it possible to lose a shadow? What is a shadow?

Scientific enquiry

Go out into the schoolyard on a sunny day and see if the children can manage to lose their shadows. Try to pick their shadows up or try to run away from them. Talk together about the children's experiences and reasons why they could not lose their shadows.

In the classroom children find out how shadows of different objects are formed using torches and screens. They can compare the shadows formed by opaque and transparent objects. They can investigate how to change the size of a shadow and whether different coloured objects make different coloured shadows.

Talking points: true, false or not sure?

- Shadows are caused when an object blocks the light.
- Shadows are caused when light passes through an object.
- Green objects create green shadows.
- Bigger objects create bigger shadows.
- We can change the shape of a shadow.

Formative assessment

Observational drawings – ask the children to draw an object and its shadow. They can annotate their drawing to show the direction of light and say how the shadow is formed.

Re-describing stage

Children's talk involves making sense of scientific ideas

The purpose of this stage is to help the children to visualise a shadow as an area of darkness where an object is blocking light.

Encourage the children to talk about why their shadows are always black or dark. Ask them to imagine what it would be like to stand inside a very dark shadow. Talk about the darkest place they have ever experienced. How did the dark make them feel? What could they see?

Scientific enquiry

Create a dark cave from opaque material and tables in the classroom. Put some dark, light and luminous objects in corners of the cave. Make it big enough for at least two children. Allow volunteers to go into the cave two at a time. When they come out ask them what they could see. Did they notice the objects in the corner? Did they recognise them?

By the end of the activity it is important that most of the children will have experienced the sense of dark and been able to talk about it. Ask the children to write about what it feels like to be in the dark. *Talk together* about why it was so dark in the cave. What would they need to do to see things more clearly in the cave? Establish that they need light to see. Allow them back into the cave with a torch to identify the objects. Establish that darkness is the absence of light; we need light to see things. Talk about how objects block out the light to form areas of darkness which are called shadows. What would it be like sitting within a giant's shadow?

Assessment and further learning

Talk again about the Peter Pan story and whether it is possible for ordinary people to lose their shadows. Where do shadows go at night? Using a strong light source, draw and look at silhouettes. Ask children to explain them and suggest how to make them sharper and change their size. Use the children's responses to assess their progress. What else would they like to find out?

Application stage

Children's talk involves trying out scientific ideas

Links to design technology and drama

Create a small shadow theatre using a box or a large one using a sheet suspended from the ceiling. Children can design and make shadow puppets to act a scene from *Peter Pan* or they can create their own stories. Use a range of opaque and translucent materials. Encourage each group to *work collaboratively* to design their own shadow scenery, props and characters. During rehearsals encourage the children to use their knowledge of shadows creatively. For example, sizes can be changed dramatically by moving the puppet closer to the light source. Giant monsters and carnivorous plants can be created this way. Talk to the children about the effects they want to create and help them put their ideas into action. Finally, children need to spend time preparing their script and rehearsing their performance.

Children rehearsing their shadow puppet show – the audience are on the other side of the giant screen
Source: Peter Loxley

Assessment

Ask classmates to evaluate performances, commenting positively on use of puppets, story, sound effects and so on. Children should be taught not to make negative comments, but instead make suggestions which might support the group's work. Discuss light, dark and shadows, and find out what the children think they need to know next.

Topic: How bees see the world

Age group: Upper primary

Scientific view

We use our eyes to see the world. The world we see is full of colours and shapes. Animals do not see the world as we do. Although we live in the same world, it looks very different to different animals depending on the structure of their eyes. For example, the honey bee has five eyes, two of which are used to create ultraviolet images of the world. The other three are used for navigational purposes.

Scientific enquiry skills

In these activities children will:

- raise and try to find answers to questions;
- think creatively to explain how living things work;
- use first-hand experience and information sources to help answer the question;
- use their scientific knowledge and understanding to explain observations.

Exploration stage

Children's talk involves trying out their own ideas

Setting the scene

Take the children to a local woodland or grassland area in spring or summer to photograph the flora and fauna. Organise the children to quietly observe and record the comings and goings of the insects, especially the bees. Record the flowers the bees are attracted to and those which they ignore.

Scientific enquiry

Back in the classroom the children can make a display from their photographs and use information sources to find out more about the bees and the flowers to which they were attracted.

Talking points: true, false or not sure?

- Some flowers seems to be more attractive to bees than others.
- Bees do not land on leaves.
- Bees can smell flowers.
- Bees prefer red.
- Bees are collecting things . . . we can say what.

Puzzle

Talk together about what the world would look like through the eyes of a bee. Does the world look the same to a bee as it does to us?

Children's drawings

Children can use their imagination to paint pictures of what they think a flower would look like to a bee. Children should present their paintings and explain why the flower would seem so appealing to bees.

Formative assessment

Explore children's drawings and responses to the puzzle. Decide what the children know and what they need to learn in the next stage.

Re-describing stage

Children's talk involves making sense of scientific ideas

The purpose of this stage is to help the children solve the puzzle by thinking and talking about it from a scientific point of view.

Children's drawings

Compare the children's eyes with bees' eyes. Children can look at each other's eyes, and draw what they see (ensure that children know that they must not shine lights in eyes). Use the drawings to talk about the pupil as a small hole which lets light into our eyes. What happens to the light after that? Use information sources to find out about the structure of the human eye.

Compare the structure of human eyes with those of bees. Children may be fascinated to find out that bees have five eyes. Why do they need all these eyes? What purpose do they serve? Bees, like other insects with compound eyes, are very sensitive to rapid movement. This enables them to react quickly to the movement of predators. If children have ever tried to catch an insect with compound eyes such as a fly or bee, they will realise how quickly their eyes enable them to react. One of the amazing things about bees is that they see the world in different colours to us. Our eyes detect the colours of the spectrum from red to violet. Bees cannot detect the red end of the spectrum but instead are able to detect ultraviolet light which is not visible to humans. As a result of their research children can identify the 'secret' colours which bees can see. They can paint pictures which compare how humans and bees would see the same display of different coloured flowers.

An important point which needs to be emphasised in the re-description stage is the part played by the structure of our eyes in determining how we picture the world. It is worth explaining the structure of the human eye in some detail.

Assessment and further learning

Use the children's drawings and explanations to assess their progress. What else would they like to find out? Children can raise and investigate their own questions.

Application stage

Children's talk involves trying out scientific ideas

Scientific enquiry

Make simple spectacles out of card and different coloured transparent materials. Ask the children to note how the world seems to change when they look through the different coloured 'glasses'. What problems do they have in distinguishing between different colours? Ask groups of children to choose one pair of colour glasses and *talk together* about the problems they would have if the world always appeared as it does when they look through the glasses.

Link to PSHE

Make children aware that the world does not look the same to all people. Children can use information sources to research the nature and causes of vision problems, including colour blindness. Discussion could focus on social problems experienced by children who wear glasses, with an examination of the motivation behind this. Provide positive role models and encourage the class to accept that sight problems create difficulties which many children live with every day.

Assessment

Use children's reports on the causes of colour blindness to assess their progress. They could also research and report how other animals see the world in comparison with humans and bees.

Information and teaching resources

Books

- Hollins, M. and Whitby, V. (2001) *Progression in Primary Science*, London: David Fulton Publishers, Chapter 4: Sound and light.

Primary science review articles (Association of Science Education)

- PSR 93, (May/June 2006). This issue focuses on *Light and Sound*.

Useful information and interactive websites

- Use this search engine to access a range of sites for light: www.ajkids.com
- Teachers' Lab – the science of light: www.learner.org/teacherslab/science/light/

CHAPTER 19
SOUND

Sound figures largely in our world. Every day we experience noise, music and voices. We use sound to communicate and entertain. Some sounds we find satisfying and enjoyable, others can be unpleasant and even threatening. At times we use sounds aggressively as warning signals, at other times to portray affection and trust. Music is one of our great cultural achievements and exemplifies how sound can be used to enrich our lives. In this chapter we look at the physical nature of sound and how different sounds are produced. We also explore the similarities and differences between the way we and other animals detect sound.

Topics discussed in this chapter:

- Historical context
- The nature of sound
- Acoustics
- Ways of detecting sounds

Part 1: Subject knowledge

Historical context

In the sixteenth century Leonardo da Vinci (1452–1519) studied hearing; he compared the sound of a bell to a stone creating ripples when dropped into water. This analogy enabled him to picture how sound could travel in waves. A hundred years later, Italian astronomer and physicist Galileo Galilei (1564–1642) noticed that vibration creates sound and that objects can resonate. As part of his study of sound, he explained everyday effects such as how a wet finger can make a wineglass ring. He also demonstrated that the frequency of sound waves determined their pitch.

Enquires into the speed of sound

In the 1600s French scientist and monk Marin Mersenne, interested in musical composition, considered the speed of sound and studied acoustics and vibrating strings. Robert Boyle (1627–91), the Irish theologian, soldier and physicist whose work on air pressure is well known, first measured the speed of sound in air in 1660. Isaac Newton (1642–1727) looked at the way sound travels, describing the relationship between the speed of sound and the density and compressibility of the medium in which it is travelling. So, for example, he knew that sound travels more readily in water than in air. Newton realised that sound can be interpreted as 'pressure' or thought of as pulses which are transmitted through adjacent particles of matter.

Mathematics, music and acoustics

The eighteenth-century Dutch mathematician Daniel Bernoulli (1700–82) studied the flow of air. He considered the relationship of music and mathematics. He found that, for example, a violin string could vibrate at more than one frequency. Such vibration consists of a series of natural frequencies, the higher frequencies superimposed on the lower. Bernoulli's understanding of the mathematical and physical nature of sound enabled him to see that complex musical sound, such as the sound made by a musical instrument, consists of a series or mix of simple sounds, such as those produced by a tuning fork.

Acoustics is the science of sound, including its production, transmission and effects. Acoustic research has led to the development of the electronic communication and entertainment systems which enrich our lives today.

The nature of sound

How vibrations create sounds

To exist, sounds need a vibrating source and a medium to travel through. To hear sounds, creatures need sensitive cells arranged to detect vibrations. Sound waves must move through a solid, a liquid or a gas. They cannot move through the vacuum of space. Sound around us is produced when the air is disturbed by vibrations in some way and these vibrations are detected as sound in our ears. The source of sound vibrations can be the speaker cone of a sound system, the air in a flute, people talking by vibration of vocal cords in the larynx, the mechanical disturbance of traffic noise, or the vibration created as a jet engine or thunder move enormous amounts of air. A cymbal creates sound. In its ordinary position, it is silent. Once it is struck, it moves rapidly to and fro. Air immediately next to it is compressed, causing a slight increase in air pressure; it then moves back *past* its rest position, causing a reduction in the air pressure. As this continues, a wave of alternating high and low pressure radiates away from the cymbal in all directions. These patterns of high and low pressure are interpreted as sounds in our ears and brain.

So it is that sounds are generated by rapid movement, or vibration. Objects vibrate in different ways to make their own unique sounds. When a gong is struck the entire object is made to vibrate. Sounds made by a violin are created by the vibrations of its strings. The vibrating strings set up vibrations in the body of the violin which amplify the sounds.

The body of the stringed instrument amplifies the sound made by vibrating the strings

Source of sound → Particle structure of a solid

Source of sound → Particle structure of air

Sound travels faster in a solid than in air because the particles, which transfer the sound, are closer together

A model to explain how sound travels

Materials are made from moving particles which can pass their energy on to others. This is how sound moves. The closer the particles are to one other the more easily they pass on sound vibrations. This means sounds travels better in liquids, where particles are close together, than in air where they are further apart. The particles of a solid such as steel have tightly packed particles, which pass on vibrations to their neighbours very readily. Sound moves more rapidly in a solid than a liquid or gas. Sound vibrations (waves) travel away from their source, radiating out in all directions.

Something to think about

Leonardo da Vinci imagined sound waves to be like ripples spreading out on the surface of water. Do you think this is a useful analogy? Could it help explain about the behaviour of sound?

Problems with the water model

The water analogy is not a perfectly accurate picture, but it does enable us to understand how the sound from a source such as a bell can be heard in all parts of a room simultaneously. The analogy breaks down when we consider the movement of the particles of water. In water waves the particles move up and down at right angles to the direction of travel of the wave. This is called a **transverse wave** and is consistent with the way light travels. Sound is a **longitudinal wave**, which means that its energy travels in the same direction in which the source vibrates.

Can sound be reflected like light?

Sound is reflected from surfaces. When sound is reflected from hard surfaces echoes can be created. Bats have very sensitive ears and use echoes to locate their prey. In effect they locate their prey by 'shouting', but their voices are at such a high pitch that we humans cannot hear them. Their ultrasound calls bounce off the hard exoskeleton of their prey, such as a moth, and are returned so that they hear an echo a fraction of a second later. Bats calculate the decreasing distance between

Ripples on water
Source: © Dorling Kindersley / DK Images

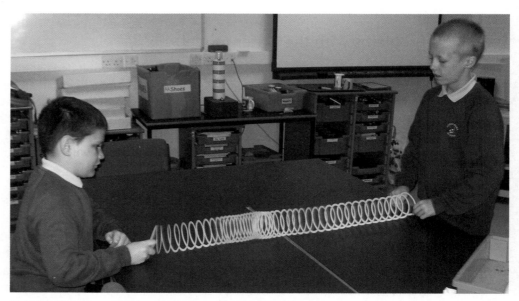

Using a slinky to model how sound travels in longitudinal waves
Source: Peter Loxley

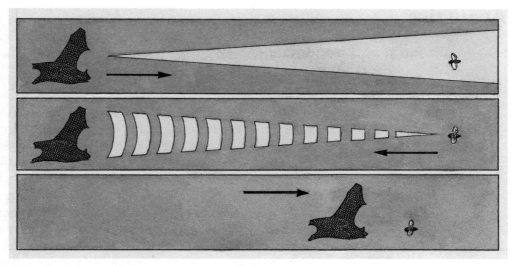

Bats use echoes to locate their prey
Source: John Woodcock / © Dorling Kindersley / DK Images

themselves and insects by listening. Some water creatures can also locate things or one another in this way. Bottlenose dolphins produce clicking sounds which they use to navigate around their habitat. There is even a Madagascan shrew that explores its terrain by echo location. We have developed technology which imitates animals' use of sound to locate underwater objects. Ships use sonar (SOund NAvigation and Ranging) equipment to detect and locate submerged objects or to measure distances underwater.

Something to think about

If sound travels better in solids than it does in air, then why do we shut doors and windows to block out unwanted sounds? It could be argued that closing doors should enable the sound to travel more easily into the room.

Which materials absorb sound?

Some surfaces absorb rather than reflect sound. Curtains and carpets make an appreciable difference to the acoustics of a room. Good absorbers of sound are often a mixture of a gas (air) and a solid. For example, woollen curtains and carpets are good absorbers; so are some manufactured materials, such as polystyrene and foam, which are commonly used as insulators of sound. Sound vibrations dissipate when they are continuously transferred from one medium to another.

Acoustics

Pitch and frequency

Sound waves have the same measurable characteristics as light waves, that is, wave-length, frequency and amplitude.

The number of vibrations produced by a source during one second is the *frequency* of the sound. We use the term **pitch** to describe how we interpret different frequencies. As the frequency of vibration increases, the sound we hear gets higher and higher. High-frequency sounds have a high pitch. If vibrations have a low frequency, the resulting sound has a low pitch. We start a column of air vibrating as we blow into a recorder; we can change the frequency of the vibrations by changing the length of the air column that is vibrating. Small piccolos have higher pitched sounds than large bassoons because they make it possible to vibrate an air column at a higher frequency. Interestingly, vibration in air columns is unaffected by the shape of the column – so we can bend and twist tubes which would otherwise be long and unwieldy to make such things as trumpets, cornets, trombones and horns with the same range of notes as they would have if straight.

How can we measure the loudness of a sound?

The loudness or volume of a sound is dependent on the amplitude or size of the vibrations. For human ears, the loudness of a sound cannot be measured with complete

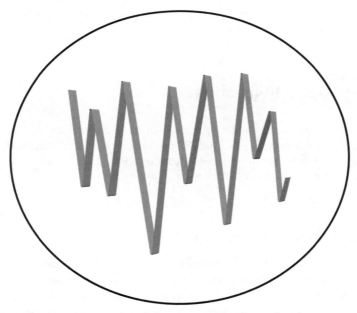

Sound wave made by a percussion instrument showing variation in amplitude (loudness)
Source: Robin Hunter / © Dorling Kindersley / DK Images

accuracy. Everyone perceives sound slightly differently, and perception of loudness by individuals is affected by the duration of a sound. However, machines can measure sound volume by measuring the amount of energy the sound wave contains. The more energy the wave contains the greater the intensity of the sound. Sound is measured in **decibels (dB)**.

The measure zero decibels (0 dB) of sound is about the lower limit of human perception. The dB scale is logarithmic: that is, an increase of one on the scale represents a doubling of sound intensity. People talk at about 40 dB; car engines run at about 60 dB; a rock concert is 120 dB; a blue whale, humming at 1 metre, 183 dB; and above 130 dB, sound becomes painful to our ears. The explosion of the volcano Krakatoa in 1883 is estimated to have been 180 dB from a distance of 100 miles in air.

Hearing sounds

Are all animals' ears the same?

The ears of mammals are specialised to detect sound and convey detailed information about direction, pitch, loudness and quality to the brains. The external shape of the ear may differ. Some animals can move their ears to track sounds. Others, like elephants, use the shape of their outer ears to help cool their bodies.

Sound vibrations are converted to electrical impulses which are sent via the auditory nerve to the brain.

Humans have well-developed brains and can use highly complex patterns of sound to communicate ideas through language. Other highly intelligent animals which produce complex patterns of sound for communication are whales and dolphins. Many other animals use systems of sounds to communicate.

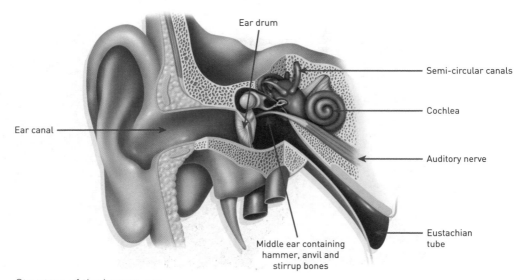

Structure of the human ear
Source: Jacopin / Science Photo Library Ltd

Although generally only mammals have large outer ears, fish, birds, reptiles and amphibians have eardrums and inner ears. For example, frogs have eardrums behind their head on both sides of their body. Sound vibrations picked up by the eardrums are sent to the brain in a similar way to a mammal's. However, frogs also use another organ to detect sound: they use their lungs. Scientists have found that frogs have an unbroken air link from the lungs to the eardrums. It seems that this link helps the frog to locate sounds and also possibly to protect the ears from its own loud calls. Frogs can call extremely loudly (up to about 95 decibels) – the sound equivalent of a train whistle. It is thought that the lungs help to protect the ears by equalising the pressure on the inside and outside of the eardrum. Since fish were the original vertebrates, and therefore have a common ancestor with frogs, it is perhaps not surprising to find that many types of fish also use a lung-like air bladder as an eardrum.

Do owls really have big ears?

Some owls seem to have tufty ears on top of their heads. Actually these feathers are not associated with hearing. Like other birds, owls have ear openings or apertures on the sides of the head. To be successful night hunters, owls need to have a highly developed sense of hearing. Some owls have the parts of their faces around the ear aperture-shaped like radar dishes to funnel in the sound. When a noise is detected, an owl is able to tell its direction because of the minute time difference between hearing the sound in the left and right ears.

The tufts of feathers on an owl's head look like ears
Source: Cyril Laubscher / © Dorling Kindersley / DK Images

Something to think about

How would an owl know if its prey was immediately in front of it? How do we use our ears to locate sources of sound?

Why don't birds have bigger ears?

Why don't owls have big ears like rabbits and foxes? Think about having a conversation on a windy day. When wind races past the ears it creates a loud roaring noise, which limits the ability to distinguish separate sounds. Lack of external ears significantly cuts down wind noise, enabling birds to hear other sounds when they fly.

Some butterflies have ears on their wings

A fascinating recent discovery is that some butterflies active at night have ears located in their wings. Previously it had been assumed that, although butterflies could detect air vibrations through their wings, they did not have specialised organs for detecting sound. As far as we understand, it is only butterflies that are active at night which have ears. Moths, which are mainly active at night, have a well-developed sense of hearing to enable them to detect the **ultrasonic sound** used by bats to locate their prey. It is thought that night-flying butterflies have evolved sound sensors to help avoid being eaten by bats.

Something to think about

The first chapter in the book explores the pleasure of finding out that the natural world may not be how we first imagine it to be. Frogs hear sound through their lungs; butterflies hear sound through their wings to avoid being eaten by bats. What other wonderful things can children find out?

Summary

Someone speaks. The vibrations set up in their larynx move particles of air. The sound wave is transmitted; the complexity of the vibration carries all sorts of information about the voice. Hearing involves the ear in capturing the vibration and converting it to neural information to be sent to the brain for processing. Sound, like light, is a physical phenomenon, a form of energy profoundly and extensively important for human life. With sound we can have language, music and story; we can be alerted to danger or ask for help; we can identify one another and learn.

Animals use sound for various purposes. They use it to locate their prey, to avoid their predators and warn others of approaching danger. Animals make sounds to attract a mate, defend a territory and challenge a competitor. In social groups animals use sound to identify others, to coordinate group activities and to generally pass on information.

Further information and teaching resources can be found at the end of the 'Ideas for practice' section.

Part 2: Ideas for practice

Topic: Detecting sound

Age group: Lower primary

Scientific view

Sound travels from its source in all directions. We hear sound when it enters our ears. Having two ears enables us to distinguish between different sounds and also helps us decide where the sounds are coming from and how far away they are. Many animals' ears are sensitive to higher and lower frequencies than ours. They notice and locate sounds we cannot hear. Animals use sound to communicate with each other, to locate their prey and to avoid predators.

Scientific enquiry skills

In these activities children will:

- raise and try to find answers to questions;
- explore using their senses and make and record observation;
- make simple comparisons and identify simple associations;
- compare what happened and try to explain it, drawing on their knowledge and understanding.

Exploratory stage

Children's talk involves trying out their own ideas

Setting the scene

Read a story involving sound, for example 'The King's Keys', and use this as a basis for games involving sound.

Story of the King's keys

The King had locked away all his gold in a room with a thick door and a very strong lock. There was only one special key which could unlock the room. Every afternoon the King had a nap on his favourite throne. He ordered the whole palace to go to sleep too, so that it was very, very quiet. To keep the special key safe while he was asleep, he always put it in a gold box underneath the throne.

One day a thief who wanted to steal the gold tiptoed into the King's room. He saw the King asleep. Without even breathing, the thief crept silently up to the throne. He knew where the key was kept. Gently his fingers closed round it . . . he lifted it up . . . and as he did so, a loud 'Ding dong! Ding dong! Ding dong!' rang through the room. The thief froze in horror. He hadn't realised that attached to the key was a small but very loud silver bell!

With his eyes closed, the King smiled to himself. As he had expected, it was his own son Prince Echo trying to steal the key. Of course Prince Echo wasn't a real thief. This was a game they played together. The King had promised that on the day his son was clever enough to steal the key he would make him King! Sometimes he used gold bells, sometimes silver, and sometimes bronze; the little bells always warned him before the thief could escape.

Scientific enquiry through play

Play the King's keys game with the children, if possible in a large space such as the school hall. Place the 'throne' in the middle of the space and choose a child who doesn't mind being blindfolded to be the King. The King sits on the throne and places the keys to the treasure on the floor underneath. The rest of the children form a large circle surrounding the throne. One at a time, the children try to sneak up and steal the keys without the King knowing. The thief is caught if the King is able to point in the direction of the approaching child. Any child who is able to steal the keys becomes the King. The game can be played in smaller groups so that more children can have the opportunity to be the King.

After playing the game, *talk together* about how the children could tell when a thief was trying to steal the keys. How did they know the thief was getting closer? How did they know which direction the thief was coming from? How did they know when the thief was behind them? Talk about how they use their ears to detect sounds.

Talking points: true, false or not sure?

- We need two ears to tell where sound is coming from.
- It is hard to listen carefully.
- Some sounds are easier to listen to than others.
- You can't hear underwater.

Puzzle

Why do we have two ears? Why are they on the sides of our head?

Formative assessment

Provide time for the children to *respond collaboratively* to the puzzle. Using the feedback from talking points and subsequent discussion, decide what the children know and what they need to learn in the next stage.

Re-describing stage

Children's talk involves making sense of scientific ideas

The purpose of this stage is to make children aware that ears locate sounds and distinguish different sounds. Start by talking about the children's responses to the puzzle.

Scientific enquiry

To explore the advantages of having two ears play a different version of the King's keys game. Again the King sits blindfolded on his throne with the other children surrounding him in a big circle. This time each child has an instrument with which to make a sound. Children are chosen randomly to make a sound with their instruments and the King has to point to where he thinks the sound is coming from and to describe the instrument.

The game continues until all the children have had the opportunity to contribute a sound. Observe how the King identifies the direction of the sound. How does he move his head? Record the number of correct responses made by the King. The King now puts a foam earplug in one of his ears and the game is repeated. Repeat the experiment with a number of different Kings. Compare the accuracy of the responses for two ears and one ear. *Talk together* about the advantages of having two ears compared with only one.

Develop the game with two children in different parts of the circle making sounds with their instruments at the same time. Are two ears better than one when it comes to distinguishing between the two sounds?

Assessment and further learning

Children can draw pictures to show how they use two ears to locate sounds. Assess their understanding by asking them to explain their drawings. What else would they like to find out about sound, ears and hearing in humans and animals? Children can raise and investigate their own questions.

Application stage

Children's talk involves trying out scientific ideas

Make a collection of pictures of animal ears for display. Include some unusual ones like those of the long-eared bat. Children compare the shape and size of a range of different animals' ears. Children can use *information sources* to compare the ears of different animals. Note that the outer ear size may be unrelated to the size or hearing capacity of the inner ear.

Talking points: true, false or not sure?

- Rabbits are hard to sneak up on because they have big ears.
- Birds can't hear sounds because they do not have any ears.
- Dogs don't like fireworks because they are too loud for them.
- Cats are good hunters because they move their ears to find their prey.
- Some animals use ears for temperature control.

3-D modelling

Ask the children how they think they could improve their hearing. Would they hear better with bigger or different shaped ears? Children can apply their emerging understanding of sound to respond to these questions. They can make simple ear models to test out their ideas. Models can be designed so they fit over the children's ears for testing.

Long-eared bat
Source: Frank Greenaway / © Dorling Kindersley / DK Images

Redesigning nature

Children can design and make simple models of an imaginary animal which can hear and locate very quiet sounds such as the movement of an ant or worm.

Assessment

Use the children's feedback from the activities and talking points to gauge their understanding of the topic.

Topic: How vibrations create sound

Age group: Upper primary

Scientific view

Sound is caused by objects when they vibrate. When objects vibrate they cause the air around them to vibrate. These vibrations travel through the air and if they enter our ears we hear them as sound. The sound we hear depends on the nature of the vibrations. For example, more rapid or faster vibrations create a higher pitch and bigger vibrations create louder sounds.

Scientific enquiry skills

In these activities children will:

- raise and try to find answers to questions;
- use simple equipment and materials appropriately;
- make systematic observations including the use of ICT for data-logging;
- use charts and drawings to record and communicate data;
- use their scientific knowledge and understanding to explain observations.

Exploratory stage

Children's talk involves trying out their own ideas

Setting the scene

Have available a range of musical instruments. Ask for volunteers to form a band. Give each member a different instrument (a range of wind, stringed and percussion) and ask them to play along with a recorded tune together. Now ask the children in the audience to close their eyes while each member of the group plays their instrument independently. The game is to identify the instrument just by listening to it. *Talk together* about how the sounds made by each of the instruments could be changed. How can sounds be made lower or higher pitch, quieter or louder, more or less tuneful? Is it possible to make a drum sound like a guitar? Encourage children to provide reasons for their views.

Scientific enquiry

Focus on how each of the instruments makes its sound. Use a drum with rice placed on the skin to demonstrate how it vibrates. Suspend a table tennis ball from a length of cotton; strike a tuning fork and bring it close enough to tap the ball so that children can see vibration as movement.

In groups children can explore a range of instruments and record their ideas as set out below.

Instrument	How do you make the sound?	What vibrates?	How can you change the loudness of the sound?	How do you alter the pitch?

Encourage the children to interpret and make sense of the scientific terms for themselves. They can *talk together* about the meanings of the terms vibrations, loudness and pitch. Check the children's understanding and encourage playing with instruments (percussion or home-made) to help make sense of scientific vocabulary.

Children's drawings

Ask children to choose one instrument and draw an annotated picture of how it makes its sound and how they are able to hear it. Children can *talk together* about how instruments are able to change the pitch and loudness of the sounds they produce. Encourage children to use comparative terms such as *high* and *low* pitch and *loud* and *quiet* sounds. Encourage children to use new vocabulary to describe how instruments work.

Puzzle

If we could see a sound travelling through the air, what would it look like? How would a loud sound compare with quiet sound? How would a low-pitched sound compare with one with a high pitch? Allow the children time to explore answers to these questions and to present their ideas through drawings and models.

Formative assessment

Explore children's responses to the puzzle and, together with the feedback from subsequent activities, decide what the children know and what they need to learn in the next stage.

Re-describing stage

Children's talk involves making sense of scientific ideas

The purpose of this stage is to provide a model that children can use to help them develop a mental picture of how sound travels through the air.

Modelling

Compare children's ideas with some alternative pictures (models) of sound. Ask them which they think makes most sense to them and whether they could be improved.
    Here are four different ways of modelling how sound travels in air:

1. Children standing in a line can model the air. Have a pile of pieces of card with the word 'sound' written on each. Children stand next to each other, close enough so that they can touch hands. One child represents the instrument and so gives out the sound. One at a time, the child passes a sound (card) to the child who is first in line. This sound is then passed from child to child down the line until it reaches the listener at the end.

2. Use a slinky coil to show how a vibrating source can cause pulse patterns to be passed along the coil. Talk about the springiness of air and how it behaves like a slinky.

3. Ask children to stand behind each other with their arms outstretched and their hands on the shoulders of the person in front. The child (acting as the instrument) at the back end of the line gives the child in front a gentle push which is then passed on down the line from child to child. The model can be developed with gentle vibrations being passed down the line. If the vibrations are made continuous then the observing children will be able to see the patterns of vibrations repeated along the line.

4. Use a line of dominoes to represent the air. When knocked over, one domino knocks over the next and so on, causing a pulse (of sound) to travel down the line.

Make it clear to the children that the models are analogies which behave in similar ways to sound. *Talk together* about the strengths and limitations of each model. Explore how the models can be used to demonstrate changes in loudness and pitch. Use *electronic simulations* of sound to help children develop mental models of how sound travels in air. There are a range of simulations for sound available on the Web and other electronic sources. It is worth downloading as many as possible to add to your library of electronic resources.

Assessment and further learning

To assess progress ask the children to look again at their own pictures which they created earlier and think about how they could be revised in light of what they have learnt. What else would they like to find out? Children can raise and investigate their own questions.

Application stage

Children's talk involves trying out scientific ideas

Links to music and design technology

Tell the children they are going to be songwriters and performers. They have to design and make their own instruments. Allow children to choose and name their own groups. Each group needs to design and make three types of instrument: stringed, wind and percussion. Provide resources such as boxes, elastic bands, ponytail bands, string, lolly sticks, thin tubes, bottles, hollow canes, disposable cups, rice, peas, fabric, spoons, etc.

Design criteria should focus on the range of volume and pitch the instruments can make. Children can use electronic data-loggers to measure the volume. Ask groups

Children playing their own musical instruments
Source: Peter Loxley

to provide annotated drawings of their instruments, explaining how they create sound and how the pitch and volume of the sound can be changed. Children can perform a favourite song or they can write their own to a popular tune. Ask groups to evaluate each other's instruments using the design criteria. What are the strengths of each instrument? How can designs be improved?

Assessment

Ask each group to create a presentation for the class in which they provide a description of their instrument, show how it works, and say what they would like to try next to improve it in terms of range of notes, volume or how easy it is to play.

Information and teaching resources

Books

- Peacock, G., Sharp, J., Johnsey, R. and Wright, D. (2009) *Primary Science: Knowledge and Understanding*, Exeter: Learning Matters, Chapter 12: Sound.

Primary science review articles (Association of Science Education)

- PSR 103 (June 2008), 'The sound of music' (Wobbly Corner).
- PSR 93, (May/June 2006), this issue focuses on light and sound.

Useful information and interactive websites

- Use this search engine to access a range of sites for sound: www.ajkids.com
- A useful simulation showing how sound travels in air: http://phet.colorado.edu/simulations/sims.php?sim=Sound

References

Alexander, R. (2006) *Towards Dialogic Teaching*, York: Dialogos.

Armitage, D. and Armitage, R. (2008) *The Lighthouse Keeper's Lunch*, Leamington Spa: Scholastic Publications.

ASE (2001) *Be Safe*, Hatfield: Association for Science Education.

Asoko, H. (2000) 'Learning to teach science in the primary school', in R. Millar, J. Leach and J. Osborne (eds), *Improving Science Education: The Contribution of Research*, Buckingham: Open University Press.

Asoko, H. (2002) 'Developing conceptual understanding in primary science', *Cambridge Journal of Education*, 32 (2).

Asoko, H. and de Boo, M. (2001) *Analogies and Illustrations: Presenting Ideas in Primary Science*, Hatfield: ASE Publications.

Barnes, D. (1976) *From Communication to Curriculum*, Harmondsworth: Penguin Books.

Barrie, J. M. (2007) *Peter Pan*, London: Penguin.

Bell, B. and Cowie, B. (2001) 'The characteristics of formative assessment in science education', *Journal of Science Education*, 85: 536–53.

Black, P. and Harrison, C. (2000) 'Formative assessment', in M. Monk and J. Osborne (eds), *Good Practice in Science Teaching: What Research Has to Say*, Buckingham: Open University Press.

Black, P., Harrison, C., Clare, L., Marshall, B., and Wiliam, D. (2002) *Working Inside the Black Box: Assessment for Learning in the Classroom*, London: King College.

Borges, A. T. and Gilbert, J. K. (1999) 'Mental models of electricity', *International Journal of Science Education*, 21: 95–117.

Brady, J. (1982) 'Halley's Comet: AD 1986 to 2647 BC', *Journal of the British Astronomical Association*, 92 (5): 209–15.

Briggs, R. (2008) *The Snowman*, London: Puffin.

Bruner, J. S. (1986) *Actual Minds, Possible Worlds*, London: Harvard University Press.

Carle, E. (1981) *The Honeybee and the Robber*, J. MacRae Books.

Carle, E. (1994) *The Very Hungry Caterpillar*, London: Hamish Hamilton Ltd.

Carver, R. (2005) 'Principles of a story', *Prospect*, 114: 32–4.

Centre for Alternative Technology, www.cat.org.uk/information/info_content.tmpl [accessed on 20 March 2009].

Cerini, B., Murray, I., and Reiss, M. (2003) *Student Review of Science Curriculum: Major Findings*, London: Institute of Education, University of London.

Clarke, S. (2008) *Unlocking Formative Assessment*, London: Hodder & Stoughton.

Darwin, C. (1974) *The Descent of Man and Selection in Relation to Sex*, Detroit: Gale Research (reprint of 1874 edition).

Darwin, C. (1998) *The Origin of Species*, Hertfordshire: Wordsworth.

Dawes, L. (2004) 'Talk and learning in classroom science', *International Journal of Science Education*, 26 (6): 677–95.

Dawes, L. (2008a) 'Encouraging students' contributions to dialogue during science', *School Science Review*, 90 (331): 1–7.

Dawes, L. (2008b) *The Essential Speaking and Listening: Talk for Learning at Key Stage 2*, London: Routledge.

Dawkins, R. (1998) *Unweaving the Rainbow*, London: Penguin Books.

de Boo, M. (2006) 'Science in the early years' in Harlen (ed.), *ASE Guide to Primary Science Education*, Hatfield: ASE.

DfES (2004) *Assessment for Learning*, Primary National Strategy, Excellence and Enjoyment: Learning and Teaching in the Primary Years.

Dyer, A. G., Whitney, H. M., Arnold, S. E. J., Glover, B. J., and Chittka, L. (2006) 'Bees associate warmth with floral colour', *Nature*, 442: 525.

Ellwood-Friery, K. (1996) 'The Moon', in M. Rosen (ed.), *Poems for the Very Young*, London: Kingfisher.

Falk, J. and Dierking, L. (2000) *Learning from Museums*, Walnut Creek, CA: Altamira Press.

Farley, F. and Rainey, R. (2006) 'Anaconda, the bulge wave sea energy converter' at www.bulgewave.com/.

Feynman, R. (1964) *The Feynman Lectures on Physics*, Reading, MA: Addison-Wesley.

Feynman, R. P. (1999) *The Pleasure of Finding Things Out*, London: Penguin Books.

Fletcher, F. D. (1988) *Life Lines 34 Darwin*, Buckingham: Shire Publications Ltd.

Goldsworthy, A., Watson, R., and Wood-Robinson, V. (2000) *Developing Understanding in Scientific Enquiry*, Hatfield: ASE.

Greca, I. M. and Moreira, M. A. (2000) 'Mental models, conceptual models and Modelling', *International Journal of Science Education*, 22: 1–11.

Gregory, A. (2003) *Eureka: The Birth of Science*, Cambridge: Icon Books.

Harlen, W. and Deakin Crick, R. (2003) 'Testing and motivation for learning', *Assessment in Education*, 10 (2): 169–208.

Johnsey, R., Peacock, G., Sharp, J., and Wright, D. (2001) *Primary Science Knowledge and Understanding*, Exeter: Learning Matters.

Johnson-Laird, P. (1983) *Mental Models*, Cambridge: Harvard University Press.

Layton, D. (1993) *Technology's Challenge to Science Education*, Buckingham: Open University Press.

Leach, J. and Scott, P. (2002) 'Designing and evaluating science teaching sequences: an approach drawing upon the concept of learning demand and a social constructivist perspective on learning', *Studies in Science Education*, 28: 115–42.

Lijnse, P. (2000) 'Didactics of science: the forgotten dimension in science education research?' in R. Millar, J. Leach, and J. Osborne (eds), *Improving Science Education: The Contribution of Research*, Buckingham: Open University Press.

Lijnse, P. (2004) 'Didactical structures as an outcome of research on teaching – learning sequences?', *International Journal of Science Education*, 26 (5): 537–54.

Livesey Museum for Children, 'Myths and Legends', www.liveseymuseum.org.uk/pdf/ TheDreamtime.pdf [accessed 16 May 2009].

Loxley, P. M. (2009) 'Evaluation of three primary teachers' approaches to teaching scientific concepts in persuasive ways', *International Journal of Science Education*, 31 (12): 1607–29.

McGough, R. (1983) 'Snowman' in *Sky in the Pie*, London: Puffin/Penguin.

Mercer, N. (1995) *The Guided Construction of Knowledge*, Clevedon: Multilingual Matters.

Mercer, N. (2000) *Words and Minds*, London: Routledge.

Murphy, C. and Beggs, J. (2003) 'Children's perceptions of school science', *School Science Review*, 84 (308): 109–16.

Naylor, S. and Keogh, B. (2000) *Concept Cartoons in Science Education*, Sandbach: Millgate House Publishers (concept cartoons are also available on CD ROM).

Newton, I. (2003 reprint edition) *Optics: Or a Treatise of the Reflections, Inflections, and Colours of Light*, New York: Prometheus Books.

NCC (1993) *Knowledge and Understanding of Science – Energy: A Guide for Teachers*, Skelderdale: NCC.

Ogborn, J., Kress, G., Martins, I., and McGillicuddy, K. (1996) *Explaining Science in the Classroom*, Buckingham: Open University Press.

Osborne, J., Simon, S., and Collins, S. (2003) 'Attitudes towards science: a review of the literature and its implications', *International Journal of Science Education*, 25 (9): 1049–79.

Osborne, R. and Freyberg, P. (1985) *Learning in Science: The Implications of Children's Science*, Auckland: Heinemann.

Poole, M. (1990) 'The Galileo affair', *School Science Review*, 72 (258): 39–48.

Poskitt, K. (1991) 'The Moon' in J. Foster (ed.), *Twinkle Twinkle Chocolate Bar: Rhymes for the Very Young*, Oxford: Oxford University Press.

Rogers, E. M. and Wenham, E. J. (eds) (1980) *Nuffield Physics*, London: Longman.

Rosen, M. (2000) *Centrally Heated Knickers*, London: Puffin.

Scott, P. (1998) 'Teacher talk and meaning making in science classrooms: a vygotskian analysis and review', *Studies in Science Education*, 32: 45–80.

SDC (2007) *Every Child's Future Matters*, Sustainable Development Commission (www.sd-commission.org.uk/publications/downloads/ECFM_report.pdf).

Simon, S. (2000) 'Students attitudes towards science' in M. Monk and J. Osborne (eds), *Good Practice in Science Teaching: What Research Has to Say*, Buckingham: Open University Press.

Solomon, J. (1994) 'The rise and fall of constructivism', *Studies in Science Education*, 23: 1–19.

Sutherland, R., Armstrong, V., Barnes, S., Brawn, R., Breeze, N., Gall, M., Mathewson, S., Olivero, F., Taylor, A., Triggs, P., Wishart, J., and John, P. (2004) 'Transforming teaching and learning: embedding ICT into everyday classroom practices', *Journal of Computer Assisted Learning*, 20: 413–25.

Sutton, C. (1992) *Words, Science and Learning*, Buckingham: Open University Press.

Sutton, C. (1996) 'The scientific model as a form of speech', in G. Welford, J. Osborne, and P. Scott (eds), *Research in Science Education in Europe*, London: Falmer Press.

Treagust, D. F., Duit, R., Joslin, P. and Lindauer, I. (1992) 'Science teachers' use of analogies: observations from classroom practice', *International Journal of Science Education*, 14 (4): 413–22.

University of St Andrews, quotations by Galileo Galilei, www-history.mcs.st-andrews.ac.uk/Quotations/Galileo.html [accessed 21 April 2006].

Wertsch, J. V. (1991) *Voices of the Mind: A Sociocultural Approach to Mediated Action*, London: Harvester Wheatsheaf.

Wheway, D. and Thompson, S. (1993) *Explore Music Through Science*, Oxford: Oxford University Press.

Glossary

adaptation The process by which creatures adapt to their habitat. Those with the most suitable characteristics survive to breed, creating creatures fitted to their habitats.

asteroid Rocky or metallic material left over from the formation of the solar system. Most asteroids orbit the sun between the orbits of Mars and Jupiter. Some cross the Earth's path and have collided with the Earth.

atom The basic unit of matter. The smallest particle of an element that still displays the properties of that element.

autotroph (primary producer) An organism that produces organic compounds from simple molecules, using energy from light or chemical reactions, e.g. green plants and some bacteria; also known as a primary producer.

bacteria Single-celled micro-organisms. Bacteria exist everywhere on Earth, including inside living organisms. In soil they recycle nutrients. In the human body some are a vital part of digestion but others cause disease, e.g. cholera.

Big Bang Model of the events at the beginning of the universe. The Big Bang considers that the universe began from an extremely hot and dense singularity 13.7 billion years ago, and that the universe continues to expand.

bile Yellowish substance secreted by the liver and stored in the gall bladder. Bile aids the digestion of fats.

biodiversity The variety of life forms within any given ecosystem, often used as a measure of the health of biological systems.

biofuel Fuel for cooking, powering vehicles and heating that comes from often specifically grown crops, e.g. wood, palm oil, corn, sugar cane.

biomass Living or recently dead biological matter that can be used for fuel.

carbohydrate Chemical used for food: consisting of carbon, hydrogen and oxygen atoms combined, e.g. glucose. Sugars or starch (potatoes, rice or bread, for example) contain carbohydrates. Glucose is used as a fuel in respiration to release energy to the body.

carnivore Animal with a diet consisting mainly of meat obtained by predation or scavenging.

cartilage Connective tissue: providing structure and support as in the nose or the ears; or cushioning joints as between the discs of the spinal column.

cell division Mechanism by which the contents of the cell, including the nucleus and DNA, divide equally. Organisms grow or repair tissue by cell division.

cellulose The material in the cell wall of green plants which gives them structure. Some ruminants have micro-organisms in the gut to digest cellulose; not digestible by humans but useful as dietary fibre to move food through the gut.

chlorophyll Green pigment found in plants and algae and contained in the chloroplasts. It absorbs light energy during process of photosynthesis.

classification Biologists group or classify different species of organisms by means of shared physical characteristics.

colloid Chemical mixture where the particles of a substance are suspended evenly within another but not dissolved: for example, fog, clouds, smoke, whipped cream, milk and blood.

comet Ball of ice and dust that orbits the Sun. As it approaches the Sun the ice vaporises and streams away from the comet, carrying dust with it to form a tail that may be visible from Earth: for example, Hale-Bopp in 1997.

combustion Combustion happens when a fuel (e.g. wood or oil) combines with oxygen through burning to give off heat. When organic substances, such as wood, burn they release carbon dioxide.

compound Chemical substance consisting of two or more chemical elements that cannot be separated by simple means. A compound often has very different properties from its constituents: for example, common salt is made from a poisonous gas (chlorine) and a highly reactive metal (sodium).

connective tissue Collagen-based substance that holds organs in place and forms ligaments and tendons.

constellation A collection of astronomical bodies, usually stars, that appear to form a pattern in the sky.

decibel (dB) Unit used to express the intensity of sound: for example, 0 dB = threshold of human hearing, 60–70 dB = spoken conversation and 110–115 dB = a rock concert.

decomposers Micro-organisms that consume dead or decaying organisms from which they get energy and nutrients for growth. Primary decomposers are bacteria and fungi.

density A physical property of matter; the relationship between the mass of an object (in kilograms) and its volume (in cubic metres). Dense metals such as lead and gold are heavy for their size whilst polystyrene has low density and is light for size.

detritivore Organisms that derive nutrients from decomposing organic matter, e.g. worms and woodlice. They form an important part of food webs in ecosystems.

diffusion Process by which particles mingle as a result of their constant motion and resulting collisions: for example, perfume diffuses throughout the air in a room.

DNA Deoxyribonucleic acid, DNA, is the hereditary material in humans and most other organisms. Contained in every cell of the body, DNA stores the genetic code that defines an individual.

eclipse An eclipse occurs when one astronomical object moves in front of another. For example, when the Moon moves in front of the Sun, the shadow of the Moon crosses the Earth's surface and we observe a solar eclipse. A lunar eclipse occurs when the Moon passes behind the Earth so that the Earth blocks the Sun's rays from striking the Moon.

ecosystem Describes the interactions between animals, plants, micro-organisms and their environment. Ecosystems can be as large as a tropical rainforest or as small as a pond.

electrical circuit A closed loop through which current electricity flows.

electrical current Flow of electrical charge carried by mobile electrons in wires.

electrical resistance A measure of the opposition to flow of electrons in a wire, depending on which metal the wire is made from. Resistance increases with increasing length and decreasing width.

electrical voltage Measure of the energy carried by the electrical charge. It is supplied by the battery and used by the components (for example, the bulb) in a circuit.

electromagnetic radiation Energy-carrying wave that does not need a medium to travel through: includes radio waves, light waves, X-rays, infrared radiation.

electron A subatomic particle. Electrons have negligible mass, orbit the atomic nucleus, and carry a negative electrical charge.

element A chemical substance made up of one type of atom: for example, iron, oxygen, carbon.

embryo An organism in the early stages of development, from implantation to birth. In humans the embryo is known as a foetus after eight weeks.

emulsion A mixture of two or more liquids that are immiscible (will not blend): for example, oil and water.

energy An attribute of objects or systems that enables work to be done. Energy can be transformed from one form to another (for example, chemical energy in food to heat energy in the body) but cannot be destroyed.

enzyme Enzymes are proteins that increase the rate of reactions that take place in organisms, remaining unchanged themselves.

evolution Changes that take place in a species over a long period of time in response to the environment. Genetic changes in a community can result in the development of a new species.

excretion The process of eliminating waste products from an organism: for example, carbon dioxide (the by-product of respiration) is excreted by the human lungs.

exoskeleton An external skeleton supporting and protecting an animal's body. Crabs and insects have exoskeletons.

exuvia Remains of an exoskeleton after the organism (generally an insect, spider or crustacean) has moulted.

fertilisation Fusion of cells, the sperm and the ovum, in sexual reproduction of animals and flowering plants.

food chain Feeding relationships between species in an ecosystem. Food chains are drawn to show the direction of energy flow, from the sun to producers and then consumers, then decomposers.

food web Different food chains in an ecosystem link up with each other to form food webs. Food webs describe the complexity of the feeding relationships in an ecosystem.

force A force is a push, pull or twist that can cause an object to change its speed, its direction of movement or its shape.

fossil fuel Non-renewable fuels such as coal, oil and natural gas formed from organisms alive around 300 million years ago; found in deposits beneath the earth.

fungi A kingdom of living things; organisms more closely related to animals than plants. Largely invisible apart from their fruiting bodies: for example, toadstools. Fungi feed on organic matter and reproduce via spores: for example, yeasts, moulds and mushrooms.

galaxy A massive system of stars. The remains of dead stars and interstellar gas held together by a strong gravitational field often with a distinct shape. Our Sun and solar system are part of the spiral-shaped Milk Way galaxy.

gastric juice Strongly acidic liquid secreted by the stomach lining to break down food in the stomach.

genetic code Patterns along the DNA molecule which define a distinct individual.

geothermal energy Heat from within the Earth, generated in the Earth's core and released via hot springs or geysers. Geothermal heat pumps can be used to extract geothermal energy to heat buildings.

global warming The increase in the average temperature of the Earth attributed to the release of carbon dioxide through human activity (for example, burning of fossil fuels).

glucose A simple sugar (produced in photosynthesis) used by living cells as a source of energy.

gravity A force of attraction between one mass and another. A property of all matter. Gravity gives weight to objects and keeps the Earth and planets in orbit round the Sun.

greenhouse gas Gas in the atmosphere (for example, water vapour, carbon dioxide and methane) that absorbs and holds thermal (heat) energy.

habitat The place where an organism lives is called its habitat. Habitats have specific conditions of temperature, water, geography, etc., which suit the organisms that inhabit them.

haemoglobin Protein in red blood cells which holds oxygen for transport round the body.

herbivore Feeds only on autotrophs (primary producers) such as plants and algae.

hormone Chemical messengers that act as a signal in multicellular organisms: for example, serotonin regulates mood, appetite and sleep.

inheritance Process by which certain features are transmitted from parent to offspring via the genetic code.

invertebrate An animal without a vertebral column (backbone). This includes 98% of all animal species: that is, all except fish, reptiles, amphibians, birds and mammals.

kinetic (movement) energy Energy an object possesses by virtue of its motion, for example a moving car, football or planet.

light year A measure of distance – the distance light travels in a vacuum in one year – about ten trillion kilometres. The nearest known star to the Sun is Proxima Centauri, about 4.22 light years away.

longitudinal wave Waves that oscillate (vibrate) in the same direction in which they travel: for example, sound waves, seismic waves produced by earthquakes.

lux Measure of the intensity of light: for example, 1 lux = full Moon overhead and 10,000–25,000 lux = full daylight.

metamorphosis Change. Complete metamorphosis is the process some animals go through when they change from the immature to the adult form, for example, tadpole to frog, caterpillar to butterfly.

meteor Small particle of debris (from sand grain to pebble) that falls into the Earth's atmosphere. Often called a 'shooting star' because it glows as it burns up in the atmosphere. If it falls to the ground it is called a meteorite.

micro-organism Often single-celled organisms, too small to be seen by the human eye: include bacteria, fungi, algae, plankton and amoeba.

mixture Two or more substances mixed together but not combined chemically (for example, solutions, suspensions and colloids). Mixtures can usually be separated by simple mechanical means such as filtering (for example, flour in water).

molecule Group of at least two atoms held together by strong chemical bonds. Some elements only exist as combinations of two or more atoms (for example, oxygen).

mollusc Invertebrates with body divided into three parts: a head, a central area containing the major organs and a foot for movement. They include gastropods (snails and slugs), cephalopods (squid and cuttlefish) and bivalves (mussels and oysters).

natural selection The process by which favourable, inheritable characteristics become common in successive generations.

nebula An interstellar cloud of dust and gas where materials clump together to form larger masses and eventually new stars.

neutron Subatomic particle contained in the nucleus of the atom that has no electrical charge and a mass slightly larger than the proton.

non-renewable energy Energy generated from finite resources such as fossil fuels (for example, coal, oil, gas). See also *renewable energy*.

nuclear energy Energy released by splitting (fission) or merging together (fusion) of the nuclei of atoms. On Earth nuclear energy is produced by splitting the atoms of uranium or plutonium. The Sun produces vast amounts of energy by nuclear fusion, using hydrogen as a fuel.

omnivore Creatures that eat both plants and animals: generally, opportunistic feeders not especially adapted to eat meat or plants exclusively (for example, bears, pigs, humans).

ossification Process by which bones are formed from connective tissue such as cartilage. Blood brings minerals such as calcium and deposits it to form hard bones.

oxidation Chemical reaction between oxygen molecules and other substances (for example, rusting); also, the loss of at least one electron when two or more substances interact.

peristalsis A rhythmic contraction of muscles that move substances through the digestive system.

phloem Living tissue in plants that transports the products of photosynthesis (sugars) to all parts of the plant. In trees phloem is a green layer between the bark and the woody xylem.

photoelectric (voltaic) effect When electrons are emitted from a material exposed to light. Utilised in solar (photovoltaic) cells to convert sunlight directly into electricity.

photosphere The Sun is a ball of gas and does not have a well-defined surface. The photosphere is defined as the diameter at which the Sun appears to be opaque. Beyond this is the corona which becomes visible during a solar eclipse.

photosynthesis Process by which plants convert water and carbon dioxide into organic compounds (especially sugars), using energy from sunlight.

phytoplankton Autotrophic plankton (drifting organisms in the oceans) containing chlorophyll and so capable of photosynthesising.

pitch Frequency of vibration of a sound. Measured in Hertz (Hz) as vibrations per second. The adult ear can hear from 20 to 16,000 Hz.

pollinator Animal which transfers pollen from the male anther to the female stigma of a flower so that fertilisation can take place (for example, bees, bats).

potential (stored) energy Energy stored within a system which has the potential to be converted into other forms of energy: for example, energy stored in the bonds between atoms or in a compressed spring.

primary consumer Organisms that obtain energy from plants (primary producers). See also *secondary consumer* and *tertiary consumer*.

primary producer An organism that produces organic compounds from simple molecules using energy from light or chemical reactions: for example, green plants and some bacteria; also known as autotrophs.

protein Chains of amino acids (found in meat, fish, eggs, dairy products, legumes, pulses and seeds) make up proteins, essential for the growth of cells and tissue repair.

proton Positive subatomic particle in the atomic nucleus with an electrical charge and mass.

radiant energy The energy of electromagnetic waves from radio waves to gamma rays and including solar heat and light.

reflection A wave travelling in a straight line 'bounces' back as it strikes a new medium. For smooth surfaces the angle at which the wave strikes will be the same as the angle at which it is reflected: for example, reflection in mirrors or echoes in sound.

relativity Theory of Albert Einstein published from 1905 to 1907 on the nature of gravitation, space and time. Presented amongst others the idea that energy and mass are equivalent and interchangeable.

renewable energy Energy generated from natural, sustainable sources (for example, sunlight, wind, rain, tides or geothermal heat). See also *non-renewable energy*.

reproduction Biological process by which new individual organisms are produced. Fundamental to all life; may be sexual (requires two individuals one of each sex) or asexual (by cell division).

respiration Cellular respiration; a process that takes place in all living cells where sugars are chemically combined with oxygen (oxidised) to release energy for growth, movement, reproduction and repair. Carbon dioxide and water are waste products.

ruminant Mammal that is able to digest plant-based foods (in particular cellulose). Food is initially softened in a first stomach (the rumen) and then re-chewed as cud (for example, sheep, cattle).

secondary consumer Organisms that obtain energy from other consumers, usually a carnivore.

solar energy See *radiant energy*.

solvent A liquid or a gas that dissolves a solid, liquid or gas solute; most commonly water.

species Basic unit of biological classification – a group of organisms capable of interbreeding.

spectrum Of light; visible frequencies of electromagnetic radiation ranging from red through to violet. A spectrum is produced when a beam of light is split into its constituent frequencies (colours). A rainbow displays the visible spectrum.

starch A carbohydrate made of long chains of glucose molecules. It is a major source of food (energy) for humans. Plants store glucose – the product of photosynthesis – as insoluble starch.

static electricity Electric charge resulting from electrons building up on the surface of an object as a result of friction (when materials are pulled apart or rubbed together).

supernova Stellar explosion of great intensity. Occurs either when an ageing star collapses in on itself and then heats and explodes or when a small, very hot star overheats and undergoes runaway nuclear fusion. Supernovas seed galaxies with material and can trigger the formation of new stars.

tertiary consumer Organisms that obtain energy from secondary consumers. They are known as 'top predators' to indicate their position in the food chain.

thermodynamics The study of the conversion of energy from one form to another. The total amount of energy in the universe remains constant: energy can be exchanged between systems and transformed from one form to another but cannot be created or destroyed.

tilt of the Earth The Earth is tilted on its axis and is at an angle of about 23.5 degrees to the vertical. This results in the seasons.

transverse wave Wave that oscillates at 90 degrees to the direction of travel: for example, electromagnetic waves – light.

ultrasound Frequencies above the range of human hearing (about 20,000 Hz). Used in medical imaging. Many animals are capable of hearing well above this limit (such as bats, dogs and dolphins).

upthrust Force exerted on a floating object by the water it displaces.

vertebrate Animal with a backbone or spinal column: includes bony fish, sharks, amphibians, reptiles, mammals and birds.

virus Sub-microscopic particle that contains DNA but no nucleus. It needs to infect a host cell to replicate itself (unlike bacteria); cause of infections such as sore throats, Ebola and HIV/AIDS.

wave motion Distortion in a material or medium when the individual parts vibrate but the waveform itself moves through the material: for example, a wave passing across a pond. Wavelength is the distance between successive wave peaks; amplitude is the height of the wave; frequency is the speed of vibration.

weight The force of gravity acting on a mass.

Index